WOMEN AT THE WALL

SUNY Series in Critical Issues in Criminal Justice
Donald Newman, Gil Geis, and Terence Thornberry, EDITORS

WOMEN
AT THE
WALL

A Study of Prisoners' Wives
Doing Time on the Outside

LAURA T. FISHMAN

State University of New York Press

Gratitude is expressed for permission to reprint passages from the following works:

Effectiveness of Prison and Parole Systems, by Daniel Glaser, p.245. Copyright 1969 by The Bobbs-Merrill Company.

Stigma: Notes on the Management of Spoiled Indentity, by E. Goffman, p.30. Copyright 1963 by Simon and Schuster.

Asylums: Essays on the Social Situation of Mental Patients and Other Inmates, by E. Goffman, p.23. Copyright by Doubleday & Co., Inc.

Social Problems, Vol. 31, No. 2, December, 1983, pp. 152-164. Copyright 1983 by the Society for the Study of Social Problems.

Published by
State University of New York Press, Albany

© 1990 State University of New York

For information, address State University of New York
Press, State University Plaza, Albany, NY 12246

Library of Congress Cataloging-in-Publication Data

Fishman, Laura, 1937–
    Women at the wall : a study of prisoners' wives doing time on the
outside / by Laura Fishman.
        p.   cm. — (SUNY series in critical issues in criminal
justice)
    Bibliography: p. 337
    Includes index.
    ISBN 0-7914-0058-1.   ISBN 0-7914-0059-X (pbk.)
    1. Prisoners' wives—United States—Case studies.   I. Title.
II. Series.
HV8886.U5F57   1990
362.8′3—dc19   88-30110
                                                           CIP

10   9   8   7   6   5   4   3   2   1

*For the women who do their own
time on the outside while waiting for
their men to come home from prison.*

*And for my "sister of many past lives,"
Jane Kates Pincus,
a gentle, loving, and good-humored woman.*

CONTENTS

PREFACE

Having a husband get "busted" and imprisoned is not an experience unique to the poor; both working-class wives and middle-class women find themselves at prison gates on visiting day. Too often I—a college teacher—found myself there, too.

During my former husband's arrest and imprisonment, my friends and neighbors who resided within my community, the Lower East Side of New York City, provided me with a strong network of support. Throughout this period of time they provided me with socio-emotional support, money whenever needed, transportation to the prison, as well as actively participating in the rearing of my son. The Hell's Angels (an infamous motorcycle "club"), who lived on my block, provided me with protection so that no one would burglarize my home or attempt to harm me or my child.

Although I had such strong support from my community, I felt something was missing in my everyday world; that is, a positive and shared feeling of social-psychological unity which could only be gained from other women who shared my status as a wife of a prisoner. Wives of prisoners, however, did not readily present themselves as I went about my normal round of activities. Nor was there, at that time, a visible network of these wives to refer to for support. Thus, I found myself, a neophyte, without access to intimate association with women who could share the problems that I encountered as a prisoner's wife and who could also provide validation that I simply was doing okay in my newly acquired role.

Prison visiting only served to frustrate this need for validation of self-worth and the "normalcy" of some of the events that I experienced as a prisoner's wife. During prison visiting, these women appeared to be remote and unapproachable. The hallways that we shared were not at all conducive to meeting one another and mingling in a relatively relaxed and congenial fashion.

I was struck by the stark contrast between prisoners and their families. The visitors' faces betrayed the kinds of troubles and anxieties that stem from dealing with too many daily responsibilities. The prisoners, by contrast, appeared relaxed, well-rested, and energetic. I found myself wondering whether or not prison was a vacation from cares and responsibilities—a time to take it easy and not worry about food, clothing, and housing, and to get some exercise. Enmeshed as I was in the daily routine of teaching, child care, and domestic chores, prison began to have a certain siren-like appeal. I sometimes yearned to trade places with my husband. "Punishment" was being on the outside and having to cope with the business of living.

When I saw the other women in the visiting room, however, I wanted to know if my feelings and experiences were unique. During these visits, I wanted to plunge into the depths of the women's lives and learn what was hidden there. Did they share similar combat stories to mine and did they also feel that they had some unshareable problems? What sustained them in these impossible places—prisons, the welfare offices, their homes, without their loved ones?

Throughout those years, I never got to know these women. I never asked the questions that kept arising during my career as a prisoner's wife. Nor did I have the opportunity to learn what lay hidden behind the eyes of the visitors. I carried these questions and my curiosity with me to my doctoral studies in the Department of Sociology at McGill University, Montreal, Canada, where I began to formulate them as an integral part of my research on prisoners' wives and their experiences with crime, courts, imprisonment, and reunion. This book on the accommodation of wives of prisoners first evolved as a doctoral dissertation. It is really to these other women that I owe a debt of gratitude for setting this project in motion.

Thirty prisoners' wives, whose histories emerge in these pages, shared their lives with me with an extraordinary generosity. They taught me how to see the humor in the pain, to persevere, and to be optimistic that painful circumstances can abate. I hope that I have succeeded in speaking for them as they wished. This book is really theirs; any inaccuracies are mine.

The credit for making this research project feasible must be attributed to Dr. James F. Short and Dr. James A. Davis who provided me with the basic methodological foundations for doing field research. Special recognition also goes to Dr. Henry Lesieur, my teacher, colleague, and friend, who enthusiastically spurred me on during the critical phases of this project.

Dr. Prudence Rains and Dr. Malcolm Spector, my dissertation advisors at McGill University, deserve my special thanks. Both were most generous with general advice and critical comments. Although I often rebelled, I am quite appreciative of their insistence that I not settle for a conventional piece of research.

Encouragement from my colleagues of the Sociology Department at the University of Vermont came in many forms. It is impossible to acknowledge by name every colleague to whom I am indebted for information, ideas, and encouragement. While many contributed, I am especially grateful to Stephen D. Berkowitz. He deserves my appreciation for helping to edit the manuscript and for providing me with crucial insights. I also give special thanks for his emotional support: especially provided at the times when I was struck by the blues. I am very grateful for the fact that my chairpersons, Jeannette R. Folta and Howard Nixon II, provided me with an environment conducive to working along with liberal use of office supplies, the telephone, copying machine, and the computer.

One colleague should receive special acknowledgment of my love. Beth Mintz has been a staunch colleague, ally, editor, and friend. I am especially touched by her willingness to share her editorial skills, feminist thinking, and astute sense of strategy. Her support and encouragement were always proffered. Without her, the task of writing this book would have been onerous.

I would specifically like to mention Elaine Michaud, who was my work study assistant for two years. On a consistent basis, she offered dedication, valuable suggestions, and a willingness to share the bad times and the good.

Once I began the project, I was helped and encouraged by a network of people who offered critical, emotional and/or practical support. One in particular is Arlo Cote (Imported Car Center) who kept my car in top condition and made it possible for me to travel the lonely back roads of Vermont on my interviewing assignments.

Two people deserve special acknowledgment for reading and commenting on the manuscript: Lisa Alther and Marty Patry. Special thanks also go to a network of friends who consistently reassured me that this study was worth doing. I am most grateful for their nurturing me along this path. These friends include: Gloria Gil, Lois Valdez, Forest Murphy, DoDo and Bruce Donovan, Jane Vitello, and lastly, Marcia Goldberg. I wish to single out Nancy Magnus, Sam Dietzel, Chuck King, and Jean Lang for their nourishment of my spiritual life during this phase of my life.

A great many more people must be acknowledged for making this work possible. I especially thank Toni Clark who with a great deal of sensitivity and a keen eye provided excellent editorial work and advice regarding the manuscript's style and organization.

A note of thanks is due to the people who banged away at the keyboards tirelessly and accurately. Special appreciation goes to Kit Andrews, Patricia St. Amour, and Sue Carol Shepardson. For expert typing and for help to meet the deadline for the printing of this book as well as for lots of hugs and back rubs, I wish to gratefully thank Janet Truman.

Special appreciation is to be given to the Vermont Department of Corrections for graciously providing me with access to the prison files and the correctional facilities. A debt is owed to the correctional superintendents and other prison personnel for assisting me in obtaining interviews with married prisoners.

As a single parent, I now acknowledge those people who provided me with some degree of freedom and/or space to get my work done. Special appreciation goes to my babysitters who not only freed me from some childcare responsibilities but from feelings of guilt about leaving my children. My deep thanks go to Linda Bloch Ayer who provided boundless love to my children and to me. I also bow in the direction of cleaning women, my garbage collector who saved me many a smelly trip to the town dump, and to Mr. and Mrs. Marble of Marble's Grocery Store, who provided me with all kinds of little personal services, from check cashing to sufficient change for the tolls in Montreal. And to Brad Miller, my deep appreciation for his support and caring amidst the fruits, vegetables, frozen food, etc. at the Shelburne Supermarket. Within this context, I count among my most unflagging supporters my oldest friends, Jane and Edward Pincus, who provided love and nourishment, and some financial resources so that I could see this project through.

Families always seem to be mentioned last. Although mentioned last, I want to assure my sons, Aryeh and Damian that they were one of the most important ingredients for making this work possible. Both almost grew up with this book. I especially thank them for providing me with the motivation to plod wearily on to the last pages of the final manuscript by refusing to indulge my urges to give up the project. They always let me know they wanted more from me. Special appreciation is due them for assuming some household responsibilities when I was overwhelmed with finishing the manuscript, for enduring the dusty furniture, and for never complaining about the clacking of the typewriter keys as I typed, many times into the wee hours of the night.

CHAPTER I

Introduction

Some women can't hack the game. Their sex lives go down the drain. They can't take the pressures, the loneliness, the feeling of isolation, and trying to communicate with their men through letters. And the prison sets up these rules for visiting. It's wrong to kiss your man. They tell you when you have the legal and moral right to be intimate with your man. And then your old man is continually saying that he doesn't want you to do this or that. You're continually pulled a thousand ways.
　　　　　　　　　　　　　　　　　　　—A Prisoner's Wife

When prison doors shut behind married men, their wives, although on the outside, also find themselves "doing time." Feelings of powerlessness, helplessness, and frustration are part of the everyday world of prisoners' wives as they share with their men the critical events of arrest, arraignment, trial, imprisonment, and release. This book is based on interviews with ordinary Vermont women who have endured these traumatic events. Their responses reveal their hardships, their struggles, their losses, but also their resourcefulness in coping with their husbands' criminality, their family and friends, and the prison system.

THE WOMEN SPEAK FOR THEMSELVES

These womens' accounts provide an introduction to the crucial but unexamined issues faced by prisoners' wives. Resistant to extricating themselves from marriages to men who participate in criminal activities, get arrested, and subsequently imprisoned, these women seek ways to explain and cope with their husbands' criminal actions and their consequences. The following discussion took place among four prisoners' wives at a support group meeting. Three of the women were neophytes. Vicki's husband,

1

Charles, was arrested and convicted for attempted rape; Susan's husband, Tim, was arrested and convicted for armed robbery; Nancy's husband, Kevin, was convicted for rape. The old timer, Tammy, was pregnant when her husband, Mark, was arrested and convicted for possession of stolen property.

VICKI. I did learn that criminals are really people who have problems. I didn't think that way before. I don't think any more, "That bastard's not any good." I don't condone what he did but I do make jokes. Like now, I say, "I'm married to rapist jokes."

People keep asking me how I can stand by Charles. I knew Charles as a person and not as an attempted rapist. He didn't violate me.

NANCY. I felt raped. I felt violated when I learned about it. I kept asking myself, "Why did he hurt me like that?"

SUSAN. I felt a little like that too. I felt that he had done a very selfish thing. He didn't let me in on his feelings. He didn't let me know that he went out and did something criminal. I felt angry that he didn't trust me with his feelings. I felt that if he had trusted me, he wouldn't have done it. He forced me into a position to be hurt. I felt inadequate. I said that I didn't pick up the signs that he was going to get into trouble and that's why he's in jail. It was my fault for not seeing the signs.

VICKI. I didn't have this to contend with. I knew that Charles has this sexual problem. I knew that there was nothing I could do to help him and it was out of my hands. I was glad that he was arrested. I prayed to the Lord that something would happen so that he would try to get some help and when this happened I was glad. I knew he had a problem. He was masturbating and at one point he didn't even care that I knew that he was masturbating.

SUSAN. It's hard for me to get angry about anything. My first reaction to Tim's arrest was the feeling that everything we had together had been destroyed. I felt really bad because I saw everything go down the drain. Then later I got angry at society and the causes that brought Tim to do these things. But I didn't get angry at Tim.

TAMMY. I felt sorry about the way Mark was brought up. He was brought up by his father who was an alcoholic and beat him continually. At eleven Mark was completely on his own. He got in with a bunch of criminals and he doesn't know anything different. I see that his problem is his hanging around this bunch of criminals.

I thought about leaving Mark. I thought about it a lot. But to me he's really a good guy. He's very intelligent and sensitive. And he now recognizes that he has to get his life in order. He has begun to recognize that he had to carry out his responsibilities and not try to escape them. He knows that he has to do it this time. I won't stand for him going back with those criminals.

SUSAN. I felt that Tim came from an economically depressed situation and he did not know how to solve his problems any other way but to get arrested. He needed to be punished and go to jail. And then he managed to come out the better for it. Tim and I are glad now that it has happened because we are coming out the better for it. He felt that I would have been pulled down by his problems if this hadn't happened.

VICKI. It's hard for the men to believe that we can wait for them. I've never resented waiting for Charles. I've never even considered going out with other men. When he was sentenced and learned that he got 4–10 years, and he hadn't even raped the women, he was terribly upset. He had to go into another room, and I went with him, so that he could change from his own clothes to the allocated clothes. He cried and cried. I've never seen Charles cry. And I was standing there crying also. I knew that he wanted to be punished. He asked to be punished. He wanted help with his problems and that was his way of crying out for "help." I told him that I would wait for him. He said, "You can't wait that long." Then he went on to say that he had always been in a prison all his life. His prison was his mind. Then he said, "When I walk out of here, I'll walk out of here a better man. I'll leave that prison forever." I knew right then and there that I'd wait for Charles and that it would be worth the wait.

Involuntary separation entails many hardships resulting from what some wives consider their worst "punishment"—being separated from their husbands. Ethel gave birth to her sixth child when her husband, Matt, was incarcerated, having been convicted of theft.

All I know is that he's been involved in possession of stolen property and attempted escape. When he was in jail before, it was for possession of stolen property. He said that he's been in and out for the past six years. But I really don't know how many times he's been in.

When he went in this time, he wasn't working. He was getting General Assistance. Now I get more. It bothers him that he's not able to support us. And that the state is doing his job. It makes him feel more like a man when he can support us. I don't like the idea of being on the State. I don't like the way they treat me. People look down on you because you're on the State. I know that I'm as good as they are. I tried to get a deep freezer on credit. The shopkeeper was all ready to give me the credit and then he asked me how I was going to finance it. When he learned that I was on welfare, the man said that he couldn't help me.

I then received an eviction notice and I had to look for a house. Here I was in Lynchburg, living in the middle of nowhere. I didn't have a car or a phone and I was pregnant and had three little kids. There was no way that I could walk to St. Albert. I got hold of some people in the CEO office and told them my plight. They started to help me. I found this place and finally had some money.

Then it took me a couple of weeks to move in. I had no one to help me. My uncle helped me to move. During the move, we had a major snow storm. All the roads were impassable and so I couldn't get the rest of my stuff from the house into St. Albert for another week. The kids and I had to sleep on the floors without beds or bedding for that week.

I was depressed, upset, and hurt. I didn't know who to turn to. My friends were never around to help me. They were always too busy. There was nothing that Matt could do. I felt all alone. My mother lives in Florida and my sister died and my brother lives in Connecticut. I was more or less alone. I was more depressed than ever. I took it out on the kids. I would argue a lot with them. I was very hard on them. I was punishing for no reason. I didn't want them around me and to be clinging to me all the time. And they continually clung to me. I guess I ignored them a lot.

I was pretty scared. I felt fearful about being alone. We hadn't even been married a year. Our first anniversary is next month. It's just so hard. This is going to be our first baby. All the other children I had with my first husband.

All I do is go pay bills, go to the doctors and go grocery shopping and once in a while I get to go to Burlington. The rest of the time I spend in this house. I wouldn't mind all this if I had someone to talk to. It's pretty boring not to have anyone to talk to. During the day my friends work and they are pretty busy. I feel closed in.

My temper has gotten shorter with the kids. I snap at them quicker. It seems to be getting harder and harder to handle them.

Maybe it's my imagination but they seem to be different since Matt has gone. They have changed. They seem to challenge me. They keep trying to see how much they can get away with. They seem meaner now and they don't seem to be minding since he's been gone. That might be their way of letting out their anger. Now they are constantly at each other's throats. They aren't minding me as good and they are fighting over nothing.

(At this point in the account, Matt has been transferred to Londonderry which is located within a few miles of Ethel's home.)

But the phone calls help now that he has transferred to Londonderry. He can now talk to them on the phone. He disciplines them over the phone. He talks to me to see what the problem is then he punishes them by not letting them watch TV or go out to play. They're straightening out. It helps because they know that Daddy is close by. When they really haven't been good, I can take them to talk with him now. They are not anxious to have that kind of talk.

I'm not as depressed as I was when he was at Newport. No ways near as much now. I have cut down on writing letters to him. I get to see him now.

When he was at Newport, we could only talk for ten minutes at a time. Now I don't have to worry about the phone bills. The kids get to see him and are happier. He's close by and I can get to him.

Now he calls me up at 6 AM in the morning and that's a nice way to start the day with his voice. Then we talk off and on during the day and he calls me at night before he goes to bed.

We both call. He calls me every morning. He gets me up. When I feel lonely, I call him. Lately, he's been doing most of the calling.

I just want to hear his voice. We have only been married a year and I feel it's our honeymoon. It's bringing us closer. We celebrated our first anniversary and we have the baby now. But this is no way to start a marriage. I know that absence makes the heart grow fonder but I do wish he were home. He has a year to go. He's been in 8 1/2 months now and it's been a killer.

CRISIS AND COPING

Each stage in the criminal justice system is crisis-provoking for prisoners' families. Wives often undergo identity crises. Families almost always experience abrupt shocks. To some extent, events such as arrest, conviction, imprisonment, and parole are *inherently* crisis-inducing because of their larger connotations. But, in another sense, the crises generated by stages in the criminal justice process are similar to those experienced by families in other cases of enforced separation.

Enforced separation itself generates a series of "crisis points" due to changes in the status and location of family members. At each point, family members must accommodate or adjust to altered circumstances by re-organizing their lives. Their ability to do this successfully depends on both external conditions and the internal resources of their family units.

The events that generate these crisis points are, of course, different for prisoners' families. Stigmatization, the conditions placed on prison visitation, the special difficulties involved in preserving marital commitments, and a variety of other circumstances make prisoners' families' crises quite different from those which impinge on other separated families. But broad similarities remain at the level of the social processes which both types of families undergo and it is important to note where and why these occur.

Almost no work has explicitly dealt with the moral careers of persons formally outside the bounds of institutions but whose lives are strongly affected by them.[1] The moral careers of prisoners' wives are largely defined by the criminalization process[2] their husbands are undergoing. To the extent that prisoners' wives are emotionally and materially dependent on their husbands, then they too become caught up in the criminal justice system. Thus they share with their husbands the implications that each stage in the criminalization process holds for the self-conceptions of those being processed by it. The moral careers of prisoners' wives parallel the changes taking place in their husbands' identities.

Several researchers have investigated the conditions under which the accused, in the course of being labelled as "criminal," become *stigmatized* and, therefore, treated as "different." According to Goffman (1963), arrest, conviction and incarceration carry so powerful a stigma that it is often difficult for families to avoid it. Thus, when one family member has been stigmatized, others may face a loss of community respect and increased social hostility as well. Goffman (1963:30) has called this "courtesy stigma" and maintains that it is attached to " . . . those regarded by others as having a spoiled identity because they share a web of affiliation with the stigmatized." The stories told by prisoners' wives show plainly that "courtesy stigma"—the pall of blame that remains behind after the period of their husbands' arrest, conviction, and initial incarceration—is often one of the heaviest burdens these women must bear. The concept of "criminalization" includes "secondary" effects, in this case, the transfer of stigma to persons not *officially* designated as part of the process.

Male prisoners' stigma extends to their wives who are vulnerable to feelings of shame and who both anticipate and encounter stigmatization within their own communities and within the prison system. In particular, prisoners' wives often perceive themselves as suffering for the "sins" of their husbands.

As prisoners' wives pass through each of the crisis points generated by the criminalization process, they are forced to assess and reassess their husbands' criminal behavior and to employ accommodative techniques to assist in preserving their marriages and making their lives more bearable. Two important strategies involve manipulating definitions of their husbands' behavior and their own relationships to it, and developing lifestyles that allow them to "normalize" their lives. Both strategies are formed in the context of continuous interaction with their husbands and with social control agencies. As such, these forms of accommodation are contingent, in certain critical respects, upon the subcultures out of which prisoners' wives are drawn, on the ways in which police and courts stage and carry out the earliest phases in the criminalization process, on the forms of interaction allowed between inmates and their wives, and on the definitions and strategies employed by social control agencies, generally, in maintaining the system.

Very little is known about the ways in which prisoners' wives' accounts vary in response to external events in their lives.[3] The present findings make it clear that wives' accounts relate to the general kinds of coping strategies they use in coming to grips with their husbands' careers. These strategies are used by the wives in their attempts to preserve their marriages, deter male criminality, and support their husbands. Some wives also devise a range of strategies to maintain the outward appearance of smooth relationships with their husbands as well as with friends and families. Few of these patterns of accommodation are, however, permanent; they are usually modified in the course of wives' ongoing interactions with their husbands. Therefore, over the course of a wife's career there are distinct patterns in the accommodative strategies employed at different stages in the criminalization process.

These wives' accounts reveal that accommodations are made within the context of their particular social milieux. Prisoners' wives respond not only to social control agents, but also to stresses and strains that stem from their socio-cultural backgrounds. Hence, they are likely to draw upon culturally specific notions in determining what they consider to be the most effective accommodations. The majority of prisoners' wives are from the working class. The kinds of accommodations they make to intermittent poverty as well as male criminality are those suggested by working class environments.

The working-class wives' accounts reveal two forms of working-class lifestyles to which they are oriented[4]—"fast-living" and conventional patterns. According to their own accounts, wives perceive "fast living" to include: (1) alcohol and drug abuse; (2) violence, especially wife beating; (3) seeking adventure in criminal and quasi-criminal activities; (4) marital instability, as evidenced by male infidelity and/or separation from their wives; and (5) frequent absences from home with peers, hanging out in local bars, etc. Wives also perceive their husbands' fast-living activities as precursors to criminal activity and subsequent arrest. These women view a conventional lifestyle as characterized by: (1) stable marriages; (2) generally steady employment among men, domestic orientation among women; (3) moderate drinking and drug use; (4) absence of domestic violence; and (5) a feeling of being "respectable" members of their communities.

These typologies provide a useful starting point for discussions of the over-all styles of accommodation prisoners' wives adopt toward the criminal justice system. Howell's (1972) observations of working class lifestyles is particularly relevant here. He observes, for instance, that these lifestyles represent ends of a continuum and, as such, are highly unstable, easily upset by external events, etc. Prisoners' wives frequently shift their lifestyle orientations towards one or another of these patterns in response to changes in their social situations which are occasioned by changes in their husbands' statuses.

CONTACTS AND COMMITMENT

The traditional conception of prison is that of a "closed system" or "total institution."[5] "Closed" prison systems are those with policies and practices that, in effect, sever most ties between prisoners and their families, friends, and communities. The thick walls which surround such prisons are thought not only to keep prisoners in, but to keep the rest of the world out. In recent years, however, prisons have begun to allow, and often to encourage, contacts with the outside world. This trend has arisen, in part, from the finding that prisoners with strong family or community ties are less likely to return to prison[6] and from the observation that inmates with family ties are more tractable. Thus, many prisons have introduced family programs which allow prisoners greater communication with their families and friends through visitation, letters, telephone, and home visits.[7] Accordingly, such reports have begun to break down the monolithic image of prisons as "total" institutions and to document the effects of such contacts on prisoners' adjustment to prison and parole.

Given this, it is important in describing the everyday worlds of prisoners' wives to examine closely the mechanisms wives and their incarcerated husbands use to maintain their relationships and how these may be reinforced by various types of prison systems. The kinds of contacts between husbands and wives during confinement and parole, and how wives handle these contacts, can influence their husbands' prison experience. Further, the conduct of married prisoners can exert ongoing influences on their spouses' lives on the outside.

Most of the current literature seems predicated on the assumption that contacts between prisoners and their families—

except for occasional visits—are minimal and that ties between inmates and the outside world are almost completely severed. However, these wives' accounts suggest that it is the continuing nature of such contacts that best explains the adjustments prisoners and their wives make to one another and to the situation in which they find themselves. Through their letters, phone calls and, in particular, prison visiting, these couples preserve their commitments to one another and maintain a thread of continuity through this most traumatic and disruptive episode in their lives.

POVERTY AND IMPRISONMENT

Grounded in the multi-dimensional worlds of prisoners' wives, this book raises important issues about women in regard to poverty, social class, and gender. Most recently there has emerged a literature that addresses the increasing poverty of women, especially for women and children who are in transition due to male desertion, divorce, death, etc. These studies are mainly quantitative studies on the "feminization of poverty" and tend to focus on structural trends in our society.[8] Only a few of these studies,[9] however, have focused on the economic consequences of divorce on the everyday lives of women and their children. The work presented here fills another important gap in this literature insofar as it contends that a segment of the population of women experiencing poverty are women and children whose status changes abruptly as a consequence of the male's arrest and imprisonment. Imprisonment itself is a socially structured experience which can have some similar economic consequences on the lives of women as well as some consequences which are unique to involuntary separation.

The findings here suggest that imprisonment, as do divorce and family life, reflects the gender-based organization of our society. Wives' accounts reveal that imprisonment exaggerates gender inequities and that imprisonment (as does divorce) necessarily comprises two parallel sets of experiences: those of the prisoners *and* those of their wives. Prisoners' wives' reactions to imprisonment reveal their secondary status in a gender stratified society; their social, legal, and economic status shapes every aspect of their lives. As a consequence, the conclusions drawn by the women raise questions about the extent to which women have been "liberated" in our society. Most prisoners' wives concur that in order to achieve conventional and manageable lifestyles, for themselves and their children, they must be married.

METHOD

This report represents a retrospective reconstruction of wives' accommodations to male criminality, imprisonment, and re-entry. It is based on material gathered from thirty Vermont women: (1) who had lived in common-law or as legally married to their men for at least six months prior to the men's arrest; and (2) whose husbands served at least six months in prison and had been incarcerated in either of two Vermont correctional facilities (hereafter referred to as Londonderry Correctional Facility, a traditional medium security prison, and as Newport Community Correctional Center, a community-based prison).

Contrary to what one might expect, wives of prisoners are not an easily identified population. Both the sources and the consequences of the stigmatization they experience are hidden; nothing, at first glance, marks them off from the great mass of those in a social welfare agency, a local bar, or a middle class neighborhood. Thus, in order to make contact with them, it is necessary to begin with their husbands.

In the present case, I decided that the most expedient method was to first define the population of "married"[10] men who were incarcerated in the Vermont prison system. From this population I selected men who had not been estranged from their wives at the time of their arrest—since I wanted to study on-going relationships—and who had been in prison for a sufficiently long period of time to become adjusted to the situation.

In order to facilitate contacts with the wives of these men, I decided to focus on a study population within a two-hour drive of Burlington, Vermont, my research base. Two facilities—the Londonderry Correctional Facility and the Newport Community Correctional Center—were most likely to hold married men whose wives would live within the specified area. My sub-group of married prisoners, consequently, was restricted to men drawn from these two facilities.

In theoretical terms, the selection of these two centers was fortuitous. Londonderry Correctional Facility is a traditional medium security prison designed to hold about eighty offenders drawn from throughout the state. It maintains three kinds of programs: diagnostic work for the courts and the Vermont Department of Corrections; medium security incentive-based programs for sentenced offenders; and short-term high security detention. Londonderry was considered the most "closed" prison in Vermont at the time the study was conducted. When prisoners in incentive-based programs have fulfilled their requirements, they are transferred to the community-based center nearest their home. Aside from visiting, emergency telephone use, and correspondence, Londonderry allows prisoners and their wives to make or receive unlimited telephone calls at specified times of the day, and, occasionally, to visit with one another off the prison grounds through the mechanism of supervised day passes. Thus, while relatively more "closed" than other Vermont institutions, Londonderry is by no means a "total institution" in the conventional mold.

As one of four community-based correctional facilities in Vermont,[11] Newport Community Correctional Center is structured somewhat differently. It holds, at any one time, approximately 132 men and women. Vermont's community correctional facilities are intended to "provide a bridge" for prisoners back into the free community. Newport is, therefore, charged not only with putting prisoners in touch with the educational, mental health, and employment resources of their communities, but with including prisoners' families in the reintegration process. In order to achieve this second goal, prisoners are granted liberal visiting privileges, unlimited correspondence, and free access to the telephone. In order to encourage prisoners to resume their relationships with their wives and families—as well as roles in the larger community—programs have been designed which include supervised day passes, unsupervised day passes, unsupervised weekend passes, work release, extended furlough and parole. As a community-based program, Newport services offenders who reside within Chittenden County so that they can be in a good position to maintain personal and work-related ties.

These two centers—the Londonderry Correctional Facility and the Newport Community Correctional Center—thus represent the range of variation in "openness" among Vermont prisons. At present, this range is obviously more restricted than in other states. In the last several years, the Vermont prison system as a whole has been informed by a "philosophy of corrections" that emphasizes the preservation of prisoners' family and social ties as a means of rehabilitating inmates and reintegrating them into their communities after release. Vermont's only nominally "maximum security" facility (Newfane prison) was closed in 1975.[12] It was a classic "closed" prison in which the routine and monotony of a prisoner's existence was heightened by strict surveillance of both correspondence and visitation. All other forms of contact with the outside were prohibited. With the implementation of the "new" philosophy, it was no longer needed.[13]

By using married prisoners drawn from these two facilities as the basis for the construction of the study sample, I was able effectively to represent the experiences of the wives of the vast majority of Vermont married prisoners at the time. Therefore, all prison records of both facilities were reviewed.

In order to define a population of currently incarcerated "married men," interviews were held with all sixty-nine prisoners so identified; sixty-five of them both signed an agreement to participate in this study and provided their wives' names and addresses. Thirty wives agreed to be interviewed.[14] They are ordinary women who come from all walks of life and represent a cross-section of prisoners' wives in America today. Twenty-six resided in urban or suburban areas while four lived in the more rural areas. The majority appeared working class and lower class in socio-economic status. Five were classified as middle class since they had at least some college education and/or held white collar jobs, and pursued a middle class round of activities. The wives' spouses were generally serving short sentences, on average, between six months and two years,[15] primarily for alcohol-related, property crimes. Few men had been convicted of crimes of violence, possession of heroin, or other more serious offenses.

Since this study concerns women's subjective perceptions and assessments of their experiences with their husbands' criminal activities, in-depth interviews were considered the single most important data source. Interviews were conducted with these women a minimum of two times over a twenty-four month period. The interviews ranged in length from three to ten hours, and were designed to elicit wives' perceptions and assessments of their experiences with male criminality, and with the crisis of enforced separation. Since the interviews conducted with the wives followed no rigid or fixed sequence, an interview guide was used to ensure that, while sequence might vary, the same basic topics were raised with each woman—for example, family life prior to arrest, husbands' and wives' history of illegal activities, wives' reactions to male criminality, arrest, and imprisonment, and reunion.

Most interviews were conducted in wives' homes. Only a few were held in my office. During each interview, I was able to take notes without apparently disturbing the wives.[16] There can be some methodological problems with collecting data on a deviant population. Due to the risk of exposure, it might seem that wives married to men who are officially labelled criminals would be less than candid with a researcher. However, my general impression is that, throughout these in-depth interviews, rapport between myself and prisoners' wives was quite good. The majority welcomed me with warmth, curiosity, and enthusiasm. In turn, I felt comfortable working with them. There were several factors, alone or in combination, that seemed to explain their openness. First, in many cases, husbands had told their wives to expect that I would get in touch with them. Hence, possible confusions about my intentions, etc., were minimized from the outset. Second, I had been married to a man who had been incarcerated in various Federal penitentiaries. I shared many experiences, feelings, and reactions with them. Wives repeatedly told me how rare it was that they could relate their reactions to someone who could appreciate the "uniqueness" of their experiences. Finally, since I was a university teacher, many felt that I would be in a good position to interpret these experiences to the conventional world and, perhaps, help others in a similar position. Many participants greeted me by saying, in effect, "Thank God somebody has discovered us! Everybody pays attention to the men. I feel that no one knows we're here and suffering too!"

Endless cups of coffee, whole packs of cigarettes, lot of talking, laughing, weeping, and sharing what was on women's minds— this captures the texture of the interviews. Talking for many hours with women makes the kind of rapport possible that allowed me to delve into places generally hidden from public view. Most wives felt that they had shared a deep part of their lives, their anguish, pain, joys, and boredom with me. I came to like these women and they knew it. And I think they came to regard me, first, as the wife of a prisoner who wanted to know more about the experiences of other prisoners' wives, and only secondly as a woman writing about these experiences.

Two other sources of data should be noted. First, a total of ten group meetings involving prisoners' wives were organized and observed. The primary topics discussed included married life prior to imprisonment, reactions to male criminality and enforced separation, and the prison system. Second, twelve wives contacted me by telephone at least every two weeks. Careful notes were kept on these telephone conversations, which typically lasted from fifteen minutes to an hour. Sometimes wives simply treated these calls as an opportunity to "sound off" to a sympathetic listener; at other times they were seeking help in solving particular problems or trying to mobilize resources.

This combination of research methods has yielded a rich source of data with which to capture the fullness of the lives of these women. Their life stories add to our understanding, not only of the crucial but often unexamined issues in the individual lives of such women, but also of criminals and the criminal justice system. The voices of these women reflect a diversity of experiences and emotional responses, and they speak for all women married to men who are less than they expected.

CHAPTER II

Women's Interpretations of Criminality Before Marriage

I, myself, go for the underdog. I feel that everyone should have a chance and that there is good in everyone and this good will come out if given a chance.

Most women who become prisoners' wives meet, court, and decide to marry their prospective husbands within a working class milieu. During courtship, almost all of the women in the study learned about their men's criminal records or activities and found ways to accommodate to these facts prior to marriage. To understand how they were able to do so, it is important to recognize that many of these women came from backgrounds in which criminal involvement was, if not totally acceptable, at least common. Peer group associations and peripheral involvement in crime early in life can exert lasting and powerful influences on later development and choices.

THE WOMEN SPEAK FOR THEMSELVES

Paula's description of how she met and courted her future husband is typical of many women's experiences.[1] Paula met Bud "on the street" and continued to woo and court him with full knowledge that he had a history of criminal activities. At the time, Paula was twenty-five years old and had two sons from a previous marriage. Bud was thirty years old and had a criminal record of such crimes as aggravated assault, armed robbery, and breaking and entering. Paula's account reveals the kind of explanations she used to view Bud in as normal a light as possible so as to preserve her commitment to marry him.

I always thought that if the right person came along, I'd live happily ever after. I felt that Bud and I were right for each other and we'd work out.

When I was married to my first husband, I almost had a nervous breakdown. He left me for a sixteen-year-old blond-headed female. I don't know why he did that. I had two boys by him. After he left, I had to go to work and I went to work in a machine shop on an assembly line doing wires for RCA and then I got laid off. Then I went to work in the hospital. My first husband has no interest in seeing the boys. He has nothing to do with them. I have managed mostly by myself and I managed mostly in tears! Some girlfriends of mine convinced me to go out one night for some beer and drinks. I ran into Bud at one of the bars we were drinking in. Things always start out so nice and end up so rotten.

When I first met him, he told me immediately that he had just got out of Newfane and that maybe I wouldn't want to see him. I told him that it didn't bother me and it didn't. I thought that people could think what they wanted to about Bud. I don't have any need to run him into the ground.

When we met he acted like a crazy person. He did things that I never saw anyone do. He did what he wanted to do and if people around him put him down, he'd do it regardless of them. I was shy and reserved and to me he did things that were different. When he was with me, he was just being himself. I liked him basically. He was exciting to me. He was working in a wood place that made cabinets. He did the set-up on the machines. We began to live together and that was fine.

It was great! He did what he wanted to do and I did what I wanted to do and then we did things together. We didn't hover around each other. When he was here, it was great to be together. We lived together for three or four months and then he was arrested and went to Bridgewater for three or four months for observation and I traveled to Bridgewater to see him.

I was pregnant with Jake then and I thought perhaps he'd straighten out with the separation and the fact that I was alone and having a baby. I thought he'd learn from that experience. I didn't feel that it was a great thing that he did but I figured he'd be in a short time and we'd have Jake. I felt that Jake would bring us closer together.

I felt that if I stick with him and if I sincerely showed him that I would wait then he'd know that I wanted him. I felt that he would come through because I'd be there when he wanted me. I felt then that he'd be able to trust me and I figured that since I was pregnant, that would help more with keeping him out of trouble. But it didn't work that way.

SOCIAL BACKGROUNDS

Age, Education, and Employment History

The women in the study group ranged in age from nineteen to forty-four, although more than 50 percent were under thirty at the time of the initial interview. Their husbands were also young, ranging in age from twenty-one to fifty-five, with more than 50 percent thirty or younger.[2]

None of the working class women found academic work pleasurable or interesting. Sixteen had not completed high school. One woman reported some college education and two had four or more years of higher education. Very few women who had not attended college or university reported having considered any other career than getting married and having children. All the women with some post-secondary education intended to pursue a career.

More of the men than the women (thirteen *vs.* eleven) had completed high school. Eleven men had less than high school training; five had some college education. Of the thirteen who finished high school, eight received high school equivalency diplomas while in prison. While the men's general level of education was higher than the women's, wives reported that for the most part, the men also found academic work uninteresting.

Fifteen women had steady jobs prior to meeting their prospective mates. Ten held jobs as factory or service workers such as waitresses, chamber-maids, nurses aides, or domestics. Five of the fifteen worked in clerical or supervisory jobs, such as administrative assistants, accountants, secretaries, etc. Three of the women had attended some kind of post-secondary educational institution. The remainder had been homemakers taking care of pre-school children.

Short-term employment seems to be the norm. Among working wives, there was little expectation of continuity or perceived need for stable employment. Work had not provided them with either status or adequate monetary rewards. Only three women considered their jobs satisfying and intended to keep them permanently. Upon marrying, nine of the working women kept their jobs.

Only five men had been steadily employed when they met their prospective spouses. Two were in white collar occupations (counselor for a social service agency, and a clerk), and two held semi-skilled jobs (factory worker, apprentice with a plumbing service), while one was self-employed in a well-established business. Nine other men worked, when they could, at seasonal or short-term jobs such as construction, house painting, farm work, and so forth. Thirteen men were unemployed at the time they courted their women.

There were, however, appreciable changes in the husbands' work histories after marriage. The number of men who were gainfully employed decreased; only nine remained employed. Of these, six worked as un-skilled, semi-skilled, or industrial and service workers. The majority of jobs were seasonal. One man continued as a counselor in a social service agency and the self-employed business man continued his work. Two men were getting money by stealing or drug dealing. According to the wives eighteen men were unemployed.

Early Family Life

The women who later become prisoners' wives usually learn about their prospective mates' social backgrounds during courtship. In many respects, these tend to be consistent with their own. However, a higher proportion of the men come from homes that had been broken by desertion, separation, divorce, or death of one parent than the wives. Half of the wives (15) in the study population reported that, for them and their men, family life had tended to be unstable, uncertain, and unpredictable. However, insofar as having two parents married and living together can be taken as a measure of stability, the other half of the wives grew up under relatively stable circumstances. But of twenty-nine men, only seven came from intact homes: twenty-one came from families broken by divorce, separation, desertion, or death.[3]

Most women in the study group had struggled with poverty and reported that they and their husbands came from families in which periods of employment alternated with unemployment or receipt of government assistance. Family violence, alcoholism, and crime had been prevalent in both the women's and men's lives, and violent episodes often erupted following heavy consumption of alcohol by one or more family members. Several women reported that they had been the targets of violent, alcohol-related attacks, and incest:

> I'm like my mother. She stuck with my father for twenty years—stuck with his drinking, beatings, and whoring around. My father was an alcoholic and he attempted to molest me when I was young. I didn't tell anyone for fear that they would blame me and it has sat with me for years. You see, there is so much incest in my own family. My father's brother has two children by his sister. Things like that went on in my family. My father was also abusive to me and to my family. I never felt that I was a good person and I still don't.

Eight of the men had also been periodically subjected to violent abuse. One woman described how her man had been abused by an alcoholic father:

> When Nelson's father was mad he used his fist. He had a cat o' nine tails that he usually kept close to him. He used this constantly on the kids. The beatings those kids got! There was absolutely no talking back to his father. He would sit at the dinner table and if a kid didn't like the food, he beat the child unconscious. . . . His father went on binges. No one ever knew when he was likely to go out on these binges. Then he would come home drunk and ready to fight viciously . . . [Nelson's] mother was beaten into submission. I understand Nelson and his father and mother. His mother had a third grade education and his father was a beaten man. They married when they were seventeen and sixteen years old, and soon afterwards began to have one child after another. There wasn't any birth control. So much poverty and children. Some people's minds break from this and the only thing that is left is cruelty. This is what happened to his father even though he was an intelligent man and lived by his wits.

Many of the women, themselves, came from families in which at least one member had spent time in jail or prison. Nine indicated that more than one family member had done so and only nine reported that no family member had ever served a jail or prison sentence. Much of this crime was described as alcohol or drug related and, typically, male-centered. Fathers, male siblings, and other male relatives tended to be involved in "disorganized," petty, irregular, or haphazard crime. In a few cases, this was true of *all* male family members. As one women recalled her family's criminal history:

> You know my family? You might have heard their name. They are notorious here in the Burlington area. The name is the Kevin family. My uncles who are twins are gay and people talked about that. I've had to fight that name all my life. I had to constantly fight to show people that I wasn't like them. . . . All my father's brothers have been in Newfane Prison for robbery, hit and run, manslaughter, child molesting, assault, you name it. But as far as my immediate family, my father has been arrested numerous times for DWI and for disturbing the peace. Once he went to jail.

Another woman talked about her brothers' involvement in criminal activities:

> My brother was arrested for selling hot guns to a detective in New York. My older brother did six months for stealing. My father has given up on another brother who is now selling drugs in New York at Russell's Point. This is where my family lives. My family has always been in trouble.

In spite of their histories of criminal activity, none of the women's families could be characterized as criminally oriented in the classic sense; some family members were periodically or episodically involved in crime, while others were not. Nevertheless, the majority of the women became acquainted with both illegal activities and socially disapproved patterns of behavior within their own families. Their notions about crime, police, courts, and jails were formed at an early age.

Many of the women reported that their men had also come from families in which one or more members had been involved in criminal activities. Siblings and other relatives, usually male, were often involved in such "disorganized" crimes as aggravated assault, burglary, bar brawls, auto theft, and armed robbery. Many such crimes were directly related to alcoholism. One woman, describing the kinds of crimes her man's family had committed, reported:

> His stepfather was in Newfane Prison in 1974 for armed robbery. His family deals in drugs. You name it, they got it. They're in

volved in stolen goods; they drive without licenses; they do B &
E's [i.e., breaking and entering]. . . . His brother stabbed two kids
and is always beating up someone.

Another woman reported:

Joe, his brother, was in Northeastern School and has been in jail.
He's on and off in jail. He writes rubber checks. Brother Greg is in
jail now. He took the firemen's payroll. He noticed that a fireman
would come into the bank and just ask for the payroll. No one
asked him for identification. So Greg disguised himself as a fireman and went into the bank and received the payroll. Paul is the
upstanding person in the family. He's an Army person. He was the
one son that they wanted. Both his mother and his father admired
him. Some of the younger nephews have been in jail for dealing
drugs. Everyone in his family, except for Nelson and his mother,
are outstanding alcoholics.

Only a few (nine women, seven men) came from relatively
stable families in which the work ethic and roots in a community were highly valued.

Peer Associations

Not only did most of the prisoners' wives have family backgrounds similar to those of their men, but in their early adult
years, they also established similar kinds of friendships. Most of
these women had been exposed to crime through peer associations. Seventeen reported that more than one of their friends had
been involved in criminal activities and/or had been arrested, although there was no discernible pattern to the types of offenses
involved. Their friends had drifted into the kinds of disorganized
crimes that involve little planning or skill, frequently under the
influence of alcohol or drugs.

The women reported that a higher proportion of their men's
friends than their own, had been involved in criminal offenses—
and, consequently, with jails and prisons. According to the
women, twenty-four men had more than one friend who had
been in trouble with the law and had subsequently been incarcerated. Moreover, the majority of men had a wide network of
friends who participated in disorganized crime. For instance,
one woman said:

We lived in Newgate and we had an apartment over a bar. I knew the guys in the bar so Earl wouldn't go there and get drunk. He drank with his friends. They were murderers and people like that. Some of them were good friends of Earl's. Not all of his friends were bad people. but those who were bad did a lot of stealing and B & E's. They went out of their way to terrify the people who they felt sucked. They'd harass or steal from these people.

Many men with previous convictions had met some of their "old friends" while in prison and had renewed these friendships. Although both the women and men had criminal associates, only a small fraction tended to "hang out" exclusively with them. Most also had friends who led stable, conventional lives.[4] Slightly more than half of the women and men in the study were familiar with criminal activity. Through their friends, they had learned about crimes, courts, and prisons. A number of women and most of the men had visited friends in jail; thus criminal activity and its consequences were not shocking. Moreover, throughout much of their recent lives, these women had been associated with men who had direct experience with criminal activity.

CRIMINAL EXPERIENCE

Female Criminality

The women in the study group were most likely to have been directly involved in criminal enterprises during their adolescent and early adult years. Twenty-four women had been involved in at least one form of delinquent or criminal behavior such as running away from home, truancy, sexual promiscuity, and occasional shoplifting. Six admitted to committing such misdemeanors as driving without a license, disturbing the peace, or loitering. Seven had participated in serious felonies such as property crime, armed robbery, grand larceny, burglary, and check forging. In general, the women's participation—in either delinquency or adult criminality—had been sporadic, impulsive, experimental, and of brief duration. Many reported that they had acted on impulse or at the instigation of their peers to relieve the boredom of "having nothing to do." For example, a young woman described how, during late adolescence, she and a group of friends shoplifted and once broke into a commercial establishment:

> I did a lot of shoplifting. I can remember one time when I was with five girls. We just decided to clean out the store. I got me a nice coat that day. I put it on and I walked out of the store with it. One of my friends wanted a wig and I just took it. It's stupid. I'll never do it again. Before I was married and living with Barry, I had nothing to do. Now I have something to do. . . . Me and two other girls—it's stupid, I don't know why we did it, it was just stupid— we were very high one night and we felt big. We had gone to a school dance and smoked some pot. So stupid. We decided to see if we could break into this garage. We broke a window in the back of the garage and then we walked out the front door. Just at that time the cops were doing their rounds. We didn't take nothing and we just did it to see whether we could do it.

Only one woman had been involved in crimes from which she derived some form of monetary gain, claiming to have been directly involved in several armed robberies and burglaries to alleviate financial problems.

There is a striking contrast between the majority of working-class women in the study who had at least a passing acquaintance with petty crime, and the eight women from settled working and middle-class backgrounds. None of the latter had ever been arrested and all claimed to have been committed to a conventional life revolving around family, school and/or work; they reported little inclination to threaten their ties to these institutions.

A considerable proportion of the women from both types of backgrounds, however, had at one time or another, consumed both illegal drugs and alcohol. Seventy-three percent of the women, including half of those pursuing middle class lifestyles, had used drugs, of which marijuana was the most popular. Only two women had used "hard" drugs such as heroin or amphetamines. This is not surprising since most of these women lived in communities where drugs and alcohol were readily accessible and recreational use was common. Only six women had been active members of drug-oriented groups prior to marriage. Four had been heavily involved in the "head" subculture, i.e., they had been heavy users of psychedelics such as marijuana, cocaine, and LSD. Two had been connected with the "dope fiend" sub-culture centering around heroin use. One young woman de-scribed her initial entry into the "head" subculture during her late adolescence:

> I lived a whole different lifestyle than his. In the middle 'sixties, drugs came to my town. My older brother got into drugs and I idealized him. I wanted to do what he did. I was in parochial school at the time and I would spy on him and follow him around in order to save him. I then met his friends and got into the drug culture of Greenfield. It was a small group of people since it was not as widely accepted as now. My parents didn't want me to be like Janis Joplin—into acid and everything. But there hasn't been a drug that I haven't tried. I've tried heroin and we had Friday night Blue Morphine parties. We would get together and take some mor-phine and just mellow out every Friday night. At that time, I was committed to the scene. I even bought my clothes from the thrift shops, I did things on impulse. I went to California for two months after I borrowed a car from my parents.

Another woman, a single parent of a pre-schooler, described her involvement in the speed subculture:

> I shot so much speed and I don't know why I'm alive today. I shot downs as well. I was sticking needles into my arm twelve or four-teen times a day. I had Shaun living with me during all this. I lived with fourteen other drug addict friends in a trailer in Alderson. We were all doing the same thing. Most of them were from Alderson and Elkhart. In order to get money, I sold speed. So fifteen or six-teen people came to my house every day to buy it and I didn't even get busted. I got it from another dealer. He fronted it to me. There is loads of speed in Lakewood. I was also drinking a lot of beer. I drank quarts of beer every day and then I added liquor to that. We all looked out for Shaun. I couldn't have taken care of him my-self. . . . I was living with a seventeen-year-old boy. He was into the same thing. I was also getting welfare. We drank speed, ate it up, and mixed it with alcohol. We were all into the same thing and got along fine. There was always enough speed to go around. I just don't know how it went on for so long. I drank so much alcohol and I'd black out for days on end.

Despite the varied histories of these women, only five had ever been arrested and only three had gone to juvenile or adult court. Only one woman had been sent to a state juvenile facility and none had been convicted of felonies. One women who was arrested prior to meeting her current husband recalled the circumstances surrounding that event:

> It had to do with Lenny, the guy I went with before Frank. Some guy broke into my house and tried to rape me. Lenny came in and beat the guy up and then shot him. Lenny was sent to Bridgewater. I blamed myself for what happened. If he hadn't shot the guy up, then he'd have been with me. Lenny wanted a gun and he asked me to smuggle it into Bridgewater. I smuggled it in and Lenny got caught. Anyway, Lenny ratted out on me and I was busted. They picked me up in Burlington. . . . I went to court and was acquitted because of reasons of insanity. They felt that I went through so much because I saw this guy shot. This was the first time I was arrested. I was cranking a lot then [taking speed]. I did a lot of cranking. I smoked pot and I feel there is nothing wrong with it except it's illegal. I've done THC and MDA. Once I dropped some acid.

Male Criminality

Crime, then, was not foreign to the women in the study population and they were not shocked to discover that it played a role in their men's backgrounds. At the time they met their wives, all twenty-two men who had previous criminal records had immediately acknowledged their criminal backgrounds. Some had informed their women not only about their past criminal behavior, but about their current status with the criminal justice system.

Seventy-five percent of the men had been imprisoned before ever meeting their wives. Eight had been incarcerated at least four times; fourteen had been in prison three times or less. Most of the convictions were for such crimes against property as burglary, possession of stolen goods, and auto theft; four were for crimes against persons; three were for paper crimes and one was for lewd and lascivious behavior.[5] These men had spent little time planning crimes or developing skills and techniques. As disorganized criminals, they committed crimes irregularly and haphazardly. However, they continued to commit crimes into their adult years and with some frequency.

INTERPRETING MALE CRIMINALITY

Meeting Prisoners

Most of the women were young when they met their prospective husbands. Some were still in high school or were recent graduates; others, not quite so young, had been previously married. Thirteen women had married at least once before meeting their prospective mates. According to the women's accounts, eleven men had been married at least once before. These earlier marriages had, in general, been difficult and problems such as alcoholism, drug abuse, violence, infidelity, and sexual deviance were common.

Almost all met their spouses within their own communities, through relatives, friends, schools, community dances, or neighborhood bars. Seven of the women met their men in prisons and three married them there. None of the women had known their husbands more than six months before marrying and almost two-thirds of the couples married within three months of meeting. Nearly all the couples who legally married had lived together first.

Of the seven who had met their husbands in prison, all perceived prisons as alternative social settings, in which to meet new men and form relationships. Some women traveled to prisons on visiting days, often accompanied by female friends or relatives, to "have a good time." Others met their men inadvertently when accompanying another to visiting hours. One woman, for instance, recalled the circumstances under which she met her future husband as follows:

> He was in the Correctional Center at St. Albert. My daughter was going on sixteen and she met a guy at Londonderry. She wrote him and he wrote back and told her that he wanted to see her. I said I could take her down to the Center so she could see him. Somehow, this kid told Matt that there was someone who came to visit with him. Matt came into the visiting room and he managed to get my phone and address. He asked like a grown-up and not a kid. He wasn't giggling and fooling around. I spent most of my time during visiting looking at him. Later, my daughter and I talked about it. Then I mentioned him to my girlfriend. After that, he was out of

my mind until I got a letter from him. I answered the letter just to
be friendly. A couple of days later, I felt like calling him and he
was waiting for me to call. He said that he knew I'd call. One
thing led to another.

Another woman told a similar story:

I took a girlfriend down to see her boyfriend at Newfane. She set
me up to see another guy. I was waiting at the bubble and I looked
through the window. I saw this tall guy with glasses. I said, "What
a hunk!" Then I told my girlfriend that I really didn't want that
son-of-a-bitch, that he was a con. No more was said or done. Then
Rudi got out and he was supposed to give me a message. He never
did. He ended up in a Massachusetts jail. He wrote me and I became a messenger for Al and Rudi. Then Rudi wrote and asked me
to write him more. I've always been for the underdog. I'm always
doing my Girl Scout duty for the underdog. I kept writing to Rudi.

From the wives' reports, it appears that the men cultivated
these new relationships in the same way they might have participated in weight-lifting or "mind building" (*i.e.*, education).
They were all ways to get by while "doing time." Romance,
courting, and intimacy flourished during visiting days. There
was the excitement of exchanging letters, looking forward to the
next telephone conversation, and having visitors (or, for the
woman, visiting new-found boyfriends). Courting appeared to
ease the "pains of imprisonment" for the incarcerated men, and
the women, perhaps flattered by the attention they received, pursued these men with enthusiasm. Three couples married while
the men were still in prison. One of the wives described her
prison wedding:

It was weird! Our best man had been in the hole for fourteen days.
He had had no bath in days. They just yanked him out of the hole
and brought him up to be our best man. We had all kinds of cooperation from the lieutenants on duty that day. We weren't
checked and we smuggled in all kinds of booze and we were married in the conference room. It was really a nice little ceremony.
They kept everybody out of the way; there were no guards involved, no guards in the conference room. My sister was maid of
honor and my sister-in-law was scared to death because she's never
been inside a prison before. But it was very nice; we were allowed
to have a few friends in who were residents, and their girlfriends
and wives.

Another woman, then recently married in Londonderry, recalled a more traditional wedding ceremony:

> When he was in Londonderry, we were married. The wedding took place in the correctional center. It was a nice wedding but it was unusual to say the least. His nephew gave me some flowers and I was all dressed up. We were married and then we had coffee and there was dancing. We had guitar music and our pictures were taken. It was nice and that surprised me.

Whether their men were found "on the streets," in prison, or hiding from the law, the most common reason the women gave for their decisions to marry was no different from that which working-class women usually give: they had "fallen in love."

Accepting the Past

No matter how they met and courted the men they eventually married, most women developed similar perceptions of their criminal activities: that crime "did not matter." This made it possible for the women to interact with their men and relate to them independent of their criminal histories.

The primary mechanism by which the wives convinced themselves—and possibly others—that their men's criminal activities were unimportant was the "sad tale."[6] A sad tale is a selective and often distorted arrangement of facts that highlights an extremely dismal past and, presumably, explains an individual's present state. The teller of the sad tale attempts to rationalize, rather than condone or excuse, unacceptable (*i.e.,* deviant or criminal) behavior. Sad tales are typically employed when it is no longer possible to cover up or deny deviant behavior. In the course of in-depth interviews, it became clear that the chief function of both covering up and sad tales was to minimize the importance of the men's criminality for the wives themselves. Both strategies were employed to create the impression, or maintain the illusion, that these men were no different from anyone else and, therefore, acceptable candidates for marriage. Further, prisoners encouraged their wives to cover up their criminal activities. Twenty-three women reported, for instance, that their men assisted them in denying their criminal status by emphasizing their more conventional roles and identities and by expressing their desire to settle down into a conventional lifestyle.

According to the women, the men frequently presented themselves either as repentant and reformed or as underdogs. The repentant was one who had sown his wild oats and was now really a "good guy" who just wanted to settle down with a wife, make babies, get a steady job and buy a house in the country. One woman who met and courted her husband in jail recalled his assurances that he was reformed:

> He felt that jail had changed him. All he wanted to do was get out and get married and settle down and lead a life like anyone else. He told me that he's learned his lessons the hard way. I had this feeling that he would stay out of trouble. He got out on May 2nd and we got married on May 20th. I love him. And that was the best reason to get married.

Other prisoners were able to win over their women by projecting the image of an underdog. Fifteen women reported that their men appeared in need of rescue from fast-living or from their "miseries" (*e.g.*, parental abuse, drinking, rootlessness, criminal behavior). One woman said that she hoped to rescue her husband from his extensive involvement in drugs and check forging:

> He kept telling me that his main problem was that all he needed was a family to support, and someone behind him, and he wouldn't go back to jail. He had never really had anyone who really cared about him. I tried to help him. I spent my whole time trying to help him. I tried to keep him away from drugs. At the time he looked so pitiful that I felt that he really wanted to have a family. I guess it was crusade time for me. It was when I felt, "Let's do something great for someone."

Since many of the wives viewed themselves as champions of the underdog, they were able to believe that, through love, patience, nurturing, and concern, they could change their men. As one women put it:

> Rex was a very hard, cold, and bitter person. The only thing he loved was himself and his car. He didn't care about anything. I felt that I had to change that. He has never opened up to people. Gradually I convinced him that there was a different life he could lead. I convinced him that there was more to life than prisons and fast women. [How did you do that?] With a lot of love and a lot of patience and I just tried to be as patient as possible.

The theme that "love can save my man" constantly ran through the wives' accounts. Two women, both of whom had formed ties with men who already had extensive criminal records, reflected on their reasons for marrying them:

> Arlene: I always liked the underdog. I felt with Frank that he was either going to rip me off or he was going to be decent. I knew that I was going to be involved with him and I didn't want to be involved with another man.

> Bea: Their family ties were bad and they only had us. . . . It was a challenge for me. I kept asking myself if I could save him, if I could help him. I'd been through a bad marriage. I felt that if I could help someone, then maybe God would forgive me.

The men reinforced these beliefs by presenting themselves as never having had anyone to rescue them from their miseries. All they needed to make it was the saving love and nurturance of a good woman. The men readily told sad tales centered on the abuses they had suffered in families devastated by alcoholism, violence, poverty, and crime. And who could have been unsympathetic to the hard years these men had growing up? There was pathos in the women's presentations of their men's family lives:

> He told me about how one time his stepfather put him in a tub for a bath. Then his stepfather held him in the tub and burned him with boiling hot water. He was about four years old then. Rex has been blamed for things he didn't do. He has a lot of hate involved and a lot of resentment.

These themes recurred constantly in the women's accounts: their men never had a chance to make good, had been victims of precarious and chaotic families, had fallen in with the wrong crowds, or had been drawn into the criminal activities of fathers or brothers. They were driven to criminal acts by external forces that they were unable to resist:

> I felt sorry about the way Mark was brought up. He was brought up by his father who was an alcoholic and beat him continually. At eleven, Mark was completely on his own. He got in with a bunch of criminals and he doesn't know anything different. I see that his problem is his hanging around with this bunch of criminals.

By accepting these sad tales, the women convinced themselves that their men were nearly blameless—that they were acted upon rather than acting. And, because of these convictions, they were better able to tolerate their men's criminal pasts. Further, they emphasized that "it's the man who counts, not his record." By adopting this position, of course, wives were able to sustain the belief that there was nothing different or unusual about their men, *e.g.*, that they were "good people":

> I knew he had been in jail before. I knew that he had a string of DWI's and B & E's. All of these he did under the influence of alcohol. These were his main crimes. He's a good person. It's hard to convince him that he is. He doesn't think well of himself. He felt he was going to hell for what he did. He figures that everything he's done is bad. These are minor things but deep down inside him is what counts. I feel that he's the man underneath all that. My concern is for the man and not the crime.

By disassociating the men from their actions, these women also avoided the fact that, in marrying prisoners or criminals, they were implicitly assuming marginal status. By defining the men as "normal," they might also define themselves as normal. Their convictions were buttressed, in many cases, by assertions that everyone had been dishonest at one point or another; the only difference between their men and all the others was that they had been caught. Their men's criminal enterprises were no more exploitative or immoral than many legally sanctioned ones. In rationalizing her husband's possession and concealment of stolen property, one wife maintained:

> That doesn't bother me at all! Whether he's been in jail or not doesn't matter. Everyone does some wrong and we all have to pay for our mistakes. He's paying for the things he's done wrong. . . . He's as good as anyone whether he's been in jail or not. I feel strongly about that.

Another woman said:

> I didn't mind his criminal involvement. I figured there but for the grace of God go I. I figured he was the one who got caught a lot more. He wasn't doing anything different from other people but he was the one to be caught.

Women also stressed that what had happened in the past was over and done with. As a rule, the women did not seek out details of their husbands' criminal activities. Rather, they focused on the men themselves and on the possibilities open to them. Asked why her husband was arrested, one wife replied:

> I think it was a B & E. Maybe an armed robbery. He hasn't told me all about it. He's told me parts of it. I figured his past is his past. I love him for him and not for his past.

Occasionally the men, or their women, presented the men's pasts as attractive or exciting—nonthreatening stories about memorable intervals in their lives.

> He was heavily into the drug scene and he thought he was the big time. But he only sold one pound a week and he tended to sell most of his drugs to his brothers in St. James. He talked about his past life as a junkie and a life of selling drugs. . . . When he came to live with me, he brought along pictures of him behind bars in all these places and he keeps the newspaper clippings about what he had done. He's very proud of this book. I thought that his stories were simply wild stories and had no reality to them. They didn't frighten me. He told me about all these wild parties he went to and that he was in a motorcycle gang and he made himself appear like he was a member of the Hell's Angels. I don't remember all of them but I know there was nothing to them. It's the way he tells the stories that makes them not seem so threatening. They appear like good, charming stories.

In marrying their men, the women for the most part accepted a deviant lifestyle. It is clear from their accounts that many had been prepared for the status of "criminal's wife" by their own social backgrounds, characterized by early exposure to crime, courts, and prisons. Perhaps the most striking feature of these women's accounts of courtship and marriage is the extent to which they parallel conventional, sentimental notions of "love and marriage" in the larger society. The overriding theme was the expectation that, through love and forbearance, they would be able to induce the men to settle down to a conventional lifestyle. In this sense, the role behavior of prisoners' wives is similar to that of other women of the same age.

CHAPTER III

Before Arrest: Domestic Life, Male Criminality and "Fast Living"

> I worked all the time and have nothing to show for it. When he worked all was fine. We looked as though we were holding our own. But when he wasn't working, then things got rough. He felt that it took away his manly dignity when I worked and he sat at home. He would have liked me to be out of work when he was. He didn't work for long because he wanted the carefree life. He wanted to run around, drink, and party.

The literature on prisoners' families has been largely based on studies that used questionnaires or structured interviews to explore the relationships between abstractly specified variables.[1] Such studies yield some information about the relationship between "pre-marital adjustment" and "marital adjustment during separation." But it is difficult to reconstruct the broader context within which these adjustments occur from the available data. Conversations with prisoners' wives reveal two kinds of marital patterns established prior to the husbands' arrest, conviction, and imprisonment: "fast living" and "square living."[2] Most women who subsequently become prisoners' wives expect that, having "sown their wild oats," their husbands will settle down and begin to live moderate, restrained lives. Instead, they often wind up with "troubles"—"fast living" and more encounters with crime and the criminal justice system.

THE WOMEN SPEAK FOR THEMSELVES

Peggy, aged 21, was married to a man with a history of theft and of receiving stolen property. They had been married six years prior to the events of arrest and incarceration and had three pre-school children. Peggy reconstructed her married life to a man who was intermittently employed, criminally active, and pursued some fast-living lifestyle patterns. Her experiences are typical of other wives who had extensive knowledge of their husbands' criminal enterprises and fast-living lifestyle patterns:

I met him in February and in September we got married. I lived with him for three months and then got married. I had just quit working at Champlain Motel as a chambermaid. He was working for the Coca Cola Corporation. He put bottles in cases.

When we lived together, I couldn't ask for a better man. We went to the movies, he took me out to eat. He then was working in a gum factory. He helped me clean the house once in a while. He bought stuff for the house whenever he had extra money. He bought us clothes. He'd go with me to pick out the clothes. He's pretty reliable. That's what I miss.

We first lived in Massachusetts and Gary got in trouble for receiving stolen property. He received two years probation. He had taken some hot calculators from some kids. At that time, everything went berserk. He left me once and went to live in St. Albert with his friends. He felt that the kids were driving him crazy. At that time we had two kids and one was on the way. His mother told me that he couldn't take the responsibility for another child and that's why he left. He was scared and left.

We got back together again and we tried to work out our relationship once more. But he started hitting me again and we started arguing. He lost his job and he felt very frustrated and took his anger out on me. It was my fault that he lost his job. Everything was my fault and I'd get beaten. I got tired of all that. At Thanksgiving, I went to my mother's house in St. Albert and I told him that I was going to stay here. He then moved here. Everything went along fine until he met up with his buddy Ernest. He then began to drink, steal, and receive stolen property with Ernest. I didn't want him to do it. I knew he was going to get caught and I told everyone about it in order to try to stop him, even Mother and Daddy. I told him to stay at home and I told him I was going to leave him again. He didn't care. We were on welfare at the time and he felt that we needed extra money. He would get this extra money one way or another and I couldn't stop him.

Just at night time the Dracula in him would come out. The monster. Not every night. Once in a while at night we'd go for a walk, or listen to the stereo, or sit on the porch together. This would happen when Ernest didn't come down. Ernest didn't come down every night and only when Ernest did come down would he go out. I had to feed Ernest and this was hard because we were on welfare. And Ernest eats and eats. He's really a eater. Once in a while, he'd pitch in some food. But when Ernest came down, they'd go out later that night. Ernest had a car. He'd only take us swimming if we had the money for the gas. "I ain't having him no more." Gary would get mad when I said that. He didn't like that. I told him that I do have some say around here and he'd say, "Who pays the rent?" So Ernest kept coming down and they would go stealing.

I told him to take this stolen stuff out of the house whenever he brought it home. He brought guns and said that we needed the extra money. I told him to get that stuff out of the house now. Who knows who's watching us? We could lose our kids. I knew and I didn't feel right about it. He wouldn't listen to me and he just put the stuff away.

Then he sold all this stolen stuff to a second hand store. The man who worked at the second hand store was working with the police. He found out that some of the stuff was known as hot and he reported it to the police.

He's had two previous arrests. In Massachusetts he was arrested for receiving stolen property. Also he was arrested for forgery. The first arrest, for receiving stolen property, he was going to court. They didn't hold him. He paid a $25 fine and then he was let out. While he was waiting to go to court, he brought some hot stuff from the mayor's office. They saw him buying the stuff and arrested him again. He got two years' probation. I was scared and I thought that I would lose this pregnancy but it worked out. My father tried to get him a job up here but he couldn't get him one. Gary's probation officer told him he could come up here and look for work. He looked for a job and he couldn't find one. We went on welfare.

In Massachusetts, we had a checking account. Our house was robbed and our check book was missing after the robbery. Gary put a stop on the checks because they were robbed. Then they arrested him and they said that he had forged his own checks. Gary said that he didn't do it and he got a year on probation. I know it was true and they did get stolen. The window of our house was broken and the checks were gone and our clothes were taken. The jewelry was missing. And we called the police.

He commits these crimes because sometimes he acts childish. He does what he wants to do. Only way he could support us on welfare was to get extra money or stuff to help make life a little easier. He doesn't really talk to me and when he gets angry all this stuff comes out. He keeps things bottled up.

He also wanted to get away from me. Once in a while I'd nag him. He wanted to get away from the house and the kids. If he wanted to go somewhere and I'd nag him to take me, he'd say, "Oh, shut up, you're staying home." He felt that he didn't have enough freedom and we didn't have the money for a babysitter. He just wanted to get out and do what he wanted to do.

I don't know why he chose this criminal stuff. He didn't tell me much about his life before he met me. I still don't know about his past.

The next excerpt comes from a meeting in which two wives of sexual offenders discuss the extent to which they knew about their husbands' sexually deviant behavior. Nancy has been married eleven years to a man who had no prior criminal record. They had one daughter ten years old. They pursued a middle class round of life, a lifestyle not typical of the other women interviewed. She described how she was unaware that her spouse had raped two women. Vicki was married one year to a man who also had no prior criminal record. They shared three children from Vicki's previous marriage (ages four, seven, and nine) and one two-year-old from their marriage. They had pursued a conventional working class lifestyle. She reconstructed how she came to learn about her husband's sexually deviant behavior and her fear that her husband's deviant behavior was a precursor to his committing a sexual offense.

NANCY. We were having some very hard times. Both of us were on opposite shifts. During the last year and a half there was a lot of shit going on. Sara and I had a bad automobile accident and I was very preoccupied with dealing with my own feelings about the accident. I began to gain weight and I got up to 260 pounds and I just freaked out. I decided to lose this weight and then I lost 100 pounds. At the same time, I was in therapy after the accident. I needed help in dealing with my feelings. I was centering on myself. As far as I knew everything at home was hunky-dory. I didn't think anything was wrong. That was the furthest thing from my mind. But we had pulled further apart. When we were together, and that was rare, we did have a good time. But it was very superficial. There wasn't any real talk. He was doing some weird stuff at IBM—exposing the corruption in management there. He got real paranoid. It leaked out who was responsible for the uncovering of the corruption and some of the people there came down hard on him. I didn't understand the pressure involved in what he was doing. He got to a point that he felt he had no one to talk to. He felt that he had real problems and there was no one to listen to him.

VICKI. Did you know about it?

NANCY. No, I didn't. Last winter he was very depressed. I just told him, "Why work there, when it depresses you?" I couldn't understand it. I saw it was very simple. He should just quit. He kept saying, "Things will change when I'm on the day shift." He kept saying that he wanted a normal life. He went like that from February to June. He was suicidal then and he went and did the second rape. The first rape occurred around February. We always had an active sex life and I didn't know that this was going on or that there was a problem.

VICKI. That's very different from what happened to me. I found Charles in the living room masturbating. He then behaved like my father and just said to me, "Go to bed!" I went off and it was like that all the time. In my first marriage, I dealt with pot smoking and heavy drinking, and then my father was an alcoholic. I knew how to deal with alcoholism and drugs but I didn't know how to deal with this sex thing.

NANCY. I think the nature of the problems were quite different. Charles had a sex problem and Kevin didn't.

VICKI. Charles would watch Channel 2 and have sex while he was watching. It's that French station. Then he started buying magazines. He'd pay seven dollars for a magazine. I said to him, "You perverted bastard! I don't want these magazines around the house for the children to see." But he would buy them and hide them. I'd find them though. He then said to me, "You have the problem. I don't have any problems." He almost convinced me that I had the problem.

NANCY. He didn't want me to know. He's not stupid. He felt that he would lose me and Sara if we knew. He did these things when he was sick and mixed up. The second one took place in June.

VICKI. Why didn't he talk to you?

NANCY. He felt that he couldn't talk to me. I was doing so well at the time—so it appeared. I had, in his eyes, everything going for me. I had this job and I was improving myself. I had both girl friends and men friends. He was jealous of what he thought I had and he felt even more inadequate. He felt so shitty on the inside and yet he looked like he was doing well on the outside.

   Then one evening there was this knock on the door and I opened the door. There were four policemen standing there. I thought that they wanted us to move our car. They told Kevin that he had to come down to the station with them. The first thought I had was that he had hit a car and left. He's a fast driver. Sara was at the top of the stairs and she saw them take her Daddy away.
VICKI. Well, when Charles was arrested I was so relieved. I accepted that his arrest was the answer to my prayers. It was the highlight of his life because he finally had to admit that he had the problem.

MARITAL PATTERNS

During courtship, most husbands assured their wives that they were ready to settle down, get steady jobs, and establish families. Thus, most women committed themselves to these men under the assumption and with the understanding that the criminal activity was going to become "a thing of the past." Only a few women entered marriage believing that their husbands would continue to be involved in crime and other nonconventional lifestyle patterns. Most also expected their husbands to be steady providers and responsible husbands and fathers. For the majority of women, however, these expectations were not fulfilled. The wives soon found themselves struggling to deal with two problematic forms of behavior from their husbands, *i.e.*, employment problems and tendencies toward fast living.[3]

   According to the wives' accounts, the most difficult problem was their husbands' unemployment. Some claimed that their men were not against the idea of working but were unemployed because of a lack of skills, education, or a history of steady employment. Other wives said their husbands did not like unskilled work because it is monotonous, demeaning, and low paying. The wives maintained, however, that the men frequently accepted such work for brief periods to satisfy their wives or parole officers. Other men seemed reluctant to work at all and, even when they did find jobs, soon quit or were fired. A few men sincerely wanted to find work and eventually found unskilled, low-paying seasonal jobs from which they were laid off. Thus, despite the fact that many men were working, wives generally reported that they still could not supply basic family needs. Only three women were married to men employed in white-collar occupations which provided their families with a "comfortable" income. Not all the women, however, attempted to rely on their husbands' incomes. A few worked outside their homes and nineteen others received some form of public assistance to supplement their husbands' earnings.[4] In some cases they were entirely dependent on it.

Fast Living in General

Wives' accounts reveal that, in many respects, their households closely resembled those of traditional working-class families. For instance, gender role segregation followed the traditional pattern: All but five women reported a clearly defined division of tasks in which women did the housework and men took responsibility for repairs and other traditionally male concerns. In other respects, however, these husbands did not conform to the conventional, working class male role. Early in their marriages, a significant number of men had been engaged in some lifestyle patterns which wives found to be problematic, *i.e.*, unemployment and fast living.

According to the wives, many husbands began actively pursuing at least two elements of fast living such as drinking and/or drug abuse, violence, especially wife beating, or frequent absences from home with peers and hanging out in local bars. Only three indicated that their men had not been involved in any kind of fast living, but had been steadily employed, had acquired some middle-class status symbols, and appeared to conform to conventional norms.

The stresses and strains of poverty took an immediate toll on most wives. They reported that when money became scarce, arguments proliferated, men became depressed and uncommunicative, marital tension increased, men "walked out," etc. These problems became more acute, moreover, when wives discovered that scarce resources were not being used to benefit their families. Eighteen women reported that, when money was tight, their men tended to squander it on alcohol and drugs. More than half of the men went on periodic binges or regularly consumed large amounts of alcohol. A small number of men used both alcohol and drugs, while a handful were primarily drug abusers.

Twenty-six wives reported that their husbands' pursuit of "fast-living" activities foreshadowed trouble. They were painfully aware that alcoholism and drug abuse could lead to more serious troubles—criminal enterprises and arrest. The majority of wives said that during their marriages the men's criminal activities were alcohol- and/or drug-related, and typically male-centered. Others were disturbed that their unemployed husbands constantly associated with their "drinking buddies" in houses, taverns, and on the streets. These wives were aware that their husbands' "buddies" lived "fast" and were sporadically involved in petty crimes. As one wife explained,

> When Rudi drinks, he doesn't want to stay home. He wants to get as far away from home as possible and not be around my parents. He goes to the bars—from one bar to another—and he gets in with some group of men and then he starts writing checks.

Another wife recalled how her inebriated husband and friends committed arson:

> He had a very bad drinking problem at that time. He was with a bunch of juveniles. Just a group of young punks. They were partying and then they drove around town. They were all drunk. They decided to burn this house down but Buddie was the only one who went into the house and set it on fire.

In some cases, the husbands maintained that they had a right to a "night out with the boys." This night out, of course, would often extend into *nights* out.

Most women worried that these unnecessary absences from home involved heavy drug and/or alcohol consumption or sexual infidelity. It is interesting to note that the men returned home after these "absences" and resumed family roles. One woman described her stormy marriage to a fast-living husband this way:

> Well, we fought over mainly money problems or the people he hung with. He was always drunk and using up the money. And he was always hanging around with these people and he never came home. He was seldom at home. He was always with his friends and he was drunk. And here I was pregnant first with the oldest one and then with the youngest one. Things got really bad with the

friends he hung around with. They were drunk and they were rowdy. He went over to New York where his parents lived and his brothers and sisters live. He got a job in construction. It was a good job. But once the winter came, he was laid off. The next day, in fact, he got into his old friends who lived around there. They also drank and were rowdy, and he ended up in jail for disturbing the peace and here I was pregnant with Tommy.

Most wives reported that they and their husbands frequently argued about their husbands' fast-living activities. It was during these arguments that many men had physically assaulted their wives. Whenever men's unemployment became chronic, the rate of violence appeared to rise. Fourteen unemployed men had battered their wives and many battering incidents occurred after heavy drinking. One wife described this pattern vividly:

But everything was really good until Russell started hanging around with Hal. Two months to three months later, he was drinking with Hal, and I'd be left alone when they went out drinking. They did what they wanted to do and if I complained, I'd get beaten. The first time that happened, I was shocked. I was pregnant and I was lying on the bed. I told him I didn't feel good and he told me he was going out anyway. I wanted him to stay with me. I was spotting and I was pretty worried. He punched and kicked me. I started crying and he said he was sorry and wouldn't do it again. I went to my mother's house until he decided to come and get me. But this was the beginning of the beatings. Every time I opened my mouth, he beat me. On Maple Street, he hit me because I tried to stop him from going with Hal. He said, "Keep your mouth shut and there'll be no beatings."

Another woman reported:

Most of the time I asked for it. If he was drinking and we'd get into a hassle, then it was likely to occur. We'd get into hassles over the kids and I disapproved of how he was handling the kids. We'd argue over the car because he wasn't supposed to drive it. If he wanted to go out, he'd take the car and I'd say that he would get into hassles. Then we'd fight. At the time I was almost convinced that it would be better to be dead than lead this kind of life and then I'd think of how he could be so nice.

Interestingly, the women who, themselves, were active in the drug subculture were less likely to perceive fast living as threatening to their marriages. Nor was their husbands' unemployment a disturbing issue. Husbands and, less frequently, wives, mainly supported themselves by such criminal activities as stealing, shoplifting, cashing "bad" checks, or drug dealing. According to these wives, couples were often preoccupied with finding money for drugs, obtaining these drugs, and avoiding the police. This woman illustrates the point:

> You can't have much of a relationship when two people are on drugs. When you're on drugs your whole life centers around obtaining and shooting up drugs. You're not as close as you'd be if you were not on drugs. Your concern is not for each other but your concern is only where the next hit is coming from and where do you get the money for it.
>
> And we always had people living at the house or staying with us. Whoever had drugs comes to the house and turns on there, and shares with the other people in the house. When you're on drugs, you have to be around people and not be alone.

For many, though, this daily round could wear thin. As one woman involved in the soft drug culture observed:

> I was getting bored with the way in which Dan and I were living. We were still just hanging around. We were getting up every day, and then we'd try to find some pot, and then we'd try to sell the pot, and at night we'd get stoned. That was our life.

When the excitement began to tarnish, and when these women wanted to leave the drug subculture and establish more conventional life patterns, they began to experience the same difficulties with their marriages reported by the other wives.

Accommodation to Fast Living

For the most part prisoners' wives tended to put up with unemployment and such elements of fast living as financial irresponsibility, drinking and drug habits, and physical assaults because they had few alternatives. Most were not well prepared to enter the labor force themselves, and, in some cases, their children were quite young and required some form of home care. Moreover, for some women, their marriages were not their first and they were determined to make them work. In many instances, the "troubles" they experienced were not qualitatively different from those they had encountered growing up. Their husbands' behavior struck them as disturbing, but not scandalizing. What concerned most women was the lack of companionship they experienced: seventeen women reported an unsatisfactory level of companionship, intimacy, and sharing in their relationships with their husbands during this preseparation period.

Square Living

A minority of prisoners' wives reported that they lived outwardly conventional, settled working-class, or middle-class lives during the early period of their marriages. They pursued what is here called, following Irwin (1970), a square-living lifestyle: (1) their husbands were steadily employed in skilled working-class or middle-class occupations; (2) consumption of drugs or alcohol was moderate; (3) their marriages were stable; (4) they acquired some middle-class status symbols; and (5) they participated in a settled working- or middle-class round of life.

Two of the three women in this category reported that, during this phase in their lives, their spouses had established roots in their communities, and that their marriages were comparatively financially secure and comfortable. However, a conventional lifestyle did not guarantee a wholly satisfactory marriage. For instance, one woman reported that she had to cope with her husband's pursuit of such elements of fast living as frequent, unexplained absences, illicit sexual liaisons, and heavy consumption of marijuana and cocaine.

Learning about Husbands' Criminal Activities

Most working class women in the study reported some familiarity with crime, jails, and prisons through family members or friends who had "gotten into trouble with the law." Most of these women saw crime as something men did to get money; they usually did not view it as outrageous, unusual, or disturbing behavior.

Glaser and Strauss's (1965) comprehensive and systematic analysis of different awareness contexts provides a useful framework here.[5] The most common form of awareness context among the wives in the study group is "open awareness." A total of twenty-six wives reported that they had some knowledge of their husbands' criminal enterprises and some of them knew because they were regular or sporadic participants in these activities. Wives also reported that frequently they overheard their husbands discussing and planning crimes with their friends:

> Q. Did you know what Jerry was doing?
> A. I was just involved in driving to the pharmacies when they were doing some jobs. I always knew what was happening. They were planned around me so they weren't any secret. I knew about Jerry's dealing. That's how we made it. People in the house always talked about the jobs they were doing and the next day after they had done their jobs, they would talk about what happened.

A second form of awareness that characterized these wives is "suspicion awareness."[6] The hallmark of this awareness context is that wives do not know, but suspect with varying degrees of certainty, that their husbands' fast-living activities will get them arrested. Wives may be extremely shrewd about the significance of their husbands' activities. This was especially true of those whose men had histories of repeated alcohol- and/or drug-related crimes. In all of these cases, these women had accumulated enough information to realize that the spiraling effects of alcoholism or drug abuse would eventually land their husbands in jail.

Confirmation of wives' suspicions occurred in three types of situations: direct confrontation, accidental discovery, and husbands criminally victimizing their wives.[7] Wives most frequently directly confronted their husbands about their suspicions. In one case, a wife became suspicious that her unemployed husband was "up to no good" since he began to spend nights out with criminally-oriented peers. She recounted a series of direct confrontations:

> I was keeping my cool and doing a lot of sensible talking. I kept telling him that he wasn't heading in the direction that he wanted to be. But new appliances and clothes for him kept appearing around the house. I then kept telling him to be honest and return those goods. One day he said to me, "I'm a lot sicker than even you suspect." I said, "O.K., I can deal with it. We'll work on these things." Then I kept asking him what else was wrong. I said,

"What is it? Have you raped some little girl, you can tell me." He said, "No!" And more new clothes showed up. He wouldn't tell me the truth. I told him that he has nothing to be afraid of. I wouldn't freak out! Then my office was broken into. I said, "Burr, tell me the truth." Finally he told me. I'd been swearing up and down that he had the keys to my office but at first he wouldn't tell me.

Many wives found out by accident. Accidental discoveries occurred when wives heard the neighborhood gossip about their husbands' criminal activities, when law enforcement agents came to wives' homes to make inquiries about their husbands, or when wives unexpectedly discovered their husbands practicing sexually deviant acts in their homes. Wives generally reacted by interrogating their husbands in order to gain additional information.

Finally, discovery sometimes occurred when husbands criminally victimized their wives. One wife first learned of her husband's illegal behavior through her bank. She found an empty bankbook and, upon confronting her husband, learned that he was forging her checks. Another woman was painfully aware of her husband's sexual deviations since he was sexually abusive to her. To gain some control over her husband's sexual behavior, she searched her home for sexual paraphernalia during his infrequent absences. Inadvertently, she discovered a set of binoculars with which she later confronted him. During this confrontation, he revealed that he used the binoculars for voyeurism.

It is interesting to note that the suspicion awareness context can be shattered when husbands acknowledge their participation in criminal activities. If the evidence (*e.g.*, emptied bank books, the stolen goods, and so forth) presented to the husbands "nailed them," then they were likely to "confess" to their wives. Although husbands generally divulged some details about their criminal activities, total revelations were rare. In these situations, wives' awareness was transformed from suspicious awareness to open awareness. In contrast, when wives lacked verifying information, husbands generally attempted a bold-faced denial, although their lies did not necessarily quell the wives' suspicions. For example, one wife recalled her husband's reactions to her unverified suspicions.

Harry would lie to me and say that he was going out so that he could work on his car engine. But he'd be out ripping something off. I'd call where he was supposed to be and he wouldn't be there. I'd ask Harry where he was and he'd lie to me. He always lied to me.

The third and least common form of awareness context is "closed awareness."[8] Only a few wives did not know about their husbands' criminal activities. These wives were committed to marriages with men who lived a conventional lifestyle. They reported that their husbands had kept their criminal activities secret. The wives, themselves, claimed not to be experienced at recognizing signs of husbands' criminal activities. Most wives whose husbands had committed sexual offenses were, in contrast, likely to be painfully aware of their husbands' sexual offenses such as voyeurism, exhibitionism, and sadism when these took place in their homes. However, none of these women were aware of these when they took place in public places.

ACCOMMODATING TO MALE CRIMINALITY

Despite the varied ways in which these women learned about their spouses' criminal activity, in general it came as no great shock. Eighteen women claimed that they were initially more likely to look upon these activities as worrisome, but not as shocking. These wives all had early exposure to criminal activities. Most had resided in working-class communities where certain types of criminal activities—such as check forging, receiving stolen goods, or shoplifting—tended to be tolerated. Many had grown up with the view that these kinds of crimes were ordinary survival mechanisms used by many working-class people.

Many wives, however, reported that they had not expected their husbands to abide entirely by conventional norms. Twelve women, in fact, indicated that they usually tolerated their husbands' illegitimate activities as long as these remained "on the street" and the wives were free to continue functioning in their roles as wives and mothers: "the less [they] know about it the better!" Husbands helped to sustain this tacit arrangement by maintaining secrecy about their activities, giving only vague details about their crimes, and lying about what they were doing.

One wife, whose husband had an extensive criminal history, recalled how he lied to her:

> I was trying to believe what he said was true and knowing at the
> same time that he did the opposite and that he was lying to me. He
> knew that he was boozing, taking drugs, and getting into trouble
> but he told me he wasn't doing these things. When he went in for
> robbing that liquor store everybody knew it except me.

Seven wives maintained that they initially tolerated their husbands' criminal activities because the money from these crimes
was necessary to meet the basic needs of their families, or because it provided their families with small luxuries they could
not otherwise have afforded. When money was scarce, there was
a tendency among some couples to combine income from public
assistance, employment, and crime in order to "get by." For example, one woman explained how her household lived better
when her husband shoplifted:

> Q. Does your financial situation get better when Frank's here or
> when he's not here?
> A. It depends. If Frank is still going straight, it doesn't change. But
> if Frank is into criminal activity, it changes a lot—we live better.
> You know, boosting food or something; it makes things a lot eas-
> ier.
> Q. At the time he does this, what is your response when he comes
> home?
> A. If we need food, I'm glad he's done it. But if it was for some-
> thing ridiculous that we don't need, then I get mad because he
> took a chance and it was stupid.

A few wives tolerated their husbands' criminal activities because they, themselves, were involved in them. Three couples had
apparently centered their relationships around dealing and consuming drugs. Other wives had occasionally acted as accessories
to such criminal acts as receiving stolen property, shoplifting, or
armed robbery. However, such participation was rare even
though most wives did not react negatively to renewed criminal
activity at first.

In general, wives came to regard their husbands' behavior as
a source of difficulty when it interfered with their own aspira-

tions for a conventional home life, *i.e.*, when it interfered with men's roles as husbands and fathers. This was most likely when either heavy use of alcohol or sexual deviance was involved. Some women felt that their men had failed to perform many of their domestic responsibilities. Others were concerned about the devastating effects alcohol could have on their families. A few viewed nonalcohol-related crimes tolerantly since they were less likely to conflict with domestic roles than alcohol-related crimes. As long as their husbands' deviant activities did not upset their households, most of these women were not likely to make a big fuss about it.

The women also found deviant behavior intolerable when it interfered with their own performances as wives and mothers, or their household schedules and routines:

> When he was drunk or on drugs, he'd come home and pass out on the chair or come in with a group of people, and they'd turn on the stereo, and party in the house. Bud wanted me with him no matter how late it was or whether I had to go to work in the morning. In the morning, there would be empty bottles strewn around the house and the house would be a mess. He always wanted me to talk to his friends.

For many women, initial tolerance began to fade when their husbands became blatantly public and/or onerously troublesome. One wife emphasized how her husband's sexual deviance began to surface within her own family:

> I knew things were getting bad. I knew that I really had to do something. The last time we were together was very frightening. I realized he was beginning to notice our daughter who was twelve years old. There was absolutely nothing sexual about her. She had not developed at all. She was outside across the street playing with some friends. She had wrapped some towels around her and she was playing that she was Queen of America and she was strutting around, rolling her hips. She was trying to imitate a beauty queen. Nelson saw her and he hollered at her that she was a "slut" and a "whore." I was aware he was picking on her. I was aware because I was raped when I was twelve years old. I said to myself, "Oh God, he's noticing her sexually!" My inner instinct of protecting her foamed up.

The majority of these wives wanted to establish conventional marriages. Instead, twenty-six had married men who were unemployed and/or actively engaged in criminal enterprises and in some elements of fast living. What becomes especially troubling for the women was not so much the likelihood that their husbands would be involved in some kind of criminal activity, but that they were erratic providers of the material and emotional support the wives believed necessary for themselves and their children. A recurrent theme in wives' accounts was their commitment to preserving their marriages, regardless of the troubles entailed, since they still believed that their spouses would provide them with the kind of lives they had hoped for at some future date. As they came to understand the potential impact of their husbands' criminal activities on their own lives, they began to search for some interpretations of this behavior and for strategies to combat crime and fast living in general.

CHAPTER IV

Before Arrest: Explaining and Accommodating to Male Criminality and Fast Living

Earl has a warm thing about kids. He becomes all soft and emotional about them. But he has another side to him. Most of the time he feels he has to come on as a macho guy. Earl is caught in a little world. Part of him wants all the good things in life but he hasn't any control. He can't seem to go after the things he really wants. He can't sit down and get them. He's like a double person. Something clicks inside him and he's the ex-con, the rip-offer.

Most of the prisoners' wives reported that, during courtship, they had not perceived their men's past criminal behavior as very important. They were far more concerned about their men's identities as suitors and prospective roles as husbands and fathers. However, during marriage but prior to the men's arrest, many wives began to deal with some stark realities. Their husbands had resumed some fast-living patterns which they believed were conducive to criminal opportunities. Wanting to preserve their marriages, these wives devised ameliorative interpretations of their husbands' activities and sought accommodative strategies with which to cope with such behaviors. Throughout their marriages, prisoners' wives seek to preserve their perceptions of their men as husbands, and incidentally as criminals. They devise a "vocabulary of motives" which explains, justifies, and answers questions about male criminality. Most women used more than one strategy to minimize and explain evidence of their husbands' criminal behavior. They also incorporated their husbands' accounts of their own behavior in arriving at a perception of their husbands as basically "good people" who were victims of bad conditions, ill luck, or physiology.

THE WOMEN SPEAK FOR THEMSELVES

A pervasive theme in the wives' accounts was their hope that
their husbands' "troublesome" behavior would change and that
tomorrow would be different.

During four years of marriage Paula's husband was incarcerated twice. In addition to the couple's son, they had two other
boys from Paula's previous marriage living with them. The boys
range in ages from eleven years to six years of age.

> We'd been married for four years now. We lived together for four
> months before we got married. When we were living together they
> came and picked him up and he was in jail that January. I was
> pregnant then and I had Jake in March. He was shipped to Wind-
> sor and we got married there. I think that he's spent more time
> with the Department of Corrections than he has with us.
>
> I thought when I met him that I could change him. That was a
> hell of a disappointment to see that I couldn't do it. I now know
> that only you can change yourself. That's one of these realizations
> that I've had. It took time to penetrate.
>
> I'm the supervisor of the kitchen at the local hospital. I did
> that kind of work at the Oxford hospital for two or three years
> and was glad to do the same kind here. I like it.
>
> When I was working and he was working, things went well.
> He would come home and he'd wait until I came home and it
> would be late at night by the time I got home. But we'd have sup-
> per and he'd be very tired. He would sack out almost immediately
> after supper and I wouldn't care.
>
> Bud would wash the floor, wash the clothes, vacuum, and he'd
> babysit with the kids. He'd do the dishes. Bud was like two differ-
> ent people. Things were enjoyable with him and he'd do things
> with the kids. But Bud also wanted to run around, party, drink,
> and do all these other things.
>
> Everything went so smoothly when he had a job. The income
> was coming in and we'd have a six pack each day and we'd have
> the money for it. Christmas time was a grand time.
>
> When he got out of jail, he always had a job, and he'd work at
> it for a while, and then he'd lose the job, and have nothing to do.
> He'd sit here and he couldn't find a job, and he'd see his wife
> working. That's downgrading for a male. And it's hard for a
> woman to work and come home and clean the house, take care of
> the kids, and see the man just sitting there doing nothing. He did

do the wash and he did take the kids when I was working on weekends. But one weekend, he got drunk and he drove his motorcycle, and crashed it and hurt his hand. And he had the kids! He's supposed to be taking care of the kids. So I began to send them to a babysitter.

He'd get frustrated and drink, and take drugs. I couldn't comprehend this. I don't know why he takes drugs. I tried speed a few times and pot a few times. I don't understand why anyone would want to put themselves into that condition. When you have kids, you have to be functioning and not sit back and nod off while they get run over by a car.

He went with a group of guys who he was in jail with. I felt that I never fitted in with his crowd. It was always party time. And when they were here, and it was party time then I had to send the kids out to play. Bud wanted to party and we did. It was easier that way. I would save myself from a fight and potential violence. Most of the times I was hit, the kids were around and they would see it. I felt it wasn't good for the kids.

People say that he's a different person when he's not with me. I didn't like to hear about this side of him and I stayed away from him when he was out drinking and taking drugs. I threw fits at him about it. He liked to party, be fucked up with booze, or smoke, or anything.

Sometimes after an argument, he'd leave the house, and go to his friends, or we just wouldn't talk. When he was sober, we didn't have very many arguments. When he was on drugs, speed, and pot, we'd argue. But he scares me sometimes. I don't like to argue with him. I've been hit by him and he's definitely stronger than I am.

I feel that booze is to blame—his drinking and his inability to control himself. And my mouthiness didn't help. I didn't approve of his friends. They weren't my kind of people. I told him that his friends had a history of getting into trouble, they were criminals and if he kept going with them he'd get into trouble with them. That's how 95 percent of the arguments started.

Where was there for me to go? I wasn't big enough to throw him out. I'd worry about his hitting and when was it likely to occur again. He threw a lot of things around too. After he hit me, he'd be real sweet for a couple of weeks and then out of the blue we'd go back to the old stuff. I got tired of going backwards. I like to go forwards.

I was looking for someone who likes to sit around the house

and play scrabble and to talk to someone. I wanted to know I had
someone backing me as a working mother. It's not what I expected. I wasn't getting any of this from Bud. He's always in jail.
That what's hard. It's a big difference between what I've expected
and what I got. Not getting what I expected is the hard thing about
his going back and forth to jail.

According to Bea, during fourteen years of marriage to Rudi,
he has been in and out of prison too many times for her to remember. She estimates that he has spent twenty-five of his fifty-
five years in jail for alcohol-related crimes. They have two
children, one boy, Todd, age 16 years and one girl, Joyce, age 10
years and she has two adult children age 22 and 21 years from a
previous marriage.

He's been in Newport before and they know Rudi real well. My
God, yes, they know him well. I couldn't even guess how many
times he's been in. I think he's been in four times since Newfane
was torn down and who knows how many before.

I figure that I have forgiven him and taken him back five or six
times. Every time he gets picked up, I always say, "This is it! I've
had it!" But that never lasts. When he's sober, he's a good provider, a good husband, and a good father. You can't find a better
man than that. But he goes all to pieces when he drinks.

Rudi is like two people. When he's not drinking, he's the best
person alive. But when he's drinking, he's terrible. Rudi is an alcoholic. I guess he told you that. When he's drinking I hate him. He
acts rotten when he's drinking. Just rotten! When Joyce was a
baby, when he drank, he'd always have to be driving about. He'd
insist that we go on these drives. When he's drinking he is very
good to the kids. He'd give them money and anything they wanted.
He wouldn't deny them anything. Just gave and gave them things.

But when Rudi drinks, he doesn't want to stay home. He
wants to get as far away from home as possible and not be around
my parents. He goes to the bars, from one bar to another and he
gets in with some group of men and then starts writing checks.
Then we get the cops sitting on my doorsteps, questioning me, and
questioning the kids.

I like to stay away from him and I don't like to have the kids
near him when he wants to drink. I have told him this. Last time
he went on a bender, he wanted the red car which was Liz's. He
got very upset when she wouldn't lend it to him and told us all to

go to hell! He stayed away for two days and then he calls me and says for me to come and meet him. He knows not to come to the house. Of course I go and meet him. Then we usually argue over his drinking. I tell him that he's put himself in a bad position and that he'll get into trouble and go to jail.

I've left him so many times when he's drinking. So many times that I can't even count them. He follows me back all the time. No matter where I move, he comes back. When we lived in Nebraska, he started drinking and he was going to stay there and stop drinking. That's what he told me! I came back here because my mother was very ill. I got here on a Friday morning and he popped up that Friday night, drunk too!

I cringe and I shake and my nerves have gone to pieces. To think what I have been going through with the children, with the cops, and with him. He doesn't pay any attention. He says that I have left him so many times that it's now a joke.

In different ways, both Paula and Bea deal with their husbands' criminality and fast living. Both search for explanations of their husband's behavior and employ different coping strategies which are directed toward improving their situations and toward preserving their marriages in spite of the fact that their husbands are unable to fulfill their conventional and expected roles.

EXPLANATIONS FOR UNCONVENTIONAL BEHAVIOR

In order to preserve their marriages, most of the prisoners' wives in the sample worked hard to maintain an image of their husbands as important members of their households—regardless of their fast living and criminal behavior. Thus, they developed rationales that allowed them to continue to perceive their husbands as fathers, decision-makers, repair men, garbage collectors—and most important—providers of economic and emotional support.

Almost all the wives tried to avoid labelling their husbands as deviants. They tried to "normalize" their husbands' behavior, to interpret it as "reasonable." Another strategy which wives commonly employed was to create a positive image of their husbands' behavior by neutralizing its negative connotations. By neutralizing these "troublesome" behavior patterns, the wives

convinced themselves that their husbands were entirely blameless: "more acted upon than acting." (Sykes and Matza, 1957:
667.) Thus they come to tolerate their men's criminality without
making a frontal assault on their lifestyles. The wives only
treated their husbands' behavior as "hopeless" in a few cases.
Three kinds of rationalizations emerged: (1) blaming the husbands' deviant activities on outside forces; (2) blaming the husbands; or (3) blaming themselves.

Outside Forces as Perceived Cause of Male Deviance

Wives' definitions of their husbands' criminality typically included both an affirmation and a neutralization of the behavior.
The husbands, they maintained, were not really responsible for
their actions, but were victimized by conditions for which they
were not responsible. Blame is thus ascribed to outside forces
and the husbands' criminal actions are seen as beyond their
control.[1] They are acted upon, rather than acting. In these cases,
the chief underlying circumstance is their lack of control over
their actions: they are driven by external forces. Three "sources"
or "causes" predominate in their accounts: (1) scapegoating; (2)
alcoholism; (3) environmental factors.

Scapegoating. Scapegoating was employed by twelve women.
Here women point to someone other than their husbands as the
direct or primary cause of the men's current and past crimes.
Common targets were parents who were deficient or abusive in
the treatment of their children, alcoholic parents, or criminally-
oriented parents. A wife whose husband had an extensive history
of burglaries blamed her husband's family:

> When we're by ourselves, he doesn't think of anything that has to
> do with crime but when he gets with his family he's always in trou-
> ble. He's easily led by them and they do a number on him.

Other women sometimes blamed their husbands' other
criminally-oriented or fast-living relatives. One wife blamed a
childhood acquaintance of her husband as well as his parents for
his current preoccupation with "*kinky*" sex:

> As I've said, his problems go way back into the past. Nelson was
> discovered by a woman who was very sick. He was discovered by

her when he was 11 or 12 years old. He was masturbating in the barn. He was sifting sand over his penis. Nelson has a deep fear of his father. He feels that his father is a cock sucker. . . . Oh, back to this woman who found Nelson masturbating. She used his fear of his father against him. She controlled Nelson through this fear. Then she told him that she was going to tell his father. When she told him that, he was scared. She then told him, "I want you to come to my apartment at a certain time." She lived on Oak Street in Burlington. He came up at the designated time and he was worried. She tied him to the bed and put an enema hose up his ass. She then ran hot and cold water into him. She used him for this for a year. He reached a breaking point one day. One part of him was enjoying it and the other part hated it. This time she put the enema hose up his ass and let it run for three hours continuously. He passed out and he was in pain. He started to shout. She then gagged him and he endured it and then he totally blacked out. When he came to he had a different attitude. He found himself more into it. She then introduced him to a man. He liked to gag me and tie me up and used these electrical cords that couldn't break. Just like she did to him. She brought this guy up. Nelson was tied up on the bed. This guy used him orally and then anally. There was a great deal of pain. The guy came. Nelson didn't want this guy. The woman then used the guy on herself and had Nelson watch. This explains why he did things like that. He was twelve years old at the time.

Just as frequently, wives also laid blame on peers. A few insisted that their husbands were easily led by alcoholic or drug-using friends who then proceeded to get the husbands involved in illegal activities. As one woman related:

Barry used to think a lot about drinking. When he's with his friends, he drinks quite a bit. When he's drunk he has this real shit attitude—he doesn't give a shit! His friends will say to him, "I know where you can make some easy money real fast." He'll fall for it. He's an alcoholic.

Alcoholism. A commonly used mechanism was to ascribe responsibility to an impersonal outside force, like alcoholism. Twelve wives who were married to husbands involved in alcohol-related crimes did this. These wives were most likely to see their husbands as "good people," but subject to a bad condition for which they were not responsible. A foreign substance, alcohol, had overpowered them and propelled them into crime. Thus their husbands' problems were simple: they would sometimes drink to excess. Only then would they commit crimes, sexual deviance, or become physically abusive. However, their essences remained untouched. For instance, a young wife accounted in the following way for her husband's forging checks:

> I worked and came home and took care of the baby. The baby is now four years old. I knew he was asking for it. He's got a drinking problem and he would get out of control and get into trouble. He was never home and went out riding in the car and went to bars. He'd come home around 1 or 2 in the morning.

Despite having to acknowledge their husbands' deviance, wives are thus able to neutralize it. In any event, "alcoholism" is not a crime and it therefore follows that their husbands are not criminals.

Five wives made specific reference to "Dr. Jekyll and Mr. Hyde" in describing their husbands, as illustrated by the following two cases:

> When Charles was drunk one time, he broke my nose. He's like Dr. Jekyll and Mr. Hyde. When he drank he'd be abusive or wallowing in self-pity. He came to my house all drunk and crying about how terrible a person he was and all that whining. It got on my nerves. I told him that I was sick of him getting drunk with the guys.
>
> Peter is like two people. He's really a Dr. Jekyll and Mr. Hyde! When he's not drinking, he's the best person alive. But when he's drinking, he's terrible. Peter is an alcoholic.

A few other wives, such as the one quoted above, asserted that their husbands' particular form of Mr. Hyde was "macho man." When they were with friends, their wives said, men who could be tender and loving at home, turned into macho men. They didn't give a damn about anything. They sought excitement and adventure, testing legal and other forms of authority. They rebelled against conventional society, acted tough, and drank or consumed drugs heavily. One woman, asked to describe the things her husband had done, interpreted her husband's criminal behavior in this way:

Stupid things like driving without a license. Petty shit like getting into fights and then he's the one who gets busted, no matter what. He's into this theory that a coward walks away from a fight. He's a chauvinist. He expects his woman to have her place and her place is to be in the home and not to go to the bars or not to work. I like that. I know he cares and he's very macho. He's the big strong man type and believes that to show kindness is a weakness.

To many women, machismo was the moral equivalent of "evil" and, to some extent, was synonymous with fast living. By ascribing battering and other crimes to Mr. Hyde, these wives were able to maintain faith in their men, the Dr. Jekylls. They were likable, lovable, and repentant, begged forgiveness, and promised never to do it again. Yet, the wives reported, Dr. Hyde did manage to re-emerge periodically.

Environmental Conditions. A third rationale presented by wives, is that environmental factors have impinged on their husbands' lives. Only five wives' accounts do this. Environmental factors— such as unemployment and poverty—they maintained, influenced husbands to commit crimes in order to supplement their incomes or reduce their frustration and anger. According to one woman's account, whenever her husband became unemployed he became depressed, drank, and then committed a series of forgeries:

When Ron got depressed or angry then he'd drink. He'd feel discouraged or he was just sitting around when he lost a job. He needed to work. He wants to keep going or he gets bored easily. When he wasn't working, he'd drink.

The combination of unemployment, poverty, alcoholism, and going with the wrong crowd, also can be disruptive for the man, as one woman reports.

I felt that sometimes, he gets into trouble because we haven't any money and so he steals. Sometimes he gets discouraged and depressed and then he steals. Sometimes he drinks and gets in with the wrong groups and goes out and steals and sometimes he steals for the fun of it.

According to another wife, the combination of household and financial responsibilities and unemployment led her husband to commit aggravated assault. Asked why she thought he got himself in jail, she replied,

> The responsibilities. He could not cope with the responsibilities and met up with so many frustrations and the pressures began to mount. He wasn't able to get a job because of his record. He couldn't perform even though he wanted to.

Ascribing undesirable behavior to environmental factors allowed wives to believe that their husbands were not responsible and that their husbands' identities as normal men were still intact. This form of justification also allowed wives to imply that their husbands' conditions were not permanent. Thus, wives could hope that, as such environmental factors were modified, their husbands' conditions are likely to change, *e.g.*, when they are steadily employed.

Internal Defects as Perceived Sources of Male Deviance

When some wives finally confronted their husbands' unconventional and/or criminal behavior, their reaction was to lay the blame on defects in their husbands' characters.[2] Their husbands, they reasoned, were basically "good people" suffering from a "bad condition." In effect, they attempted to encapsulate some character flaw—and thus see it as something separate from the men as individuals. By doing so, they were able to shift blame away from their husbands who, after all, were simply being driven by uncontrollable *internal* forces. Wives reported three defects which could affect their husbands in this fashion: (1) immaturity; (2) character "weaknesses"; and (3) mental illness.

Immaturity.   The most frequently employed rationale was immaturity. Nineteen of the working-class women asserted that their husbands were immature since they had been slow in developing emotionally. In describing their husbands' criminal acts, these women often described their husbands as having acted like "boys." Or they would simply assert that their husbands had never grown up: they were "just big babies." In this fashion, the women were able to convince themselves that the men's behavior was governed by physiology or biology. One woman, whose husband had been cashing her checks, had this to say about his behavior: "Earl ended up being another child and he was like a hyperactive child that you have to watch every second to keep out of trouble."

Still another wife used the following rationale to explain her husband's repeated involvement in alcohol-related check forging sprees:

> Sometimes he acts childish. He feels that no one is going to stop him. He does what he wants to do. The only way he could support us on welfare was to go get extra money or stuff to help make life a little easier.

Implicit in this interpretation, of course, is the idea that their men's condition is not permanent. "My man needs time to sow his wild oats before he settles down." But until their men grew up, these wives were able to describe their husbands as spoiled, lacking will power, and acting like babies. This rationale was probably drawn from the surrounding working class subculture. Within this milieu, it is often expected that men will live "fast" during their adolescent years. Once they have had a chance to do this, they are then expected to settle down, establish families, and assume adult roles.

Character Weakness. In attempting to maintain a positive image of their husbands, wives sometimes ascribed their husbands' criminal behavior to specific character defects such as "bad tempers," "meanness," "lack of self-control," and so on:

> Joey always has a bad disposition. He's always thinking that someone is out to get him and he's always looking around and saying, that person is after me, this person is after me. He has a bad temper. And he never lets you finish what you're saying when he's angry. He cuts in on you and just goes off into a screaming fit.

Another wife places the blame on her husband's need to have constant attention:

> He needs a lot of attention and he's not selective about how he gets this attention. He doesn't care what he does but he cares that he gets attention from it and the attention be completely focused on him. He wants attention from the people around him and he wants to know that they're watching him. When he gets in "trouble" he really doesn't get attention from the people around him—they don't care—but then he gets a different kind of attention from the courts.

This was true of ten women in the study population. These character defects are perceived as "mild," but recurrent. Only some of their husbands' characteristics were offensive. Thus, while their husbands were wrong, they committed criminal acts due to inherent character weaknesses which were beyond their control.

Mental Illness. Whenever the wives used mental illness to explain their husbands' deviance, they also tended to denounce their behavior. Only four women provided this rationale, and only on those occasions when their husbands' behavior was so bizarre that they could not avoid other people's perceptions of it as completely "crazy" or "sick": As the victim of her husband's crimes, one wife accounted for his forging checks in this way:

> It didn't bother him in the least. He has a thing about checks. He's a pervert. He loves checks. It's thrilling for him. it's thrilling for him to steal them, make them out, and cash them.

Another young woman whose husband was involved in sexual offenses offered this explanation for his behavior:

> I think he's not right upstairs! Normal people don't do the things he does. I mean there must be something different about him. He needs help!

Under these circumstances, wives were prepared to assert that the person they thought they knew was no longer there. Once women defined their husbands as mentally unbalanced, they were able to describe them as ordinary, conventional husbands in their previous incarnations. Once wives came to believe that their husbands were "sick," they frequently accepted their condition as permanent and hopeless.

Wives as Cause of Male Deviance

The final strategy, reported by eight women, was to place the blame on themselves.[3] Here, husbands' behavior was explained, justified, or made acceptable by the fact that the wives themselves caused it, *e.g.*, that they did not do enough for the husbands. Interestingly, all the women who offered this explanation indicated that their husbands encouraged them to assume blame. As illustrated by one wife's lament, these wives considered their husbands' accusations to be valid, and subsequently did blame themselves for varying periods of time:

> He felt that everything was my fault. It was my fault that he lost his job, it was my fault that we had kids. And it was my fault that everything wrong happened to him and then bam, bam, bam. He'd hit me. He'd stay up late at night and he then couldn't get up in the morning to go to work. If I couldn't wake him up in the morning to get to work on time, and that could be an impossible task, he'd hit me. I'd get beat.

Accepting responsibility for their husbands' acts tended to leave many wives tense and bewildered. For example, one young wife, explained her reasons (or lack of reasons) for blaming herself for her husbands' sexual offenses:

> At first, I thought that it was because of me. I put the blame on myself. I don't know why. I didn't really know why he did it. But I figured that there must be some reason. His mother blames herself too. It's just like why do I blame me? Because I don't have any other explanation.

A few other women reported that, the more their husbands reinforced them for doing it the more likely they became to search for additional areas for self-blame. Thus, they made every effort to become the kinds of wives their husbands expected them to be. But, typically, no matter what they did, their husbands' deviance persisted. One older woman (married for fourteen years) related that she was in a quandary as to how exactly she was to blame for her husband's alcoholism:

> We've had disagreements and I ask him if he goes out to drink to punish me and he says, "No!" But I do feel that he's punishing me. I feel that he's saying, "I'll hurt you and I'll drink just to show you that I can drink." When he does drink, I go through my mind— what have I done, what have I said, and I never come up with the right answer. Sometimes I feel that if we had an argument, he'll use it as an excuse. So I've stopped arguing with him.

By employing this justification the women involved were able to isolate a single factor which was responsible: They, themselves. Once again, the men were not responsible for their acts because they were driven to them by their wives' failures. The reason that all of these rationales were employed, of course, was that it is not easy to go about applying criminal labels to one's intimates. Wives of criminally involved men want to postpone assigning this identity to their husbands—especially if their marriages are their lives, jobs, and careers. Beyond this, many wives sincerely care for their husbands. Once married, they in no way want to threaten their marriages. While their husbands may be irresponsible fast-livers, they are better than no husbands at all. All these rationales, then, were employed to make their marriages more bearable, and to allow wives to stick by their husbands "for better or worse."

These rationales were made more plausible by the fact that few wives perceived their husbands' situations as unalterable. Most wives did not denounce their men as "rotten eggs" who had had every opportunity to make something of themselves. Nor were the men generally seen as requiring permanent care. Rather, wives searched for sources of change in outside forces, within themselves, or any other place except within their husbands. In searching for evidence that their husbands were really nice guys, they hope to find some accommodative mechanism which would allow them to establish the kinds of marriages they wanted in the first place.

PATTERNS OF ACCOMMODATION

If I'd known he was really drunk, I would have walked away from the verbal harassment. You just use whatever "tricks" work; what seems to be the most advantageous thing at the time. Sometimes it's a sexual overture; sometimes just walking away and changing the subject; sometimes just saying you're sorry.

Defining and rationalizing criminal behavior is not enough. In their everyday world, wives must learn to accommodate to male criminality and fast living to make their lives more bearable and preserve their marriages. These strategies differed depending on variations in their husbands' behavior. Many wives reported that they were likely to change strategies when they proved to be ineffective in curbing their husbands' criminality. Sometimes, they reported that they used an array of strategies until they found one that worked, at least temporarily. The strategies most frequently employed were (1) nurturing, (2) active resistance, and (3) passive distance. Another coping mechanism, less often employed, was participation in the husband's criminal activity, although in some cases this was done reluctantly.

Nurturing

Nurturing was employed by almost all the women in the sample at various points in their marital histories.[4] In general, wives whose men had histories of repeated alcohol- and/or drug-related crimes less frequently employed this strategy than wives of first-timers who had gotten themselves involved in some criminal pursuit. When wives engaged in nurturing, it was usually to avoid physical battering, or to deal with their husbands' heavy drinking, or sexually deviant behavior, as well as with the criminal activities. Nurturing works on a very general level, *i.e.*, with the hope of controlling or stopping the causes of the problem. Nurturing assumed several patterns.

Many wives said they treated their husbands as child-like spouses who needed to be encouraged to grow up. These wives gave their men emotional support and manipulated situations in the hope that they would mature. They spoke to their men as if they were troublesome children, rationally presenting the consequences of their acts, lecturing them about their behavior, and even offering them rewards for "good" behavior, *e.g.*, sexual intimacy, more personal wifely attention, special treats, and so on.

Nurturing also involved providing husbands with socio-emotional support, initiated when husbands appeared to need understanding, patience, or love. In this case, nurturing consisted of building up the man's self-image, listening attentively to problems, and being generally supportive. As one wife said:

> He kept telling me that his main problem was that all he needed was a family to support and someone behind him and he wouldn't go to jail. He had never had anyone who really cared about him. I tried to help him. I spent my whole time trying to help him. I tried to keep him away from drugs. At the same time he looked so sad and pitiful that I felt that he really wanted to have a family.

Nurturing could also take the form of trying to manipulate the environment in order to prevent husbands from pursuing criminal and fast-living activities, or physically and/or sexually abusing their wives. Some women worked hard to manipulate the behavior of other family members toward the men. Others went to great lengths to control as many external factors as possible. For instance, they expended time and effort in decorating their homes, preparing special meals, and putting the kids to bed early so that their men would have their homes and wives to look forward to, rather than street activities. That is, they attempted to make their homes and themselves more attractive. Beyond this, they also often arranged as many social activities as possible in an effort to keep the men so busy that they had no time for crime. According to one wife:

> Earl was into shooting downs. He wasn't having a problem with downs at the time. Thoughts about the downs did run across his mind though. When he'd tell me, I'd say, "Stay at home for the week-end and we'll do something." I always tried to put something else in front of him to do so he wouldn't get into drugs. There was always beer and casual drinking and no one really got drunk.

Another wife, whose husband engaged in a series of burglaries, reported how she became a "social director":

> I'd try to keep him occupied and not bored. I'd sit around the house and play cards and go to the movies. Or I'd say to him that there was a good movie on the TV or I'd suggest that we go and take a walk. This usually worked. But trying to find something for him to do was a full-time job.

Active Resistance

Generally, the wives studied here employed other accommodative strategies before turning to active resistance.[5] As their husbands continued to pursue criminal activities "on the streets" with their male cliques as well as heavy alcohol and/or drug use, seventeen conventionally-oriented wives reached the point at which they could no longer tolerate this behavior. Two other women, who had occasionally formed criminal partnerships with their husbands but now wanted to settle down to conventional lifestyles, also resorted to active resistance.

Hoping to stabilize their marriages, many women fluctuated between nurturing and active resistance. As time went on, they found that nurturing did not prevent further criminal behavior, and they increasingly resorted to its logical opposite: active resistance. Both strategies are typically employed with recalcitrant children. Hence, we can infer that these women treated their husbands as children who were "up to no good." A few reported that they argued, screamed, nagged, or pressured their husbands as they would their children. An older woman explains her reasons for doing this:

> Men do things like a kid. They will do anything for attention in order to see if you care. If you scream at them, if you're madder than hell at them, then they know that you care. It's their security.

Arguments centered around their husbands' failure to provide satisfactory incomes and around their inability to fulfill their dreams for a conventional lifestyle. Marital conflicts also erupted around the wives' fears that their husbands would get arrested. Accordingly, they tended to escalate their demands as time went on. Their increasing frustrations were often expressed in angry outbursts and statements that came as a surprise to their husbands. In some cases, the more argumentative the women became, the more their husbands turned to fast living which provided them with criminal opportunities.

Active resistance assumed many forms. Wives frequently initiated direct confrontations with husbands, spending countless hours reasoning with them, pointing out the likely consequences of their actions, etc. When this stopped working, they resorted to nagging, berating, and arguing with their husbands. One woman, afraid that her husband's "nights out" with his male friends would land him in jail related how she responded:

> When he's not working, as he got closer and closer to going to jail, he would stay away one night here and two nights here and there. I'd stay awake waiting for him and then I'd fall asleep on the sofa. It aggravated me that he'd arrange it so that he'd come home and leave home without seeing me. He'd manage to leave home before I got home from work. I was not capable of staying calm and waiting for the time to discuss it with him calmly. I would jump on him as soon as I saw him.

Some wives reported that their husbands responded by ignoring them and continuing their criminal activities. Other men reacted to the nagging and arguing by pretending to acquiesce.

Eventually, wives reported, their husbands attempted to hide their activities. All the men in question began to lie to their wives. One wife said:

> Mark would lie to me and say that he was going out so that he could work on his car engine. But he'd be out ripping something off. I'd call where he was supposed to be and he wouldn't be there. I'd ask Mark where he was and he'd lie to me. He always lied to me.

In response to their husbands' lying, wives typically escalated by playing out a full-fledged spy game. They came to feel that they could no longer trust their husbands. Hence, they attempted to keep track of their husbands' whereabouts, the kinds of friends with whom they were associating, etc. If the men were spending household money for their own purposes, the wives might attempt to control the money, hide their checkbooks, etc. One woman explained her reasons for attempting to control the household money:

> We got married the end of October and the night before New Year's Eve, he beat me up. I was paying the bills. Earl, probably during the whole time he was with me, got all of four paychecks. I convinced him to give up his money and he gave me the checks willingly. I wanted to control the money so he wouldn't get drunk. Then he went out and cashed checks all over town. He didn't like getting up and going to work. He did share the household chores though.

Women also resorted to hiding the wine or whiskey bottles, drugs, knives, or the car keys, in an effort to block future moves their husbands might make. Asked how she attempted to prevent her husband from "getting into trouble," one wife replied:

> When he went to Burlington, I would hide his car keys and I even would hide his spare tires so he couldn't find them whenever he had a flat tire. That didn't help. He'd find it or he'd hitchhike. He knew all my hiding places. I fought, begged him, and held on to him. He didn't like it. He'd say to me "Either I go or you get a beating!" I'd save myself and he'd go.

And another wife reported her reasons for hiding her husband's knives:

> Earl likes knives. He had them all over the house. He had all kinds of knives. I started hiding knives because I knew that he wasn't sane. He'd throw a lot of things around and yell and scream. I'm afraid of Earl. You bet your sweet bottom, I'm afraid. I remember once his being mad at me and flashing these knives around. I'd hide the knives around when he was asleep.

Often the women, when arguing and nagging were perceived as ineffective, resorted to violence. The men, themselves, often physically battered their wives in response to their active resistance. At times, both spouses acted violently. One woman recalled how she resorted to violence in response to her husband's heavy drinking and hanging around with criminal associates:

> The last time it was really bad. We were both drinking, which is really bad news. I really got mad because he was drinking and I wanted these people to leave my house and they wouldn't leave. The kind of people he hangs around with when he is drinking are different than the kind of people he hangs around with when he is sober. He finds the dregs of society when he is drinking; people that come in and destroy my house. I called my neighbor and asked him if I could borrow his gun, and he said, "Why?" and I said, "Cause I'm going to shoot Sam!" And he says, "Not today, Lucy!" I pulled a knife on Sam. I threw stuff at him. I could have killed him that day if he hadn't knocked me cold. I'd had it.

Still another woman employs violent means in order to keep her husband home:

> It means that Louis believes that being macho is being able to steal from people, to have guns, getting mad and throwing an iron, TV, and stereo, and breaking them into millions of parts. But once I hit him with a liquor bottle on the head. I wanted to stop him from going out. He had the keys to my car and I didn't want him driving my car.

In most cases, wives indicated that they felt a mixture of relief and intense shame, when these incidents had passed, at having deviated so far from the "behavior of normal women." Acting in the role of "active resisters," two women arranged for their husbands to be committed to the state mental hospital. Another informed police about her husband's criminal activities.

Frustrated by their husbands' continual pursuit of fast living and crime, they believed that the only thing to do was to enlist professional help. One woman, whose husband's heavy drinking and battering had escalated, told why she did this:

> Either some asshole would come along and bring him some booze, or he would have to go out and get it. He was going from a Dr. Jekyll to a Mr. Hyde type of personality, begging me one minute to help him, and the next minute he was trying to rip my face off. I had him committed to Bridgewater, and I was afraid that he wouldn't understand, but he thanked me for it after he sobered up.

If all else failed, the women were likely to resort to threats, usually threatening to leave their husbands if criminal activities continued. Ten women separated from their husbands one or more times. Several of these had done so repeatedly. Flight was one seemingly logical way to control what they perceive as their husbands' failures to fulfill their dream for a conventional lifestyle. One woman, whose husband hung around criminally-oriented friends gave the following explanation:

> The friends he hung around with have all been arrested at one time or another. One friend did an armed robbery. I kept telling him that the reputations they had I just didn't like and he'd wind up in jail like them. I threatened to leave him and that didn't do any good. When we moved to New York, he immediately wanted to go off with his friend over there. I told him in no uncertain terms that I'd leave him if he went. A friend of his came over and egged him on to go. I said, "Reggie go and I'll leave you now." He left. I got the kids ready to go and as I was walking out of the door, he came in. We had one of our few talks and he promised not to go out so frequently with his friends. Things were a little better after that. But when we went back to Vermont, the same thing began over again.

Still another woman, involved in the "hard" drug subculture, reported her reasons for separating from her drug-using husband:

> We argued about everything. But mostly our arguments centered around my feeling that he shouldn't be doing this to himself. Sometimes the arguments became violent. He became violent with me like hitting me. After he hit me once, I left him and went to my

parents. We had been arguing about drugs. He had left me alone for a couple of days while he searched down his drugs and I got mad. I went and stayed with my parents for about a week. We talked on the phone and he said that he was sorry and he'd try to be different. He hasn't hit me since.

By separating from their husbands, the wives thus hoped to "teach them a lesson" and hoped that, having lost their most valued relationship, the husbands would return to a straight and narrow way of living. In most cases, threats to separate and actually separating did have the desired effect. Husbands temporarily abstained from their criminal pursuits. In a few cases, however, threats to separate led to physical abuse:

One time I was going to leave him and I called my grandmother to come and get me. As I was talking with my grandmother, he came into the room with an ax and he chopped the telephone wires to pieces. I got so mad that I threw the phone at him. He then hit me and he almost broke my neck. He threw me upstairs and hit me against the door. He kicked me. I wanted to go to the hospital because I knew that I was badly hurt. He didn't want me to go to the hospital because he didn't want them to know that he kicked me. I went anyway and then when I came back, he kicked me again. I was on crutches and he kicked me on my hurt leg.

Whether or not the wives became fully active in the spy game—complete with interrogation ("Where the hell have you been for the whole night?")—or threatened to leave their husbands, the net results were the same. There was a loss of trust when wives discovered over and over again that their husbands were up to their "old tricks." However, for a period of time, household money would be managed more effectively; husbands, reminded that they could be returned to prison for parole violations, sometimes stopped their troublesome activities. Yet the costs of actively resisting were high: husbands became increasingly resentful, further alienated, and eventually resumed crime and fast-living activities.

Passive Distance

Fourteen wives resorted to "passive distance" when they discovered that other accommodative strategies neither made their lives

bearable nor deterred male criminality.[6] Most of these wives indicated that they tended to use passive distance whenever they
detected that active resistance resulted in marital discord or
physical abuse.

After an extended period of criminality, wives were likely to
behave like women in classical literature: that is, to throw up
their arms to the sky and bemoan their fate. By withdrawing, the
women reported, they could not communicate with their husbands about pressing household concerns or dissatisfactions with
their activities. Instead, they became absorbed in themselves and
their children, kept their mouths shut, and did not attempt to
interfere with their husbands' enterprises, or have any knowledge of them. They seldom questioned the men about their associates or "business" activities. They withdrew whenever their
husbands brought drug deals, stolen goods, criminal associates,
etc., into their homes. In response to her husband's unexplained
absences and receiving stolen property, one wife eventually withdrew in this fashion:

> I told him to take them out. He brought guns and said that we
> needed the extra money. I told him to get that stuff out of the
> house now. Who knows who's watching us. We could lose our
> kids. He wouldn't listen to me and he just put the stuff away. After
> a while, I just didn't do anything. If he went out, I went to sleep
> and didn't get up when he came home. I told him later that I didn't
> want to know anything about what he was doing. I didn't care
> about the stuff.

Another woman reported:

> We lived in Devonshire. He and his friends more or less figured it
> all out. I was there when they were planning it. I was watching TV
> as they were planning it [a burglary job]. I was scared and I didn't
> want him to do it. I told him and he said that I shouldn't worry
> about it. I just kept my mouth shut. When he does something stu-
> pid, I don't talk to him. I just more or less sit in my corner.

Once wives employed this strategy, they had given up any
responsibility for their husbands' actions. As far as they were
concerned, their husbands were out of control.

Passive distance was an effective strategy if husbands kept
their criminal activity on the streets. Wives could more easily

remain absorbed in their own worlds and felt less need to scrutinize or challenge their husbands.

Husbands can react violently to their wives' active resistance. As a response to battering, most wives, for varying periods of time, isolated themselves from their husbands out of fear. They kept their mouths shut and retreated into silence; fear was a major response to battering. As in the case of one young woman, many came to believe that there was nothing more they could do: "I won't argue with him any more. I won't take another beating. He can go to jail for all I care."

Wives reported that they derived certain satisfactions from employing passive distance. It allowed them to control the kind of information they could acquire about their husbands' activities, information which might possibly threaten their perceptions of their husbands as "good" guys. Wives generally attempted to observe only what they and their husbands deemed safe. Passive distance also reinforced the wives' determination to preserve their marriages. By acquiring scant information about their husbands' criminal and fast-living activities, they could concentrate on their roles as mothers and minimize those aspects of their wifely roles which might threaten the stability of their marriages. When their men continued to pursue criminal activities on the streets, for instance, the wives intensified their activities as home managers, as disciplinarians for the children, and as decision-makers: they became "domestic controllers." As wives, they held on to their obligations to service their husbands; they fed them, did their laundry, kept their homes according to their husbands' standards, and had sexual intercourse with them. What the wives derived from this strategy, then, was the illusion that husband-wife-children roles were viable and intact.

A deep sense of powerlessness is reported by wives who employed this strategy. Their husbands still continued to shape the wives' behavior and the structure of their households and the wives realized this. This sense of powerlessness was also reinforced by the belief that there was an inevitability to their husbands' "troubles with the law." Unlike other accommodative strategies, passive distance does not end or control husbands' actions. However, by withdrawing from their husbands' troublesome activities, wives trivialized the behavior, and made their own lives bearable, and preserved their marriages.

Co-Participation

Eight women had established criminal partnerships with their husbands, primarily involving property crimes, such as burglary or shoplifting. Two couples had dealt in drugs, one in check forging, and one in armed robbery. Four women in the study population had independently participated in criminal activities such as shoplifting, check forging, burglary, or drug dealing. As co-participants, these women usually played secondary or supportive roles in criminal activity. Seven women had engaged in a variety of criminal activities in roles which reinforced their husbands'. Only one woman had played a leading role in planning and carrying out crimes initiated by her husband.

Generally, husbands first taught these wives the techniques used in particular crimes. Wives most often acted as accessories by carrying weapons, driving get-away cars, acting as look-outs, and hiding stolen property. However, the husbands were not always in positions of dominance. All these women reported that there were times when they also planned, initiated, and enacted crimes in which their husbands assumed secondary roles. For example, one woman recalled how she initially learned to do burglaries from her husband, but eventually planned and carried out her own:

> I helped him on a few jobs. He did other pharmacies, too. I went with him one night and chickened out on it. But I did do one with another guy. I drove him there and I planned it. . . .
>
> We broke into the pharmacy without making any noise. I planned how to get the stuff and how to get out and where we would meet. It was a simple break and entry job. I wasn't caught. . . .
>
> We must have done a few of them. We needed money for narcotics and this was the best way to get it.

Another wife related that her husband taught her shoplifting techniques which she then used on her own:

> When Frank boosted, I would go along sometimes. He boosted when the money was really bad, we just didn't have any money. I

began to boost and I showed him that I could lift better than he. I worked in a team with a girlfriend. She'd lift cigarettes and she'd drop it and I'd come along and pick it up. If she got caught she would have nothing on her. We'd split up the goods. This was Frank's idea. I said the hell with bills, I'm going to eat. I'd never done it before, and Frank told me how to do it. I got four or five shirts one time and the next time I tripled my take. I got into a kind of competition with Frank to see who could lift the most. I guess I did it because I was bored and when I got bored I'd go out and lift.

Wives co-participated in criminal activities for several reasons. For some, co-participation was an accommodative strategy used in demonstrating their loyalty and love to their husbands and hence was helpful in preserving marriages. But in addition, co-participation provided wives with certain personal satisfactions, notably heightened excitement, adventure, and challenges missing from everyday domestic roles. As this wife related:

I guess in a sense it was exciting because there was something new going on all the time. The last time I did anything was because I was pregnant. When I realized that if I got caught, the state could take my kid away and after I realized that, I didn't do anything. When I was pregnant was when I hid Randy and Art and held the stolen property in my house. The only thing that I didn't become involved in was the B & E at the warehouse. Randy was involved. I knew about it and I had this feeling that he was going to jail. I just had these weird feelings.

Crime—especially drug use—can also be a form of recreation. As members of the drug subculture, three wives reported that all drug-related activities could be satisfying, since the drugs bring euphoria and pleasure. Those wives who abused drugs reported that the whole process of securing money, finding drug connections and getting high, could bring them and their men "closer together." Since their relationships were based on drug consumption, they could share a mutual orientation. Finally, a few wives reported that they were involved in crimes for immediate tangible reasons, *e.g.*, money and material goods. These women reported that they primarily acted as co-deviants or as independent criminals in order to secure money to support their households or their drug habits. One woman asserted that she forged checks primarily for economic reasons. However, she also derived other satisfactions from it: excitement, fun, and the challenge of "beating the system." Asked why she participated in criminal activities, she said:

> When it was a necessity. When we were broke and needed money. Like checks. We'd cash checks when we were broke. I was scared shitless when I did it, but it's like a disease. You can't stop! It's a fever! But how you can con some people!
>
> There are all kinds of ways to beat the system. There is always a way to get around the system. It's fun to use your mind to get around it. It's the excitement of getting away with it. You first wonder if you're going to get away with it or not. All your senses become alive. You're alive! I lived it. But since I am older now and have more responsibilities, I don't do it. I think that we're all excitement oriented.

Many of these wives who participated in crime eventually decided to establish more conventionally-oriented lives for themselves and their families. At this point their husbands' persistent criminality became problematic, and they then turned to other accommodative strategies previously analyzed.

Reluctant Co-Participation

Three wives reluctantly engaged in their husbands' fast-living and criminal activities, under threats of physical harm, i. e., as a consequence of actual physical battering or under such forms of threatening coercion as shooting off guns in their homes, brandishing knives, destroying household furniture, and so forth:

> I wanted him to stop drinking and I've given up on him. He won't stop unless he wants to. Nothing I can do about it, but I'll just watch him drinking the rest of his life and I'll just be watching him drink for the rest of mine, I expect. When he starts to drink, he picks up a bottle. I get so afraid that he's going to hit me. I don't say anything and I am so scared that I just sit quietly and drink my coffee and smoke cigarettes. Sometimes I go to the store and buy him more beer. I don't know why I go. I'm scared and wonder when the first punch is going to come. When I told him I wouldn't go to the store and get his beer, he punched me. After that, I got him whatever he wanted—beer, pot, or whatever drugs he wanted.

Poorly trained and uneducated, they felt that they had few alternatives to remaining in their marriages and participating in deviant behavior they found offensive, *e.g.,* receiving stolen goods, securing drugs for their husbands or being sexually abused by their husbands:

> Nelson was a sexual deviant. His idea for sexual fun was using whatever he could. I told him at the end that what he needed was a corpse. I came out and said that to him. I told him that, "You want me to function as a housewife and mother during the day in perfect fashion and then at night you want me to come into the bedroom and be a corpse. What kind of life is that for me?" He did all kinds of things. He would build himself up to a frenzy.
>
> During the day and then at night we would do these things. He strangled me, put stuff inside of me that didn't belong. I let him do all these things because I didn't want the children to know what was going on. I wouldn't scream even though there were times that I could barely help myself from screaming. But I didn't want to wake up the kids or he'd kill me. There was no place for me to go. There was nobody for me to talk about Nelson. I was always afraid that he would kill me. Around my thirtieth birthday, I got very tired of all this. I began to plan on leaving him, but I wanted to wait until the kids were grown.

It is their husbands who planned and initiated these enterprises. As time progressed, men's insistence upon their wives' participation escalated: one wife's home was more frequently used as her husband's base for receiving and selling stolen goods; marital rape became more frequent while loving sex became more rare; and lastly, trips to procure drugs become more frequent.

Reluctant co-participation neither curtailed nor limited husbands' criminal behavior. Instead, by using this strategy, wives avoided further "hostile" confrontations with their husbands. This strategy was a compromise used to prevent further verbal and physical abuse and thus to make life more bearable.

None of the accommodative strategies were as effective as wives anticipated they would be. At best, wives were able to achieve a temporary attenuation of some of the fast-living or criminal activities they found most difficult to cope with. The majority experienced an overwhelming sense of powerlessness as a result of trying to deal with their husbands during this stage in their lives. Linked to this was a sense of inevitability about their husbands "getting into trouble with the law." This undermined the effectiveness of the strategies they adopted, and made the task of steering the men away from criminal acts and fast living—and thereby preserving their marriages—even more difficult than it might have been.

CHAPTER V

Arrests, Lawyers, Courts,
and Sentencing

I don't think that anyone understands the degree of loss that I feel
about his going to jail. I can't talk with my friends. It would be
so different if Danny had died. When someone dies, people see it
as a legitimate reason to act weird, but they don't see any
legitimate reason to be weird because your husband goes to jail. I
feel a sense of loss and they don't realize that. They don't realize
that he was torn away from me. My friends see his arrest as
something you have done willingly. They see my relationship as
my blame. I've made my bed, so now I lie in it. They see it as if I
did something wrong, too. It's absurd. When they say, "How do
you devote yourself to him?" they don't realize that I can't turn
my feelings off like a water faucet. It's not the kind of thing that I
can be objective about.

Two crisis points in the experiences of wives whose husbands
are passing through the criminalization process are arrest and
sentencing. Wives' accounts reveal that, at each of these crisis
points, they were confronted with multiple tasks which they performed to support their husbands.

Accommodation to their husbands' criminality meant being
willing to cope with the unfamiliar and sometimes frightening
aftermath of arrests and sentencing. The wives assessed past
events to explain their husbands' new identities as "accused offenders," and attempted to reconcile this status with images of
their men as "husbands and fathers."

THE WOMEN SPEAK FOR THEMSELVES

Tammy had been married for three years to a husband who was
charged and sentenced for possession of stolen property. This
segment of Tammy's account describes first how the police, with

warrants to arrest her husband, gained entry to their apartment which they shared with her husband's mother.

We were both sleeping when the cops came in. Two creeps with shotguns came into the house first. All of a sudden the house became a madhouse with cops swarming all over the place. We were told to sit in the kitchen. Mark's brother and sister were quite afraid and we were busy trying to calm them down. They searched the house. The house was a mess. They looked through everything.

They wouldn't let me get dressed. I asked them if I could go into my room and put on some clothes. They wouldn't let me. They got their jollies out of seeing me nude. For most of the time they were here they had me sit in the kitchen nude. They let me get dressed when they got good and ready. And then they insisted that one of the cops had to be in the room with me when I got dressed.

They went so far as to go into my toilet bowl. The toilet bowl is an old one, Mrs. Green [her mother-in-law] put a coke bottle in the toilet to keep the toilet from running the usual amount of water. She had been told that if you put a coke bottle in the toilet it prevents it from running a lot of water. They threw this coke bottle at me and told me it was dope. It was filled with water. I tried to explain to them why the coke bottle was there. There were a couple of nice policemen and the rest of them were pigs. They intended to go down stairs and search the apartment of Mark's aunt and grandparents. They are in their eighties and nineties. I tried to explain to them that these people were too old to be harassed and they had nothing to do with our lives. They didn't go.

They were going to take what they wanted. So much they stole from us and never returned. They tried to tell me that a package of poppy seeds was opium. If I knew my legal rights at the time they could never have done what they did. I would have had them out of here. But I didn't know my rights.

They threatened to have Mrs. Green involved and arrested if we didn't let them search the basement. They searched the basement and tore it apart.

They took Mark away first and then they said that I had to go with them. We went to the police station and they asked me all sorts of questions. They first said that they were going to arrest me. They kept me there all night asking me questions about where the stolen goods came from and where was the dope they were supposedly looking for. I was kept in a little room which had no windows and they just badgered me with questions. They asked me who were Mark's friends and who of these friends deals in dope and who deals in guns. I told them nothing.

In the meantime, they arrested Mark for possession of guns and stereo equipment. They told me that since I lived there, I was just as much a part of this as was Mark. They were going to put me in jail and somehow Mark talked them out of it.

They placed bail for $2,800 on Mark and we did not have the money. If it wasn't for Mr. Keeny we wouldn't have been able to get Mark out. Mr. Keeny is a big man in Derby. He owns Derby. For three days we fought them. We offered all our property up instead of bail and they wouldn't accept it. They wanted cash. The City Clerk's office rubbed our faces in shit constantly. When Mr. Keeny came down there they were so nice to him. We've learned how much money counts. When he put money up for bail, they kowtowed to him. He owns the town of Derby and they know it.

It was awful. Everyone was against us. We were all so uptight during this time. Whenever anyone knocked on the door, we expected it to be a pig. We were frightened all the time. I remained a bundle of nerves. Mark thought about committing suicide because he was so despondent. He felt that his life was over. We had long talks with Mark then: trying to keep his hopes up. When he went to court, he had tears in his eyes. We felt that he was not guilty. We were pretty close during this time. We did fight, but it was because we felt caged together in this thing. I hated to see him be caged and so did he.

Louis Jackman was appointed to be Mark's lawyer. He was good to us. He was really fighting for his client. He knew it was a setup and even though we had no money, he fought. If it was not for Jackman, Mark would be sitting on a life sentence. He had three charges for stolen property which placed him in the habitual offender category and they wanted to give him life.

I went to court with Mark every time. He was surprised when the judge dropped the habitual criminal charges and he only got 4–10 years suspended sentence and he had to serve 2 years. They wanted him to go to Londonderry and then to a halfway house. His probation officer made up this plan. He was supposed to be doing so much for us, and he kept telling us that he would do good for us. He kinda tricked us because he got this halfway house tacked to his sentence. If he had done straight time, without the suspended sentence deal, he would have less time to serve. Jeff Lewis, the probation officer, came here and talked to us. He said he'd do anything to help. He said that he was going to help Mark and didn't do anything.

When the sentence was given by the judge I didn't understand it. I asked Mr. Jackman and he explained it to me. I was shaking because I didn't know what was going to happen. Once I knew, I began to feel better. The sheriff let Mark and me talk a few minutes before they took him away. That was good.

I went home after court. I felt lost, completely lost without Mark. It was so strange, such a strange feeling, after having him around here and not to have him here so suddenly. I felt as though I was hanging in the air. I still do.

The next account expresses well the kinds of fears women experience when they, themselves press charges against their husbands. Penny, married less than a year, begins her account by describing the circumstances surrounding her husband's arrest.

The first thing that went rotten in our marriage was his cashing my checks all over town, and his getting drunk every day, and then he broke into OEO [i.e., Office of Economic Opportunity]. He called my kid a rotten puke. I'll never forgive him for that. I'd be taking Shaun off to day care when I went to work and Earl would say that I should keep him home all day. He'd take Shaun on his little jobs and give him pot.

One day I went into a store and the man gave me some of my checks. He told me that they had all bounced. Earl had signed my name to these checks. Every day I went home and there were more checks. It came to over $500. I made them all good. Every day he swore that there wouldn't be any more checks. At this time he had all these guns in the house and he wasn't going to work and he was just staying at home and getting drunk.

More checks came back to me and then he beat me in the face. One night Earl got drunk and I told him that I was going out to get something to eat. He then grabbed me by the neck and beat the royal piss out of me. That time I had bruises on my cheekbone and cuts on the inside of my mouth. I was bleeding in two or three places on my face. I had big bruises on my legs and my back. One of my wrists was cut up. I didn't go to the hospital. I didn't want to face that kind of humiliation.

I was trying to get to my apartment. I was beating on my door and there were three guys in my apartment waiting for me. They opened the door. One took Earl outside and told him to get lost. They helped me clean up. Earl came back and they sent him away.

I couldn't believe it could happen to me. I spent four years with an alcoholic and he demolished me. He probably beat me one hundred times. That's no exaggeration. And he never changed. People don't change like that. I said that if Earl beats me once, he won't stop and it fits in with his type of life. No way am I going to take a chance like that again. I told him before if he beats me, I'd leave him. He didn't believe me.

After he did it, I felt that he would do it again. He was drunk and I didn't want him to have the car. The check thing was coming out. He knew I was getting pretty fed up with that.

Earl needs a lot of caring. There was no way he could get it quick enough from me and that was pure frustration for him. So he'd continue to beat me. No way I'd forgive and forget him. Not for one second did I make that mistake.

The next day, I called the police. After I had a few cups of coffee I tried to figure out what to do with this maniac. If I had felt he would leave me alone, I'd let it be. I couldn't see that. I was afraid that Earl was not going to let me go easily. He wasn't going to make it easy for me. I said, "Fuck it" and dished it right back!

I had the checks with me when I went to the State's Attorney's Office. I didn't want him running on the streets loose and I was worried about Shaun's well-being with him around. When I got to the State's Attorney, they told me that they were after him for forging $250 worth of checks and I just fell into their hands.

Finally I pressed the charges. He likes going to jail. He doesn't have any pressures there. He gets his meals, sleeps, and he can finally feel superior because he can accomplish things there that he can't seem to accomplish on the outside.

Three days later we talked. He called me from the jail. He couldn't believe I did that to him. He wanted to continue our relationship while he was in jail. He just wanted some visitors.

June Bollo is his friend and she'd keep in touch with me. I kept calling her and she me. She kept telling me that Earl wanted me. I started thinking of his friends walking the streets. I was worried about his friends. I knew that word had gotten out that I had ratted on him. Somehow it got around that I had ratted on a friend of Earl's and then they said I was ratting on everyone. I felt that it was very important to show I wasn't doing anything nor was I about to do anything so I went to see Earl. I felt that if they saw that Earl and I were continuing our relationship, they might then feel assured that I wasn't going to rat on them.

I felt that his friends were going to beat my brains in. They would follow me around in their car and send me dirty messages. One message said, "You're going to get it." I was afraid. Through word of mouth I got another message—if I didn't say anything to the cops, they'd be happy. I was going to testify in court but I backed out because I was afraid of what his friends could do to me.

I went to court all the times he went. The cops would bring him in and they'd ask me why am I here for this turkey? I'd say, "I don't know." And I really didn't know why I was there.

Earl would come in with the suit that he had won from a poker game and he'd say, "Hi honey!" I'd say to myself, "You fucker, you thrive on this game and you love it." The rest just bummed me out. John Heller [the prosecutor] would see me with Earl and see me holding his hand. He'd say, "What was I doing?" He asked me why I wouldn't testify. I wouldn't tell him because he could tell Earl's lawyer and then it would get back to Earl that I was playing with him. I would look around the court and I would see people that I knew who did the same things over and over again. I'd say to myself, "Look at these turkeys and I used to hang with them and they do the same thing over and over again."

I am now a constructive person. When I did drugs, I was fucked up. But I'm not that kind of person now. I believe in doing constructive things and I tend to set my goals higher than do other people. This is not for me. For some women, this is for them. It's like you're throwing your life away. I'm not going to do it. I could see doing the prison thing and he will get out in four months and then do it again. No way am I going through that!

He got 1–5 years. I felt why couldn't they give him more. In a year, I'm going to have to contend with this turkey. I knew that if I'd testify, he'd have gotten 15 years and then when he got out, I'd be in bigger trouble.

He's coming out in the spring. I'm very worried that I'm still going to be his wife. I just want this divorce to go through. I don't want to talk to him. I hope he will stay away.

ARRESTS

Whether or not wives knew about their husbands' criminal activities, their arrests came as a rude awakening in which all wives experienced disorientation, *i.e.*, bewilderment, shock, and disbelief. Of twenty-eight women who had been living with their husbands for six months or more at the time of their arrest, seventeen were aware that arrest was imminent—but all experienced some degree of surprise. Nine were "old timers,"[1] *i.e.*, they had previous experience with their husbands' arrests, convictions, and imprisonments. Old timers were more likely to believe that arrest was imminent than were neophytes. The remaining eleven wives, who did not anticipate their husbands' arrests, were all neophytes.[2]

Two major factors seem to determine whether wives anticipate "troubles with the law": whether or not their husbands were "living fast," and the type of criminal activities in which they engaged. When the men were living "fast" and were involved in criminal enterprises, their wives anxiously awaited their arrest. The wives of men with previous criminal records believed that their husbands *were* going to be arrested. This was particularly true if the men had histories of repeated alcohol- and/or drug-related crimes. An old timer whose husband had committed numerous alcohol-related crimes reported how she responded to her husband's heavy consumption of alcohol:

> I knew then that he was on the verge of trouble. I just knew it. I tried to get help from AA, the State Police, Waterbury, and Mental Health. All of them said that they couldn't do it. If he didn't come in voluntarily then they couldn't help him. He must show that he wanted help. Then two days later he got into some guy who was cashing checks. The cops, as always, began to follow me, to sit out here in front of the lawn, always asking me questions. I told them that "I didn't know where he was. I'm not paid to follow him and you are! So you find him! I didn't know where he was."

And another old timer explained how she knew her husband was about to be arrested:

> It depends on what he's done. When he's down at the police station, I know even though nobody has told me. I have a sixth sense about it. It's always when he's been drinking and he usually does some dumb, stupid things. If he's innocent, then I fight like hell for him. But if he's guilty, I become quiet.

The extent to which wives were able to anticipate their husbands' arrests varied by the type of offense involved. Most of the wives whose husbands engaged in property or "paper" crimes reported some knowledge of their husband's activities.

> I knew what he did before they arrested him. I had a sense of what he was going to do. He and another guy came home and they had money in their pockets. My husband had just a little bit of money, but enough so that I asked him, "Hey, where did you get that money?" And he said that he and another guy had participated in a robbery. The first thing they said was, "Heh, we got some odd jobs." I knew he lied. I knew that he hadn't gotten any odd jobs. I became scared. The next day, two detectives came and asked questions. They asked me if I knew what he had been doing the other day. I told them that I didn't know anything but I thought he would be coming home at 6:00. And they said that they would return in order to talk with him. I took the children out and went to my mother's house and when I came back he was gone. The detectives had come back when I was gone and they picked him, my husband, up.

Most of the women whose husbands were arrested for crimes against persons were aware that arrest was likely. A few of these women pressed the charges against their husbands for either physical abuse or both physical abuse and forgery. A wife whose husband had a history of battering, described a battering incident in which he was arrested:

> The first thing I remember was that I was laying on the ground. We were at my mother's house. We were drinking and it was a hot day so we were all inside. All at once Rocky comes in and says that we're leaving immediately. He was mad at something. He had been drinking too. We got into the car and Joanne, my little girl, began to fuss. He turned around and slapped her in the mouth. I got mad and I ran out of the car. He grabbed me and I was out on the ground. The next thing I knew he was beating my mother. Then he took out a knife and tried to slash his wrists. This I learned later. Then the ambulance came and took me to the hospital.
>
> He was arrested the same night. They first took him to the hospital to have the slash in his wrists attended to. He cut his wrists with his knife. I think that he wanted to commit suicide.

Few wives were completely surprised by their husbands' arrests. Almost all of these were wives of first timers, who had, without warning, gotten themselves involved in some criminal pursuit. None of the wives of "square johns" were aware of the imminence of their husbands' arrests. One wife reported that her husband's drinking had been the reason that he had committed a crime against a person. Of the three men arrested for sex offenses, two wives had not anticipated troubles with the law. The other wives were tied to men arrested for some form of property or paper crime. A few wives reported that they had not been suspicious about their husbands' activities, because they had been living apart at the time.

Seventeen women were present at the time of the arrest, while eleven were not. Generally, when women witnessed their husbands' arrests, they defined them as both dramatic and very traumatic events. Most arrests took place in their homes, on the streets, or in cars. The wives recalled that most arrests were handled by the police in a routine, fair manner. There was usually no particular hostility involved. Typically, this wife of an accused sex offender recalled the arrest as matter-of-factly enacted by the police:

> Then one evening the police came and I answered the door. Sara was in bed. There were two male cops and a female cop. I found out that the woman was from the rape squad. I asked them what was going on. Rape was the last thing I could imagine. They told me that they came to arrest Kevin for rape. My picture of the rapist was one of a monster. It was only later that I found them to be criminals who are people with problems.
>
> The police were there and Kevin asked them if he could go get a shirt to put on. I said to Kevin, "What is going on!" He said, "It's called rape!" I couldn't function at all. Kevin left immediately.

Movies and television tend to portray arrests as dramatic moments, often involving violence or at least a threat of it. The actual threat of police violence was present in only a few cases:

> The last time he was picked up at my mother's house. They slammed him against the banister and beat him. They wouldn't let me talk to him. I said to the cops, "Piss on you!" and then I ran down the stairs after him to give him his cigarettes. They wouldn't let me see him because he was still married to his first wife. I called a lawyer. They gave me a hard time. They disliked me from the beginning because I gave them a hard time.

Even when arrests were routine and nonviolent, most wives found the event to be devastating. This was true even when the husbands had severely assaulted their wives or forged their checks. In one case a husband had attempted to murder his wife and children.

Those wives who were not present learned about their husbands' arrests from their husbands, friends, other family members, the police, or in the case of some separated couples—from newspapers. Some old timers reported having to telephone the local hospitals and jails when their husbands did not come home for a night or so:

> Randy went out with Ken one day at 9:30 in the morning. They went to fix the blinkers on car. They went someplace. At 11 o'clock in the night, they weren't here. Then 1 o'clock came by and they still had not returned. I stayed up waiting for Randy and then I went over to his mother's and he wasn't there. While I was sitting here, and it was dawn by then, the lady upstairs asked me to come up for some coffee. She suggested that I call the jail and find out if he was there. I called one of the inmates at the jail and he told me that Randy was back there. I cried and that's how I found out.

The women who were not present generally treated their husbands' arrests as routine or unexciting events. Several wives who were aware of their husbands' criminal activities reported that they experienced a sense of relief because the dreaded event had finally occurred.

Most wives believed that their men were guilty of the crimes for which they had been arrested. For these wives, arrest was the most important event in the judicial process; their husbands' cases were virtually "over" when arrest occurred. Only one wife believed that her husband's arrest was entirely unwarranted. Consequently, she perceived the next stages of the judicial process to be critical. Whether or not wives thought that their husbands should have been arrested, they found that they were forced to come to terms with the formal labelling process as well as the more direct consequences of their husbands' arrest.

Willingness of Wives to Raise Bail

Immediately after their husbands' arrests, wives were confronted with the problem of securing bail money. They soon learned that, as the wives of accused offenders, this was their responsibility. Husbands first informed them of this; only two men took direct charge of raising the necessary money themselves. Sixteen women actively attempted to raise bail, while twelve women did not. Of these seven neophytes and five old timers, eight simply did not have the necessary funds, nor could they raise them from friends or family. A neophyte related how she reacted to the amount set for bail:

> The judge read what the charges were and what the consequences of these charges would be. Then he set the bail at $50,000. It didn't look like I'd be raising bail. [Laughs here] I wasn't laughing then and they sent him back to jail.

The reason given by these old timers for failing to attempt to raise bail was their husbands' histories. They described how they actively supported their husbands when they had had their first encounters with the law. After repeated arrests, however, they refused to respond to them as emergencies which required immediate attention. Instead, they assumed a position of passive distance: they withdrew. Accordingly, they neither called lawyers nor provided bail money:

> Q. Did you cry the last time he was arrested?
> A. I didn't cry. I'm trying to remember how I found out. I probably did cry, but it wasn't the same—Bawl! Bawl! Bawl! I probably cried and said, "Barry, you fucked up again!" and that was it. All I think about now is my work. If he gets into trouble, go ahead. I've given up. I've given up on him. I've helped him all I can. His father came and told me that Barry wanted to see him at the court and he needed bail. I might have cried but then I went back asleep. I had to go to work the next day and that was more important than Barry's needing bail.

Another old timer reported her reasons for refusing to raise bail for her husband who has an extensive history of drug use and crimes against the person:

> Once I borrowed money from my father and that was the only

time I got bail for him. I don't deal with banks. The time I borrowed money was the first time he needed bail since we were married. He didn't go by all the rules. He fucked the bail up. He went back to the center. He almost got my father's money forfeited. You don't walk over people who help you. He gave his word and he broke it, and it was my father's money. So I never got him bail after that. Other times, I told him that I don't have it and there is nowhere I can get it. That's it for him.

Four other women did not make an effort to raise bail. They were either simply unwilling to raise bail since their husbands' imprisonment guaranteed that they would be out of their homes, or they were not around: one was hospitalized and the other was out of state.

Obtaining bail is costly and places additional financial strains on wives who want to secure their husbands' release from pre-trial detention. Often large sums of money are required for bail, lawyers' fees, and incidentals. These amounts involved were usually beyond the means of these wives. Thus the crisis of arrest was often exacerbated by wives' lack of cash reserves for bail money. As in any crisis, almost all these prisoners' wives sought support from their personal networks; particularly their close families, and sometimes extended kin and friends. Twelve women sought bail money from relatives. Neophytes were more likely to ask and receive family support, while old timers were less likely. A neophyte, married to a man who had previously been arrested, described how her family got her husband "out on bail" after his first arrest:

> I tried and I couldn't get it up. The bail was about $5,000. They wouldn't let Gary out. My father went down and said he'd sign this paper that Gary would be in his custody and then Gary got out. My grandmother put her house up for us. He got out after a month. It took a while because the lawyer had to get so many things together. He tried to get Gary's bail reduced and other things and as a last resort he used my father.

Old timers, by contrast, were less likely to receive support from families. Three old timers and only one neophyte asked their families for support and were denied. Of the nine neophytes who made no effort to raise bail, most of them explicitly stated that they had not tried to ask their families.

The general reasons for not asking for or receiving family support were similar. With each arrest, trial, or sentence, the women usually made heavier demands on their husbands and/or their own families. However, when arrests were repeated, families' reserves of good will tended to dry up. Hence, families became less reluctant to let the men remain in pre-trial detention, and wives more reluctant to ask for help.

Ten wives were successful in getting their husbands released on bail as a result of family help. One old timer reported that she got her husband released in her custody. Only a few of these men had sufficient cash reserves and did not need their wives' help. Some wives, who were members of the drug subculture, turned to other drug users for help:

> This time I went to court. I told him that I was going. He was out on bail. I had bailed him out. Some friends helped me by giving me money. That's what happens in the drug scene. When one person goes to jail, the others do attempt to raise the bail money for that person. So he had been out on bail for six or eight months. At that time we were living on drugs. He wasn't working and we still got our money through drugs.

Thus, a little over half of the men have remained in pretrial detention. While wives' willingness to raise bail money played a role in determining who would be released and who would not, the accused's economic standing also was important. For instance, when square janes discovered that they could not raise bail money, their husbands' families were likely to come to their assistance. All husbands of square janes met bail, while most working class husbands did not.

It is clear from wives' accounts, then, that they were the ones most likely to assume major responsibility for their husbands' release. Wives' initiative, perseverance, and assertiveness were important factors in determining whether or not this occurred. In doing this, wives had to balance a multitude of responsibilities: the care of their children, homes, jobs, as well as their husbands. The critical differences between those women who obtained their husbands' release from pre-trial detention and those who did not were: (1) the wives' willingness to make the attempt; (2) the wives' status as neophytes or old timers; and

(3) their ability to marshal resources in the form of a cash reserve or family support.

Wives' Reactions to the Crisis of Arrest

Arrest can be a crisis-provoking event in the lives of prisoners' wives. In general, wives are abruptly confronted with both involuntary loss and the kind of status transformations inherent in this stage of the criminalization process. Their husbands are officially labelled as accused offenders. This carries with it implications for these wives as well, and conditions their reactions to the events going on around them.

Many wives reported feeling disoriented at the time of their husbands' arrests. Many had a sense that events were suddenly out of context. Wives who were unaware of the imminence of their husbands' arrest were more likely to report that it had nightmarish qualities since they had no information about what their husbands had done to deserve being treated as they were:

> When I got home, I just freaked out. I cried and cried and cried. Everything was ruined; my world was ruined and my house was torn apart—all my clothes were on the floor. Some of them had been ripped. The police took my personal things like rings and I didn't get them back for a year. They said that they assumed that they were stolen articles and had to hold them until they were sure they weren't stolen. This was all so big. It was happening around me and I just watched it. It was happening and I was part of it but I had no say in what was happening. This was overwhelming.

Most wives recalled that they experienced feelings of shock, denial, disbelief, helplessness, and personal loss at the time the arrests occurred.[3] Many women indicated that they have felt both uncertain and fearful about what the future would hold. However, this was clearly more true of old timers. As wives became aware of the ramifications of their husbands' arrests—jail, trials, and likely convictions—the tears flowed and then the floundering began. As one old timer whose husband was arrested for possession of stolen property related:

> It was during the Christmas season. We were living then on Manchester Street. We went up the street Christmas shopping. My father was driving by our house and he saw that the lights were on

in the house. The house was ablaze with lights. He told us that when we dropped in to see him after shopping. He said that someone was in the house, and that state police cars, and city police cars were surrounding the house. Soon after he told us, a cop knocked at the door and told Gary to come down to the house. We went down to the house. We left the kids with my parents. When we got there they advised Gary of his rights and told him that he could have a lawyer. They had knocked down the door because no one was in the house. They kicked the door in with its chain locks. They ripped the door. All the doors and windows of the house were wide open and the furnace was up to 90 degrees. It was winter time and every light was on in the house. Gary had a fit. They took truckloads of stuff away. They even took some of my own stuff because they didn't know that it was my stuff.

The house looked liked a hurricane came through and hit it. They tore everything up. It took me three days to clean it up. While I was there, the next day, someone tried to break into the house. I told him that I'd call the police and he went away. I was scared to stay there. Well, my sister moved out of this house and I moved in. I was in hysterics. I didn't know where I was going to stay, how I was going to live with Gary and I knew that he was going to be in for a long time.

One neophyte whose husband had just been arrested for sale of regulated drugs illustrated these reactions:

I was up all night. I found it was hard to sleep under the circumstances. I was trying to figure out what had happened to him. Early that morning, I was trying to get him a lawyer. I called all sorts of people to find out the names of the lawyers who'd likely take his case. I also wanted to find out what to do about my car and how I should handle myself. I wanted to know if I had to get a lawyer for myself as well as for Grant and what to do.

Neophytes were more likely to feel disoriented since they had few guidelines as to how to act. Old timers more frequently anticipated their husbands' arrests; they experienced shock and personal loss, but soon were resigned to their husbands' guilt and eventual conviction. What ran through old timers' accounts were such responses as anger, resignation, relief, or a "Here we go again!" attitude. One old timer expressed this well:

Fifteen minutes after they picked him up, Rudi called me on the phone to tell me where he was. He told me that he loved me. I said to myself, "Here we go again!" He doesn't remember that he called me. Then he called me again from the police station. He told me that he had been arrested. I told him that I knew that. He had called me before and told me. Then the police dropped over to the house and told me that he had been arrested. They always come over and tell me when Rudi's in. Rudi told me that he wanted me to know first.

Beyond this, old timers were more likely to know what to expect, more likely to assert their own and their men's rights, to refuse to sign statements, to call their lawyers immediately, and to start raising bail money, if possible:

The minute he gets busted, my first reaction is to call the lawyer because I know that the first hours are the most important ones. So I keep busy with the lawyers.

The predominant reaction among old timers whose husbands were alcoholics or drug users was one of relief:

Sometimes it's such a relief to see them go back to jail. You know that at least they will dry out and that they can't get into even more trouble. I know that I'd worry and worry about Frank. I'd worry that he was going to get himself into some kind of big trouble. But it's when you stop worrying, that's when they go off to jail.

Feelings of relief were also expressed by two wives of sex offenders. In most cases, this relief was based on the expectation that prison personnel would be able to control and/or cure their men of aberrations and turn them into normal citizens.

A few wives, however, were relieved to see their husbands arrested for other reasons. As victims of their husbands' crimes, they welcomed their husbands' arrest and subsequent detention as a viable solution to an intolerable marital situation. In effect, jails and prisons became the final solution for their deteriorating marriages. As one of the women whose husband had criminally victimized her recounted:

I was relieved to get rid of him. I still cared about my well-being and there was no way that I'd feel bad for him. I had been stupid once but I wasn't going to be stupid twice.

I felt a little guilty about putting him there. But I didn't have any feeling of loss. I felt that I had gained a lot. I had gained my sanity and peace and quiet. Things made more sense than when Earl was around doing all kinds of crazy things.

Women who experienced this sense of relief usually did not feel anger and resentment. Some old timers, however, reported that they reacted this way since they believed that their husbands committed the crimes with which they were charged and they were angry and resentful at the possibility of being left to manage on their own. In these cases, the wives in question seemed more resentful about their husbands' apparent "desertion" than the fact that they had committed crimes.

No matter what offenses the men committed or how many times they had been arrested, the majority of wives reacted with concern for their men's predicament. What the wives tended to feel was that being supportive of their men was their wifely duty.

Aftermath and Rationalization

Once their husbands had been arrested, most wives found that they were forced to come to terms with the formal labelling process. Wives reported that, for days and sometimes weeks after the arrest, they were preoccupied with the events leading up to it. Many life concerns were brought up for review. The wives sometimes investigated their husbands' past or, just as frequently, examined themselves and any possible role they might have played in their husbands' "downfall." "Accounts" can flourish during this period, and the women usually referred to those explanations their husbands provided. Hence, husbands' own assessments frequently become incorporated into wives' accounts.

It was usually at this point that the wives first devised a comprehensive account or a history of the men's criminal behavior, *e.g.*, a sad tale to explain what had transpired. These sad tales differed in several ways from those presented by women during their courtships. First, in these instances the sad tales generally focused on a few significant events or themes to demonstrate what had gone wrong in their men's lives. Second, these

sad tales were devised to reassure the women themselves that
their marriages were really worth while.

Tales created during this critical period also included situational justifications. Some wives placed their husbands' behavior
within the context of extraordinary situations that were not
likely to happen again. For instance, one neophyte recalled how
her husband committed his first rape:

> He got into the routine of jogging every evening if he found that he
> couldn't sleep in the evenings. He had developed a prearranged
> jogging path that he followed every time. As he went along, he got
> into the habit of looking into people's windows. This looking acted
> as a release for him. He had all these tensions and stresses. In
> one window he usually saw a woman who was parading around
> her house without any underwear on. He got into stopping and
> watching her. I don't know how long he watched her. It must
> have happened one weekend. I don't know how he got into her
> house, but he got in. He cut the telephone wires. When he got
> into her house he went into the bedroom and said to the girl,
> "Don't be frightened, don't holler. I need someone to talk to. I
> don't want to hurt you but I will if it's necessary." She was scared
> to death. Then he said, "I want to make love to you and talk to
> you." She said, "No!" He said, "I don't want to be mean." She
> then told him that she was afraid that she would get pregnant. She
> asked if she could use her diaphragm. He said, "Yes!" He took her
> into the bathroom where she got her diaphragm and put it on.
> They made love. He had to do it so he could be close to her and
> talk. But he couldn't come. He made her perform oral sex and then
> he finally reached orgasm. She was quiet and made it clear that she
> wouldn't struggle.

Other wives elaborated their sad tales by placing their husbands' crimes within the context of disturbed marriages, overwhelming job pressures, car accidents, and so forth. One young
wife placed her husband's involvement in armed robbery within
the context of job frustrations:

> He was getting discouraged. The drinking began. At that time he
> was working with an organization that gets jobs for teenagers who
> are economically deprived. He was not getting too much response
> for this program. The program was not going anywhere. The direc-
> tor, who ran the program, was always in the bar downstairs and

left Tim to run it. Everything started to snowball. He became frustrated and humiliated and he began to lose sight of himself. I guess he lost control. I guess he got into this state that he was in and he was terribly irrational.

Still another wife ascribed her husband's attempted rape to his history of unusual sexual situations:

... But when he was arrested, a lot came out of him. Things that I never knew about Charles came pouring out. I didn't know that he was charged with rape during the service. He was with a woman in his apartment and attempted to have sex with her and she cried rape. The charges were dropped. One by one I started learning things about him. Also when he was in the service he got some girl pregnant. She went back to her home town. When he got out of the service he found that she had given up the baby and married another man. He didn't know that as she hadn't told him. He wanted that baby. He's never had any good experiences with women and he doesn't trust them ... I also found out that he was raped in the service by five or six guys. A girl had set him up for this. He had all these problems with girls, and he felt that he couldn't trust anyone.

As in the sad tales they devised during courtship, these wives found outside forces to blame for their husbands' criminality. The men themselves contributed to this by presenting themselves as being "wronged" by environmental factors. The wives' tales reinforced their own belief that their husbands were victims of circumstances. In twenty cases, alcoholism and broken homes, drugs and unemployment, and criminally involved friends or family members were presented as the factors which drove their husbands to commit the crimes they did. There was anger and frustration in this woman's placing blame on her husband's criminal associates for his involvement in armed robbery:

He's a stupid idiot. If his friends are doing it why can't he. He follows his friends and before he knows it he ends up in trouble. In jail they see you as a piece of dirt and yet he goes off willingly. He deliberately hangs around those people who like him and don't see him as dirt and then he starts drinking with them. Things start to hassle him—anybody can become a hassle. He doesn't feel that he can fit in with anybody except these friends. He doesn't feel that he knows what to talk about with other people. I don't have anything in common with his friends.

Another woman married to a man arrested for an alcohol-related crime, ended her sad tale by blaming her man's arrest on alcohol. As do many other women whose husbands are alcoholics, she believed that the spiralling effects of alcoholism would eventually land her husband in jail, but also that her husband's involvement in crime was a "cry for help":

> He was mean. I never knew enough to shut my mouth and he got mean. Our arguments were 10 percent his fault and 90 percent mine. Neither of us knew how to deal with his drinking. When he couldn't handle it any more, he'd do something stupid and make sure he got caught. He wanted to get caught. He thought that this was the only way he had to stop drinking.

Similarly, some women attempted to interpret their husbands' behavior in terms of character flaws and defects. As during courtship, they tried to ascribe the men's present criminal behavior to some previously unrecognized character flaw. However, in the aftermath of arrests, their scrutiny of their husbands' character defects usually was much more thorough. The same women who denounced their husbands' behavior during courtship and early marriage, continued to do so after their arrests: their husbands are "hopeless cases" and beyond reform. One wife whose husband had attempted to murder her and the children described how a psychiatrist's evaluation validated her perceptions:

> Dr. Marvel told me there's no cure for Nelson. He's a homicidal maniac. There is absolutely no cure for that kind of disorder. Nelson can be quite charming when he wants to be. . . . Maybe he'll find someone as sick as he is. He should find a woman who is sexually compatible with him. I've told him that. I don't see bondage and sadomasochism as fun. He enjoyed the fear that it instilled in me.

Finally, another wife whose husband has frequently been arrested for severely battering her, blamed drugs for his "crazy" behavior:

> He's been on drugs. He takes anything like pot, downs, speed, and

stuff like that. Not heroin. He used to smoke pot every day. He doesn't use pot any more. He got burnt when he did THC which had some strychnine in it. He went crazy and every since then he gets weird when he smokes pot. He gets wasted. He just can't handle it. He was into pot and drugs before he was arrested. The week before his last arrest he had taken this THC. I think that this is why he was so weird, the THC just whacked him out.

Prisoners whose wives regard them as hopeless can no longer break through the interactional limitations imposed by their master status as criminals or as mentally unbalanced. By denouncing their husbands, these wives had, in effect, begun to dissolve their marriages. It is interesting to note that a larger proportion of wives blame themselves for their husbands' arrest than ascribe blame to themselves prior to this. Fourteen wives saw themselves as chiefly responsible for their husbands' arrest.

Arrests seemed to challenge, in a number of fundamental respects, many women's conceptions of themselves as responsible and devoted wives. A typical rationale was offered by one young wife whose husband had been charged with rape:

> I blame myself for over half of what happened. I was selfishly into my own job and into my weight problem. I put my energy into myself and not into him. And when I don't put energy into him, he goes and rapes women.

Wives of men charged with alcohol-related and sexual offenses tended to assume blame in their sad tales. It seemed as though they could not continue to think that their men, who had declared their love for them, could be as brutal and violent as their crimes revealed:

> I thought it was because of me that he did those things. He told the cop that he did it because he didn't get enough at home. I thought that I had failed him as a wife and why else would he show himself to a girl. He's not happy but I guess he had this thing about showing himself and playing with himself. I'm not proud of it.

In turn, many men provided the ammunition for the wives assumption of blame. These men blamed their wives for their criminal involvement:

> . . . We started arguing. He lost his job and he felt very frustrated

and took his anger out on me. He felt that everything was my fault. It was my fault that he lost his job, it was my fault that we had the kids, it was my fault that everything wrong happened to him.

By creating these sad tales, most women appeared to be reminding themselves how frail and insecure their husbands were. Their men in turn, reinforced this perception. In these sad tales emphasis is given to how much the men need their wives, how sick and in need of help the men were, and how their dismal pasts had virtually undone them.

In order to reinforce the notion that their men really needed them, some wives included their fears that their men would commit suicide in their sad tales. The men reinforced this by centering their frailties and insecurities around this issue. Suicide was not an idle threat; a handful of the men validated their sad tales by attempting to commit suicide. Many wives, as a result, came to believe that their men were so mutilated by past events that suicide was a "normal" solution to their problems. These kinds of rationales served to create the impression that these men were really no different from anyone else, thus, wives were able to perpetuate the image of their men as basically "conventional" or "normal" husbands who deserve the continuing support of their wives.

LAWYERS

Wives' Perceptions of Lawyers

Not only was it necessary for prisoners' wives to care for their children, cope with the issues of everyday living, but they also had to learn how to deal with their husbands' lawyers. In Vermont, all felony defendants must be provided with a lawyer, *i.e.,* either a public defender or a private attorney. When a defendant is indigent, the courts can either appoint a public defender or a private attorney to represent him. According to the women's accounts, twenty-four men were represented by court-assigned public defenders, while five retained private lawyers.

Twenty-nine women believed that their men were guilty and ought to be punished. Since this was the case, they did not expect their husbands to be acquitted. Thus they expected their husbands' lawyers to do a variety of other things, *i.e.*, to protect their men's interests and dignity and to negotiate minimal sentences for them.

In most cases, reality differed sharply from wives' expectations. The majority expressed disillusionment with their husbands' legal counsels. This was more likely to be the case with court-appointed lawyers than with private attorneys.[4] This disenchantment began for most wives when they realized that their lawyers were relatively inaccessible to their men. Most women reported that busy public defenders spend little time with their husbands and received minimal information from them. Usually, wives reported, these lawyers only met with their clients for five or ten minutes before a court session. One young woman observed:

> A month later, there was a hearing to lower the bail. Grant finally met his lawyer. He was so well prepared for the case that he didn't know Grant's step-parents who were part of the case. He was so together that he had to ask the judge what the bail had been set at. My intuition told me that things were going to be bad. The D.A. read his past record and took the position that Grant was a bad risk. Dick Thomas was Grant's lawyer. And Dick Thomas more or less agreed with him. They lowered the bail to $5,000. But this still was an impossibility. I didn't have the $5,000.

Another major factor in the women's disenchantment with court-appointed lawyers was that they only appeared to be interested in "the deal" the prosecution would make in return for a guilty plea to a lesser charge. Hence, the lawyers' brief conversations with their clients usually focused on deals and not on the details of the crimes, mitigating circumstances, or husbands' motives or backgrounds. Therefore, many wives believed that public defenders were on the state's side, since they directed their energies towards plea bargaining rather than understanding their clients as individuals and interpreting their behavior to the criminal justice system. In treating their husbands in this way, public defenders appeared to be helping to create a system of assembly-line justice.

By contrast, five wives reacted favorably to their husbands' private attorneys. They felt that these lawyers were "on their husbands' side." Private attorneys seemed to be interested in their welfare as clients' wives, had fought hard for their men, and were willing to provide wives with information as to what was going on.[5]

Wives' Relationships with Lawyers

Most wives perceived themselves as having had a separate or direct relationship with their husbands' lawyers, but these relationships were generally disappointing. Most women did not understand court procedure and wanted answers to scores of questions about what was going on. They felt they had a right to answers to their questions, both as members of the accuseds' family and as emissaries for their jailed husbands. In most cases, such answers were not provided.

Most women also expected their husbands' lawyers to provide them with the technical information needed to understand their husbands' legal situations: (1) information about the progress of the case; (2) chances of acquittal; (3) possible lengths of sentences; and (4) chances for parole. Instead, most wives claimed, it was almost impossible to obtain answers to these questions from court-assigned lawyers, although no such observations were made about private attorneys:

> Jerry had a public defender. I couldn't get anything out of him. I couldn't get hold of him because he was always busy or just not available. Jerry's parole officer was very helpful and concerned at the time. Jerry had to report in to him every day because he was still on parole. This parole officer told me that if I needed anything, I should just get in touch with him. He tried to keep us informed of what was happening and he was always trying to be available if we needed anything.

Most wives needed to obtain legal information for their husbands. Since their husbands were often in jail, it was up to the wives to convey information between the lawyers and their husbands. Since the men had little personal autonomy, many placed continual pressure on their wives to act for them. Lawyers were often unavailable and this was a continual source of strain in the relationships between prisoners and wives:

I had to keep calling his lawyer and keep staying on his lawyer's back, because this lawyer took his sweet time in doing what should have been done. We found out that I could get things done far quicker than my husband primarily because I was on the outside and he was on the inside.

Some wives mentioned that court-assigned lawyers encouraged them to help pressure their men to negotiate "the best possible arrangements under the circumstances," *i.e.*, to plead guilty rather than stand trial. These wives complied. This, in effect, meant that they had become agents for the court system rather than their husbands' advocates.

COURTS AND SENTENCING

Court Sessions

It has been well documented that, to outsiders, courtrooms appear to be "closed clubs" in which the major interactions take place between legal experts who have handled similar cases together over a long period of time. This small group of judges, prosecutors, and defense lawyers have more in common than they do with most defendants. Accused persons pass through the system, while court personnel remain, and no one appears to want to change the status quo. The wives' accounts reveal a similar perception of the judicial system.

Twenty-two wives indicated that they attended court sessions as frequently as possible, but were often bewildered, frustrated, intimidated, or disoriented by them. These feelings emerged primarily as a result of wives' lack of knowledge of courtroom procedure.[6] For instance, as one wife said:

It was weird. I had never been through that kind of thing. It was weird hearing everything and seeing the lawyer sticking up for Tony and the D.A. being against him. I couldn't see that they had much evidence against him but then again, I don't understand law. I don't see that with the evidence they had on him how they could put him away.

And just knowing he was going through it was weird. It was hearing everything against him that struck me. It was long and boring and it was way over my head. I sat next to Tony during the time in court.

And one wife expressed her sense of helplessness this way:

> When in court, I felt more or less like an outsider. I couldn't un-
> derstand what was happening. I sat there and listened. I felt like
> one of the kids because I didn't understand so there was no way I
> could help my husband. I felt left out and I really felt bad. I
> wanted to help but I didn't know how.

Only two of the old timers claimed to have understoodlegal
terminology and court procedure well enough so that they did
not feel disoriented. Both had been in court more than four
times before. Some prisoners' wives reported that they had felt
intimidated by the judges; six neophytes and three old timers
mentioned that they were awed by their symbolic power.

In general, courtroom procedures reinforced wives' sense of
powerlessness. Many of the neophytes repeatedly expressed the
feeling that they had no direct control over the circumstances of
their husbands' lives or their own. Only a few old timers reported similar responses to courtrooms. For example, a few
wives told how the state could publicly symbolize its power, and
the consequent moral inferiority of the accused, by bringing the
defendant into court in manacles. A symbolic message was thus
conveyed to the women, who thus believed that there was no
way to alleviate their husbands' predicament:

> When court time came, I was pretty tired. In court they didn't
> paint too bright a picture about Beany. When he came out of the
> elevator, he was handcuffed to another person. This freaked me
> out. It looked so inhuman—to know someone as you know them
> and here he's seen as a different person without the qualities that
> you know. This freaked me right out.

The only time that wives felt they were doing some good was
when they could act as character witnesses and/or "good wives."
They could be a "moral credit" for their men and lawyers to
draw upon. Eight old timers and five neophytes reported that
they had acted as loyal wives so that their husbands could amass
moral credits. They did this by: (1) holding hands with their husbands; (2) throwing loving glances at them; (3) speaking and be-
having in a helpless manner; and/or (4) wearing clothes that
accentuated their pregnant condition:

> ... Then when he goes to court, I go with him and I play the grieving wife role. I know that the judges like to see the family together. I would even take Lilly with me and usually the judges would act more leniently. Frank is now sick of using the family in order to get him out of his difficulties. The last time I didn't go with him to court and he refused to use us.

However, not all of these wives employed this strategy with enthusiasm. Old timers were more likely than neophytes to "put on a performance" reluctantly. As their husbands' appearances in court became more frequent, wives became reluctant to employ this strategy. One old timer explained her reasons for not attending court sessions:

> I didn't like being there to show the judge that Bud has a wife who's going to stand by him no matter what. The more the judge says he's glad that Bud has a good woman who takes care of him and Bud should stay out of trouble because of that woman, the more antagonistic I feel. So I stopped going. I'm not his mother and I don't want to be presented as though I am his mother.

Whether they could play out these roles or not, most wives were fully cognizant that they were present as spectators at their husbands' inevitable convictions.

Sentencing

Although sentencing day was naturally a crisis-provoking occasion for most women, the outcomes were not unexpected. Most wives knew that their men had pleaded guilty in exchange for a reduced sentence. What became important was whether or not the men would receive the sentences negotiated by their lawyers.

Twenty-two women believe that their husbands had been sentenced unfairly. According to these women; (1) the sentences were not according to the going rates; (2) the judges were to blame; or (3) the lawyers were at fault. Nine old timers and six neophytes measured their husbands' sentences against what they considered to be the "going rates" for the particular crimes involved. A sentence which exceeded these rates was considered "unfair."[7] As a rule, wives learned about these rates from their husbands, lawyers, and from knowledgeable people in their communities.

Feelings of injustice about the sentences were most frequently expressed by the wives of sex offenders:[8]

> . . . the sentence wasn't fair, it was too harsh. He should have got-
> ten two to four or two to six. Other guys that were convicted of
> actual rape got less than Storm did. And other guys that were up
> for murder got the same thing that he got. It seems ironic because
> he would have served only 18 months, which I don't feel would
> have been enough. But I feel that four to ten was too harsh.

Wives expected individualized justice. That is, they expected
their husbands' lawyers, the prosecutor, and the judges to take
the individual involved into consideration. As a result, many
wives concluded that their husbands' sentences were unjust since
they were not the product of individualized attention. They expected both the court system, in general, and the judges, in particular, to pay attention to their men as individuals and,
therefore, take their social backgrounds, the circumstances of the
crimes, marital histories, family backgrounds, etc., into consideration. A few wives thought that this individualization would result from their husbands' willingness to cooperate with the
police. One neophyte described how her husband reluctantly
agreed to plead guilty after being pressured to do so by the
police and his lawyer:

> Reggie wanted to take a jury trial. I pleaded with him not to and
> the lawyer and cops told him that Tim Bowen [his partner in the
> armed robbery] had already pleaded guilty and he was advised to
> do the same. I don't know Tim well but I saw him once before.
> Anyway, Reggie pleaded guilty because he believed them. He found
> out later that he had been tricked because Tim had not pleaded
> guilty. They had done the same to Tim. Reggie got 7 years for
> armed robbery and 3–5 years for the antiques. I didn't expect him
> to get so much. I felt it was unfair. He was doing okay before this
> happened and the fact that he had a family was not taken into
> consideration. I was really surprised and my heart went to my feet.
> I went back to my mother's house. They asked what he got and I
> told them. They didn't say too much about it.

Seven old timers and three neophytes blamed the judges specifically for failure to individualize sentences. Some wives asserted that the judges had not been concerned about what was

"best" for their husbands: the harsh sentences meted out had little to do with rehabilitation or individual treatment, but mainly with punishment:

> When Kevin was sentenced, the room went up into the air. I was shocked and I saw it worse than before. He was angry. He felt that he was honest to do what he had done. He was getting help, he has signed a confession and things like that. He had learned that he won't be afraid to ask for help again and he had spared the women and the state from having a trial. The sentence was stiffer than what was recommended. He knows it's the system and it's run by people who don't know him. The judge made the decision—all this was laid on this judge who plays God. The judge had to weigh what people told him. And all these people know that Kevin's changed. It's unfair and there isn't much there to help him in jail.

Some old timers, instead, blamed the judges for creating a kind of multiple jeopardy in which their husbands continued to pay for what they had done in the past. Most of these women saw the judges as passing sentence solely on the basis of their husbands' past criminal records. These wives firmly believed that the judges determined the amount of time their husbands were to serve by the number of their previous convictions:

> Almost eight years ago, Frank pulled an armed robbery and kidnapping, too. He used to do these bad-assed things before I knew him. They judge him by these things he did then. He can't be judged now by his previous record and yet they do.

A few wives concluded that judges also took their husbands' families' reputations into account:

> The judge also knows Matt's father. They have a record on his father and I don't know what he's been in for. Matt has been in and out of jail six or seven times for possession of stolen property and for attempted escape. I think that's why [the judge] doesn't have a high regard for the Denton name. I think that once the judge hears the Denton name, it sets him off.

Another circumstance that indicated to the wives that their husbands' cases were not being treated individually was the judges' apparent sensitivity to "public opinion":

It was hard to catch all that was going on between the lawyers and the judge. Prosecutors said, "Look, these people are upset by what he did. There have been a lot of armed robberies all over Burlington. They want to see these people who do these crimes in jail for a long time." That was basically the same thing that the judge said. Tim gave a speech. He tried to talk the judge out of sentencing him. The judge laid four to six years [on him] and I feel the judge intended to give this sentence before the trial. It looked like everything was predetermined.

These two wives of sex offenders conclude that sentences can vary simply on the basis of judges' individual personalities:

NANCY. I wish that they could see it as a cry for help. I now fully understand how much a cry for help it is. They gave him a long sentence. Much longer than we expected. Now I read everything in the newspapers, especially the "Day in Court" section of the paper. And I read the other day that some guy received 4–8 years for receiving stolen property. Some seem to get these long sentences while other don't who do the same thing.

VICKI. We figured out that there was no justice. It's just how the judge and the others want to do with you.

NANCY. They don't take into consideration all the other factors surrounding the case. I don't know how they made these decisions. I guess it depends on the judge's personality.

Ten neophytes, in contrast, concluded that court-assigned lawyers were primarily to blame for the situation with regard to sentencing. Although their husbands had pleaded guilty, these wives felt that their lawyers could have negotiated a more favorable sentence. They felt double-crossed. Neophytes, naive about lawyers as well as the rest of the court system, were most likely to lend credence to the lawyers' confident and bland assurances that their husbands were going to receive light sentences once they had pleaded guilty. According to the wives' accounts, lawyers also frequently claimed to have "inside knowledge" about the intentions of the prosecutors, police, probation officials—or to have direct access to them. Based on such assurances and inside knowledge, many wives urged their husbands to cooperate with these officials. On sentencing day, when wives heard their husbands' sentences, they felt that their attorneys had "conned," manipulated, or tricked their husbands into "copping a plea" by promising them a sentence less than the going rate:

> We went to court that day. I had told the lawyer that I was preg-
> nant with Charles' child. The lawyer assured us that Charles
> would be out on the street in seven months. We thought we could
> handle that. When we went to court we expected that Charles
> would get the sentence that would allow him back home in seven
> months. We really believed the lawyer. Charles knew he had a
> problem. He found it was easy to talk to the doctor. He had con-
> fessed. The judge gave him four to ten years. I was shocked. We
> believed the lawyer.

In general, wives who reacted this way did not realize that
lawyers could only negotiate a promise from the prosecutors to
recommend a sentence in exchange for a guilty plea, and that
judges normally have sole authority to pass sentences.[9]

Finally, a number of wives based their notions about the fairness of sentences on more subjective criteria. These women had
been aware that their husbands were going to serve some time in
prison. Yet, they initially expected that their men would receive
minimum rather than maximum sentences. It might be that these
wives' notions of "fairness" derived from their sense of how long
they could manage by themselves:

> I was going in circles about all this. I didn't want to see him in jail
> and we both knew that this time he would be sentenced for sure.
> That morning, when I heard the sentence, I was knocked out. I
> couldn't believe it. He got zero to two years. We depended upon
> him and we needed him. What were we going to do? I didn't know
> what was to happen to us. We just needed him around. Just having
> him around was important. Any problems that come up, he would
> handle.

Eight women believed that their husbands had been sentenced fairly, that is, either their men got a good deal—something less than what they might have gotten, or the going rate
for the offense. Neophytes were more likely to conclude that
their husbands' sentences were fair when they conformed with
the going rate than when they did not. The three old timers in
this group believed that their husbands' sentences were fair because they were light:

> This time I was very pleased. I was pleased as punch. I figured that

he would be shafted. I felt that he was going to get the book thrown at him. But he didn't. He had two lawyers who worked for him very hard and I feel that he had a fair sentence. They were talking about 15–20 years and giving him the habitual criminal conviction. He would have died there. He's no young kid now.

Women who had been the object of their husbands' criminal acts tended to be ambivalent about sentences. On the one hand, they believed that the courts had acted in a "just" manner since their husbands were going to prison for an extended period of time. On the other, they believed that the sentences were not fair since their husbands had often received less than the "going rate."

Responses to Conviction and Sentencing

Regardless of the severity of their husbands' crimes, most women were unprepared for the sentences they received. At the time of sentencing, wives' identities were abruptly transformed: they became prisoners' wives. They had lost their spouses as active partners in their households and were losing the social definitions they associated with marriage. One neophyte reacted in this way:

> I felt that this was longer than my entire life had been so far. I was nervous about whether I could commit myself for that long a time. I didn't want to abandon Grant and no one ever came to see him except me. I still felt the same way about him and I just couldn't see him being there. At first, we talked a lot about what he was to do—how he should handle being in jail so that he could get out as soon as possible—then we laid great plans for our future. It was too far off to tell whether these plans were workable. It was so stupid. It would be stupid to ask people for jobs for him five years from now.

Another woman said:

> I was scared. How can I do it when he's gone. I could do it for seven months, but how could I do it for four years at least. He won't be with me when I have this child. The kids are going to be hurt. Here they are used to having him as their Daddy and then he suddenly disappears. They love him now and they'll be hurt. Then

I thought that if he learns something from all this then the rest of our life should be good.

For most of the women, arrest and court sessions had been disorienting. They had been extracted from relatively orderly and familiar routines and thrust into an unfamiliar and often seemingly chaotic environment. For all intents and purposes, wives felt themselves in limbo while the judicial process determined the parameters of their lives. When they heard their husbands' sentences, many wives reacted with relief: there was a definite end in sight to the process of arrest and imprisonment:

> We both waited and waited to see what would happen. How long he would be gone. What would the separation be like? It's over with now. We know the best and the worse. Now he can deal. He can do the best that he can. The pressure is off me because I felt that I had something to do with it. Now I have the pressure of how to pay bills. It's less stomach pressure. Now it's the pressure to get us through. Now it's the day-to-day coping. Now I have to shift for Jill and I and it's all on me. Now I shift from focusing on Kevin to focusing on us and how we're going to survive. I have to have my own program for me and for getting Jill through it. But I don't have this program yet.

Those women who wanted to remain married, especially neophytes, felt relieved because they thought that the prison system would be able to help their husbands to deal with their problems. Old timers were more likely to feel relieved because they were free of their husbands' most serious demands on their families' monetary and emotional resources. A few old timers also welcomed the separation with relief since they had previously discovered that their relationships were more satisfying when their husbands were in prison. But relief was mixed with grief for both neophytes and old timers. Several wives lost their appetites or began eating compulsively, could not sleep, or were depressed and lonely. As one woman, whose husband was sentenced for possession of stolen goods, noted:

> I was hurt and upset. I held it all back until I got home and then I let it all out. I cried like you wouldn't believe! I felt that it wasn't right for him to serve time for what he didn't do. He didn't steal that stuff. It wasn't right to serve time for someone else who did

steal the stuff.... [As time went by] I was even more depressed and hurt. I wasn't able to get in touch with him. I was more or less in a state of shock. I went about my everyday things. I did do my housework. I did everything automatically. I was pretty numb until the day before Thanksgiving.

In contrast, the four wives who had wanted to get rid of their husbands offered different reasons for feeling relieved. In these cases, their marriages had been conflict-ridden before separation. Hence, imprisonment offered them an opportunity to begin the process of dissolving marital ties. In many instances, it also provided them with a respite from the fear of physical abuse or financial disaster. For these wives, imprisonment meant sanity and peace and quiet.

However, wives who were using the time their husbands were in prison to break off marital relations also reported that they were afraid. The husbands who had committed crimes against their wives continued to threaten to harm them. They thought their husbands would try to retaliate against them in some way. Consequently, all of these wives had decided to wait until their husbands had "cooled down" before filing for divorce. One woman also prepared to defend herself:

> I then got a gun—a 38 special. I told the guy I bought it from I wanted the biggest bullets possible. He sold me the biggest and I went out that day and it took me one-half hour to learn. I cried and cried. I took hold of myself and got to the point where I knew how to shoot it. Next time he called I told him that if he hassles me, I had the means to handle it. He told me that he had some guys who would be coming to get me. I said, "Let them come! I'm ready!"

Although enforced separation can primarily engender either relief or unhappiness, it may also be the beginning of a new situation which holds promise for rewards as well as the pains of separation.

CHAPTER VI

Stigmatization and Prisoners' Wives' Feelings of Shame

> I made this point of not watching the news because I knew he would be in the news and I didn't want to hear it. When I read it in the papers, it was a real weird feeling. . . . It was hard to read it in the papers. I feel the problem was a lot more me than anything else. My name is still Abbott and no one has yet said, "Are you related to that guy?" It's me fearing the unknown and of the people changing their opinion of me. But I did feel that if they did, fuck them! But no one has ever done that.
>
> —A Prisoner's Wife

The effects of arrest and imprisonment reverberate throughout the lives of prisoners' families. Such events are, at once, forbiddingly confusing, shameful, disturbing, and sometimes tragic for their wives and children. While some attention has been directed toward observable effects of such events on family members, stigmatization and perceived hostility among prisoners' wives has not been examined in depth.

Prisoners' wives frequently perceive themselves as suffering for the "sins" of their husbands or perceive themselves as contaminated. They express feelings of shame and embarrassment, and report stigmatization from family and friends, as well as from representatives of the criminal system. Such accommodative strategies have been employed by women to explain their husbands' institutionalization in mental hospitals and by parents to reduce stigma transferred from their handicapped children.[1]

WIVES SPEAK FOR THEMSELVES

From the wives' accounts a theme emerges. Prisoners' wives are not simply "separated" from their husbands—although they share similarities with others facing crises of separation. They must also continually deal with the problems of minimizing opportunities for stigmatization—particularly in the various prison towns and prison systems. The first segment offers a few typical descriptions of the kinds of stigmatization that prisoners' wives encounter as well as how wives attempt to manage their feelings of shame. Two old timers recount facing hostility from families and members of their communities and how their children managed to cope with encounters with stigmatization.

Bea, an old timer, has had extensive encounters with such prisons as Newfane Prison and Newport Correctional facility. During her husband's incarcerations she resided in a small town on the outskirts of Burlington, Vermont. Arlene, an old timer, cannot recall the number of times her husband has been arrested and sent back to jail. She has had extensive contact with all the correctional facilities in Vermont and has been a resident of two Vermont prison towns. Her husband's most recent conviction, which was highly publicized, involved such offenses as kidnapping and aggravated assault. During his incarceration in a Federal penitentiary, she resided in a Vermont prison town for a short period of time and then moved with her daughter (10 years old) to a small town in central Vermont.

> ARLENE. Cranshaw told me that once a woman comes in to visit her man, she's a criminal too and is to be treated like a criminal.
>
> BEA. I feel like a prisoner when I enter those doors. When I first went to Newfane, I found that there was no smoking there. And you had to talk to your man through a screen. You couldn't hold hands at all. At Newport you can go in and hold hands and kiss. The atmosphere there is way better. But I still don't like it.
>
> ARLENE. I love St. James. It was like my old home. They dealt with the whole family there. The families went to counseling together. The whole family had a say in what happened to the prisoner. It was a family jail. At Christmas time, they had Santa Claus come to visit the kids in the jail. The jail really cared. They wanted to work with the families. They felt that the guys were in trouble and therefore the families were in trouble.
>
> My daughter has been brought up in prison. We've always told her what's going on. She's had to learn how to deal with it. But what a life it's been for her. Not so great.
>
> I was worried when Frank got busted back in St. James for driving without a license because of people talking and she was

going to kindergarten. It was a very small town, and the people didn't want the jail there. We went to the laundromat and this little kid said, "My Mommy said that your Daddy's back in jail." And Lilly said, "I love him and don't you say things or I'll slam you in the mouth!" So I said to myself, hey, she can handle it. I don't know how frequently it happens though.

Everyone thinks that I'm wrong for telling Lilly about her father. She knows why he's in jail and all about my arrests. We don't lie to her. She knows she was born before we got married. We're always honest with her. Everyone says we don't have a healthy relationship with her. They think that she shouldn't be told. I feel that she should learn how to deal with things now. She was at first embarrassed at school. She didn't want to tell the kids. She told the kids that he was working for the government and that's why he's not home. For the first time, the other day, she told a kid that he's being punished and even though Daddy is in jail, she loved him. I think that she got over the stigma and shame, and the guilt feelings that she had.

People freak out when they hear her say things like that. It freaks them to hear her say that it's his fault that he's in jail. I feel that when you protect and lie to your kids, they are kids that you're going to have trouble with. My mom feels that Lilly is too young to tell. I said that she's learned how to deal with it and learned not to pass judgments on other people. She understands criminals but doesn't pass judgment.

BEA. You know most of the communities hate the prison and the prisoners. When the Newfane community wanted Newfane closed they learned quite a lesson. The prison closed. They got what they wanted. Then they found that they had lost their major revenue. The families moved out, the guards moved out. All of a sudden they realized that the prison was the best thing for them. They realized how much money they made from it.

ARLENE. The St. Albert landlords won't rent to the wives of prisoners. Most of the prisoners' wives have to lie to get an apartment. In St. Albert, it's a hostile town and it's a cruel, vicious place. When the men escape, the townspeople retaliate on the families. I had rocks thrown through my windows because I was a prisoner's wife. They told me to leave town. I couldn't let Lilly out to play alone. I wouldn't move back there if Frank returned to Londonderry. There is no way I could put myself and my daughter into that situation.

I had girls coming in and out of my house. I'd put them up for the night and on Sundays. We'd eat together. We're all alone and

we knew it. We all felt like outsiders. We were in a prison ourselves. We've been treated more like trash than the guys inside.

And then the strip searches. I knew it was unconstitutional.
They told me that Frank was dealing in contraband. The strip
searches got grosser and grosser each time. It was the most degrading, filthy, vile thing I've gone through.

I'm going to have to move again. I know once I tell landlords
that my husband is in jail, they won't rent to me.

BEA. Don't tell them that you're Frank's wife.

ARLENE. I feel I can't deny that he's my husband.

BEA. Well if I wanted that house I would just say he's related and
let it go at that. I've done that because people wouldn't rent to me
because of Rudi. Just say, "We're separated." It's a little fib but it's
not lying. After all you are really separated. You don't have to tell
them everything.

ARLENE. The repercussions have been really bad for me when I've
done that.

BEA. My kid don't tell them where her father is. She won't tell anyone. When she's at school she just says that he's away. The minute
you give her his name, you can forget it! Just say you're related.

INVESTIGATOR. Arlene, what have been the repercussions?

ARLENE. I always pick the best people to lie to. I rented this house
in St. Albert and I told the woman [the landlady] that my husband
and I were separated. I told her that we might get together some-
time in the future but I didn't expect it to happen very quickly. I
had this great house and I really fixed it up. Come to find out she
was a State Trooper Dispatcher. They have resumes on all the inmates at Londonderry and their families. She was in the process of
updating the resumes when she came across Frank's.

There was my name and Lilly's and the address of the house
that we rented from her. Well she found out and come to the house
and was furious. And she wanted me to get out immediately. I
wasn't behind in the rent and I got mad—really mad. I made her
evict me. And here his case is eight years old and people don't ever
forget! But then it was a sensational case.

BEA. Do your folks object to Frank?

ARLENE. They'd love me to separate from him. It's subtle. They
don't come right out and say it. But I know what they're feeling,
"Why do you put up with it, why do you go back with him each
time?" My brother said, "He's never been good to you." He has hit
me but I deserved it. I have pushed him back. But they feel, "He's

no good! He's a criminal." They don't realize that when he's with us, he can let the softness come out. When he's with his friends he has to be macho. If he shows any kind of compassion then you're dead in prison.

EMBARRASSMENT AND SHAME

For both husbands and wives, feelings of shame were most likely to occur when the husbands' criminal acts received the most public attention through the media, at the time of arrest, and when sentences were handed down. Women reported experiencing feelings of shame because of what they felt to be society's general stigmatization of the offense or imprisonment. The extent to which they did so depended on: (1) whether they were neophytes or old timers: and (2) the kinds of crimes for which their husbands had been arrested.

At the time of their husbands' arrest and subsequent sentencing, the majority of wives reported that they experienced feelings of shame independent of other people's reactions. Most of the neophytes recalled that they were ashamed from the beginning, whereas old timers felt embarrassed that they no longer had their men living with them. Without their husbands, old timers felt a loss of status within their communities. Wives of sexual offenders were especially likely to recount feelings of shame. For instance, a wife of a sexual offender recalled:

> I began to be aware that I felt embarrassed by his being in jail. I didn't want people to talk about me in terms of my husband being in jail. I worried about how all this would reflect on my family. I worried about how it would hurt my job. And then I worried about how it hurt me as a person in terms of my taking the responsibility for this relationship.

Many wives reported that they felt especially ashamed and embarrassed when their husbands' criminal behaviors and convictions were reported in the local newspapers and on the local TV news programs. These women also reported that they felt somehow guilty, or that they assumed some guilt for their husbands' offenses, even though they were completely innocent. As one wife of a sexual offender reported:

Before the story was printed, I worried about whether it would be in the newspaper. When I saw it the next day I felt very guilty because I felt as if it was my name in the newspaper. I didn't go out for a couple of days. I stayed here in the house and tried to figure out how I was going to face people.

And a neophyte speaks about her feelings of disgrace:

I felt ashamed that I let my husband do these things and I felt that I could have stopped him but I didn't know how. I felt ashamed I knew him. I felt weird going out and everyone seeing me. I felt they were saying, "There goes that girl whose husband stole that stuff." I didn't want to live like that. Gary told me to move.

Other neophytes were also likely to feel ashamed since they had few guidelines as to how to act and were less likely to know what community reaction would be. They felt uncertain and fearful about what the future would hold:

I made this point of not watching the news because I knew he would be in the news and I didn't want to hear it. When I read it in the papers, it was a real weird feeling. It was hard to read it in the papers. I feel the problem was a lot more me than anything else. It's me fearing the unknown and of people changing their opinion of me.

In contrast, old timers tend to be resigned and relieved that their husbands were arrested and incarcerated, since their husbands' arrests often were expected. They also were more likely to know what to expect from the community and to go about the business of coping with arrest and imprisonment:

The minute he gets busted, my first reaction is to call the lawyer because I know that the first hours are the most important ones. So I keep busy with the lawyers.

Twelve neophytes and two old timers recalled that they worried about encountering stigmatizing situations. These wives generally were most fearful about being the object of gossip, ridicule, rejection, and hostility. Wives of sexual offenders were most worried and anxious about neighborhood gossip. A wife of a sexual offender recalled her fears:

After Joe was arrested, I felt that everybody knew about him. I didn't even want to cash a check because I didn't want to see their reaction when they saw my name. Now I realize that people only pay attention the day they see it in the news. I felt that everybody knew.

Feelings of shame were a real presence in the lives of most wives. These feelings, however, did not overwhelm them, for other issues demanded their attention: taking care of legal matters; child management or domestic concerns; and extending support to their husbands during arrest and incarceration. Moreover, the ongoing physical separation from their husbands was a constant background against which all other factors had to be judged. What the wives missed most acutely was the financial support, sympathy, and companionship of their husbands. They were therefore more concerned with being deprived of their husbands than with the stigma associated with imprisonment.

Community Reactions

As a public event, arrest serves to bring the wives of accused men into the public view. Other people learn about men's arrests through the media and word-of-mouth. In response, people acquainted with these men's wives often expect them to account for their husbands' criminal acts. Many wives reported vivid recollections of unsubtle stigmatizing situations during arrest, conviction, and initial incarceration.[2] For instance, some wives recounted hostile encounters with shopkeepers, service men, and landlords. One wife recalled:

> The bill collectors threaten you when they wouldn't dare to threaten a man. The repairmen charge you outrageous prices. Then there is trouble renting a place. These landlords ask, "Where is your husband?" I tell them, "He's in jail." They ask, "Has he been in before?" I then tell them that he has paid his time and this is not any of his business. But before I know it they are asking me if I'm going to have wild parties and boyfriends constantly coming into the house. I tell them that only my daughter and I are going to live in the house. Or they say, "I'll rent to you if you get friendly with me." Some landlords are nice though.

Wives anticipated derogatory evaluations from community members more often than they actually encountered them. However, some wives recalled neighbors avoiding them, making derogatory comments, and in general, expressing their disdain for women married to known criminals:

> People look down on me because of Matt. It doesn't come out in so many words, but I get the feeling that people think it's awful that I'm married to a guy who's in jail. I feel it through the reactions I get and the way they treat me. They treat me in more or less the same way that they treat me when they knew I was on welfare. They think that they're better than me. A lot of people don't want to associate with me. They don't hear my side of it. They believe the newspapers.

And a few mothers of school-age children reported that their children were periodically subjected to hostile behavior by other children and/or teachers:

> There is a teacher at school who won't let Lilly go to the bathroom. When the children are out on the playground and she's in charge of the children, she refuses to let her use the bathroom. She is the only teacher who refuses her. She's the niece of the family that Frank robbed and kidnapped. I might be paranoid but I feel she's taking it out on Lilly. Too many days, she comes home with her underwear soaking wet. She has to remain at school feeling wet and uncomfortable.

The stigmatization that prisoners' wives actually experienced was not continuous or general, but episodic and situation-specific. Thus, wives reported that community reactions to their husbands' criminal offenses were neither uniform nor predictable.

Usually, families, friends, and co-workers reacted to the husband's arrest as a disaster or crisis event. Friends and neighbors offered emotional and practical support. This barrage of attention and sympathy from significant others clearly played an important part in undercutting the wives' own feelings of shame. In many cases, it seemed to reassure wives that they were not blameworthy, i.e., that they had not done something terribly wrong to have caused their husbands' criminal acts.

The extent to which wives reported positive or hostile community reaction is partially explained by the kinds of communities in which they lived. Arrests are not extraordinary events in most working-class communities.[3] People are in and out of jail.

In some communities, being officially labelled as a criminal's wife is so common that it becomes personally irrelevant. When wives live in such crime-familiar communities, they do not tend to recount stigmatizing events. One wife, for example, described her neighborhood in the largest urban center in Vermont:

> Most of the people around here weren't so bad. The neighbor next door had been in jail and so had her husband. The people across the street have been in jail. Charlie Buy knew Harry for a while and he was a deputy sheriff and when he knew that Harry was an escapee, he didn't turn him in. A lot of people around here have been in trouble. I like this neighborhood. They don't think that if you've been in jail, you're going to be a criminal for the rest of your life.

In these communities, arrest was considered to be more crisis-provoking than stigmatizing by many residents.

Within middle-class communities, however, arrests were not treated as ordinary events. There were, moreover, no apparent guidelines for how one should respond to a husband's arrest. Wives indicated that, within these communities, friends and neighbors were unlikely to know how to respond. Friends were more likely to be supportive. Neighbors were more likely to withdraw. One young woman who lived in a middle-class neighborhood observed that:

> It was uncomfortable with the neighbors. When someone dies, people know what to do. But when someone goes to jail, it's not socially acceptable. They don't know what to do. The neighbors didn't call or come over and I felt that was strange. I got real paranoid. I realize now it was probably more my feelings than what happened. Because when I did see them in the normal course of events, they expressed how concerned they were about Kevin and me and asked me if he was okay. At first, I had this fear of the unknown. When Kevin came home on bail, he talked with the neighbors. It was not uncomfortable for us to be in the neighborhood. We're not uncomfortable about what happened to Kevin and the people take their cue from us.

Nine prisoners' wives lived in some of the towns where Vermont's prisons were located. All nine reported that people in these towns were generally hostile to both prisoners and their families.[4] These wives, in particular, found themselves facing various forms of stigmatization: they were frequently treated as "suspicious," "irresponsible," or "psychologically disabled." As prisoners' wives, they felt discriminated against. They reported being denied jobs when employers learned who their husbands were. Landlords refused to rent to them. They were subject to petty acts of vandalism. Shopkeepers refused to serve them. Neighbors avoided them and their children were taunted by their peers. An old timer, whose husband had been heavily involved in receiving stolen property, recalled the hostile treatment directed at her:

> After the bust, the neighbors snubbed me. They wouldn't have anything to do with me. They would call the police when my dog barked. I felt it was time for me to move because I couldn't live in that hostile area. The kids didn't go out too much and we all stayed in the house.

Another old timer recalled:

> A bunch of us women moved up to St. Albert to live near our guys. One townsperson said "You're nothing but trash." Others up there feel that anyone who is married to a man in jail is trash or hookers. They see our kids as juvenile delinquents. Any town that has the centers has this attitude toward us. When the escape happened at Londonderry, the people there said that the women should be sterilized—all women who are married to men in prison should be sterilized! These are the Christian people who are supposedly full of love and forgiveness. If this is the way that the good people live and feel, then I don't want any part of their way of life.

As a rule, community reaction did not vary with the kinds of crimes that men committed except for cases in which wives, themselves, had been their victims or when the husbands' families had been previously labelled as troublemakers. Whether or not they lived in crime-familiar communities, women who had been victims did not encounter stigmatization. Instead, several women recalled overwhelming support from friends and community members:

> I received no negative reaction. People tried to give me money. They wanted to help me pay back on the checks he had cashed. They were super to me. My neighbors didn't really react. For them, it's typical around here to see guys go in and out of jail.

They all knew what Earl was like anyway. He was stealing everyone's welfare checks and so the neighbors just said they were glad they got the sucker. People were relieved to see him go because their welfare checks stopped disappearing. Earl is a social problem no matter where he goes.

Families in which several members had already spent time in jail were frequently labelled by the community as "troublemakers," "jailbirds," or "a bunch of hardened criminals." Wives reported that they encountered hostile reactions because they were affiliated with their husbands' families by marriage. According to these wives, community reaction appeared more hostile in prison towns. A wife, whose husband and his relatives were frequently in "trouble with the law," recalled the hostility she encountered in a prison town:

> A couple of stores I just don't like. I have a hard time shopping there. When I want to pay for something, they ask my name and I tell them and they ask me if I'm related to him. Then when I tell them that I am, they say that I can't do business there. I don't like them running down my husband.

Although wives expected hostile reactions from friends during these initial crisis points of arrest and incarceration, they were actually likely to receive support from friends and community members. Hostility and stigmatization were only the predominant reactions in prison towns.

Family Reactions

The majority of the women's families were quite familiar with the possible ramifications of arrest and incarceration. This was especially true when family members knew at least one close relative who had been arrested and/or incarcerated. What perhaps was most problematic was wives' families' emotional reactions to the husbands. Families' hostility toward husbands initially dispersed to the wives and then dissipated. It tended to emerge: (1) prior to the women's marriages to their prospective husbands; and (2) at the time of husbands' arrests. After arrest and initial imprisonment, families were likely to be supportive.

Not all family members reacted to the women's impending marriages in the same way. Some were supportive, while others were cool, indifferent, or hostile. Initially, parents' reactions to their daughters' impending marriages to men with previous records were likely to be unfavorable. Twenty wives reported that their parents reacted in this way. For instance, one young wife recalled her parents' initial reaction to her husband who had a criminal record:

> My father thinks he's a criminal. He thinks that Leon is no good. He doesn't know him or understand his problems. Leon and I get along fantastic. They feel that he won't be any good for the rest of his life. I don't bring up Leon with them. I don't give a shit how they feel. I'm looking out for my own happiness and for the kids. No one else. I don't care.

According to most wives, those parents who reacted negatively to their men seemed threatened by their past criminal behavior. They funneled all their evaluations through the man's master status. Thus, in some sense, they reflected values in the larger community. What seemed most threatening for parents, however, were doubts this master status raised as to their prospective sons-in-law's abilities to provide an economically viable and conventional lifestyle for their future families. While these men assured their fiancees that they had done their fast living and were ready to settle down, parents were sure that they would continue to do the opposite. Moreover, parents were sure that the men's criminal behavior would generate stigma which would affect their daughters. For instance, one woman recalled that her mother believed that her man, who had an extensive criminal record, had crime "in his blood."

> They were very upset because I was going with a jailbird. They felt that I'd get hurt and that he was using me. I don't have much to do with my family because of it. My mom and stepfather—they don't get along with him at all. My mom and I are very close . . . She says that it's my life and she's afraid that I'll get hurt. She doesn't see that Rex is going to change. She feels that as often as he's been in jail and the things he's done that he hasn't been caught for shows that crime is in his blood. I say that it takes the right person to change him.

Parents who had been exposed to crime were the most likely to react with disapproval. As one wife recalled:

They called him a no-good bastard and a thief and more. Most of them have been busted for one thing or another. My dad was busted for aggravated assault against the Chief of Police, and my uncle has been busted for writing checks, jacking deer, stealing cattle. But they feel that their crimes aren't as bad as Frank's. That's bull shit! Everybody does something wrong whether you steal a car, whether you steal somebody's money, whether you jack deer— it's all against the law. It doesn't make any difference.

Families that had achieved some degree of stability in the conventional world also tended to be upset since such a marriage would threaten their tenuous hold on "respectability." A little less than a third of the families were reserved but supportive. Some family members took the position that whatever their daughters did was right. They reassured their daughters that they would not treat their prospective mates differently from anyone else.

The initial tendency was for almost all women's families to react negatively to their prospective sons-in-law. However, these reactions tended to be relatively short-lived. Family members often had opportunities to observe the men performing in a "normal" manner, *i.e.,* not as stereotypical criminals. With no visible stigmata, most decided that the men were not radically different from themselves. Normalization occurred. However, there were residues of their previous reactions irrespective of the men's performances as suitors, workers, or conventional community members. The women in the study population, of course, went ahead with these marriages despite parental reactions. It was, therefore, not surprising that when the husbands were arrested and imprisoned, parents were likely to respond to these events as crises. Ten neophytes and two old timers reported that their families were more likely to rally around them during arrest and initial incarceration than old timers' families. The most common forms of assistance were to give their daughters a place to stay for the first few days immediately after the arrest, meals, help with child care, and, in some instances, financial assistance. Neophytes also were more likely than old timers to report that these offers of assistance were not coupled with reproach.

Some family members, however, offered the same assistance, but remained hostile to their sons-in-law. Four women reported that some family member acted in this way. This was most often true when the husbands had criminally harmed their wives. By contrast, eleven old timers and four neophytes encountered unsympathetic and unfriendly responses from their families. These hostile reactions did not appear to diminish as husbands served their sentences. These women reported that their parents continued to refer to their husbands as "no good," "jail birds," or as "hardened criminals." They continually pressured wives to leave their husbands.[5]

Only the old timers also reported that they rarely received emotional or practical support from their families. One old timer, whose husband had been incarcerated twice, spoke about her parents' response to her situation:

> When I needed money for Pampers and stuff, they wouldn't give it to me though. Right now I have trouble getting my mother to babysit for me. She doesn't want to watch my kids. There has been no support for me when my man is in jail. They believe that it's not their problem. My father puts Gary down as a stupid kid. My mother wanted me to leave Gary and get a divorce and I told her to keep out of my life. I'd do what I wanted to do.

Wives generally felt strongly that they were being betrayed by families who refused support since they tend to view the family as a last resort or refuge.

Managing Stigma

Whether or not arrest was common in their social milieu, most women felt exposed and uneasy. The wives' chief concern was impression management: "How can I project an image of normalcy to others despite my husband's criminal status?" Behind this question was another: "How much information can I disclose to others about my husband's situation?" Who and what to tell thus became critical. How wives controlled information about their husbands depended on the management strategies they used to present what they considered to be "normal" faces to others. The most commonly used strategies were: (1) affirmation; (2) misdirection or avoidance; (3) covering up; and (4) jailing. The particular strategies used depended on the community responses anticipated. New encounters demanded new efforts at normalization. Wives found themselves almost continuously engaged in utilizing whatever strategy they felt would achieve some reduction in stigmatization.

Accommodation: Affirmation, Avoidance, Covering Up, and "Jailing"

Affirmation was a widely used technique, with old timers more likely to affirm their husbands' situations than neophytes. When the women made their acknowledgements, they usually provided cues as to how significant others could continue to relate to them as "normal" wives and mothers. When they were successful and the preferred definitions were accepted, wives could continue to sustain normal relations with those with whom they came in contact. One old timer described how a strategy of affirmation is carried out:

> I say, "Hey look, my husband's in jail. I love him, I support him. You have your views, I have mine. I'm open to listen to your views, but I won't change mine and I know you won't change yours."

Affirmation can assume a variety of forms. It frequently does not involve full disclosure of potentially stigmatizing detail. One woman, who had been physically abused by her husband, explained how she decided how much information to disclose and to whom:

> I just told them he was in jail. I don't want to keep the truth from them. Everyone saw it in the newspaper anyway. People just asked factual information and asked if I was going back with him when he got out. For those who haven't read it in the newspaper, I just told them why and where he was. With some people I tell them he committed a violation of his probation. I didn't want to go through all the questions.

Wives generally received some help from others, in the form of tactful inattention, in insulating themselves from their husbands' spoiled identities. This made it easier for wives to reject the application of labels to themselves and their children and allowed them to maintain a sense of themselves as "normal."

Avoidance or Misdirection

Another device used was questioning people about their own crimes and misdemeanors, thereby reminding them that they, too, had once been potentially subject to stigmatization. This strategy limited other people's opportunities to draw lines between themselves and the wives, and allowed the latter to redirect the encounter in other directions. In some sense, this strategy relied on the same principles as those used by magicians: it focused viewers' attention on things that were not damaging to the illusion and away from those that were.

At one time or another, seven old timers and three neophytes avoided the application of labels by denying their relevance. This technique involved acknowledging the arrest and its circumstances, and yet being indifferent to other people's reactions to it. They recognized that this strategy might not always protect them from stigmatization. One old timer talked about this:

> I don't bother to read [the newspaper] any more. People let me know that they've heard Frank got busted, they heard it on the radio or something. I know it. I don't have to read it.
>
> I don't let it [affect my everyday life]. I could be afraid to walk down the street or curl up, but I say, "To hell with it. Frank did it and Frank's doing time for it. I'm not going to let them infect me that way."

Even when these women did not "accept" other people's definitions of their men's behavior, they were forced to respond to other people's reactions by maintaining distance. Yet these wives avowed their "differentness" precisely because it implied an outcome of less differentness, not more.

Some wives avoided contact with neighbors who might want information about their husbands. Others reported that this was unnecessary since their neighbors avoided them. A neophyte, whose husband had been heavily involved in receiving stolen goods, told why she moved away from her old neighborhood:

> After the bust, the neighbors snubbed me. They wouldn't have anything to do with me. They would call the police when my dog barked. I felt it was time for me to move because I couldn't live in that hostile area. The kids didn't go out too much and we all stayed in the house.

Covering Up

Another accommodative strategy, covering up, was employed by thirteen wives. In its most common form, this strategy involved withholding information about husbands. Wives simply rearranged their round of activities so as to conceal their connections with their husbands, and made their appearance and lifestyles even more conventional than they might have been. For example, one prisoner's wife moved back to her parents' home in another state:

> Because I was kinda a dual person at the time, when I went to work at my father's business. I always tried to be as conservative as possible. I tried to give an innocent and naive appearance. I was very conservative. I didn't want them to know about Grant. I was having my own problems there. In the travel agency, the girls and Mr. Forman, who was my boss, didn't know how to relate to me because I was the boss's daughter. It took them a while to get them to trust me. I felt that their knowing about Grant would just place greater stress in my work world. So I kept it a secret.

Covering up was generally used in situations in which "official" identities were at stake, *e.g.*, applying for jobs, talking to landlords about renting houses or apartments. Neophytes were more likely to withhold information from friends and relatives.

> I wanted him to move to Greenfield because I knew he could get a job there. I knew though that if people knew, he would be ruined here. Manny had told me that the only reason he didn't get anywhere in Vermont is because he had a record. I moved to Greenfield to protect him. I didn't want people here to see him as a person just out of jail. I did not want his entrance into my world to be as a "jail bird." I wanted to give him a new entrance to the world. I didn't want people to be saying, "Here is this wild, crazy guy from Vermont." I just didn't want him to be a legend in town. I felt that this was the best way to handle it.

Covering up required uninterrupted vigilance on the part of the wives. They therefore tried not to respond to or encourage even friendly inquiries about their husbands. They carefully watched every word and gesture when they were around strangers. As long as they could conceal information, they assumed that community members or significant others would regard them as "normal."

Jailing

The least frequently employed strategy wives used to cope with potential and actual stigma was "jailing." "Jailing" involves cutting oneself off from the outside world and attempting to construct lives around the prison. Wives who "jailed" were likely to acquire other prisoners' wives as friends. They centered their lives around prison gossip and expressed scant interest in events going on in the larger community:

> Frank says that I'm the only woman in Vermont who does time. A lot of the women have lives that are unrelated to their husbands and they just go their separate ways and meet occasionally. Mine is wrapped up in Frank and Lilly. I sit home and other women are out partying. I don't want to party. Women can get cliquish up here. But the society encourages that; society turns on the women. If they stay with their husband, they are a son-of-a-bitch. If they don't, they're a son-of-a-bitch also. So the women will stick together. A bunch of us women moved up to St. Albert to live near our guys. One guy said that we're nothing but trash. Others up there feel that anyone who is married to a man in jail is trash or hookers. They see our kids as juvenile delinquents. Any town that has the centers has this attitude towards us.

Wives devised these strategies to cope with potential public reactions and to convey an appearance of normalcy. However, permanent normalization was difficult to achieve. As their husbands passed through the criminal justice system, their progress deeply affected their relationships and daily lives.

CHILDREN

Many wives realized, often with shock, that they were on the threshold of a new style of living from the point at which their husbands were arrested. They were going to be alone with their children for whom they would now be solely responsible. All these wives had to assume the role of single parents at a time when they also had to cope with the legal system. At the same time, they were aware that their children needed both emotional support and some explanations about their fathers' disappearances. Again, these wives had to engage in impression management. Information had to be given to the children that might preserve their images of their fathers as "just normal like anybody else's."

Almost all the women in the study expressed fears about their children. What concerned them most was that the children not suffer as a result of their fathers' arrests. Consequently, wives reported, they were quick to react to possible community hostility. No matter how tolerant the women's communities were, they anticipated that there would be some people who would act in a hostile manner toward their children. Therefore, a large proportion of wives wanted to prepare their children— especially if they were of school age—for any possible form of stigmatization.

During arrest and initial incarceration, the women had to decide what and how they would tell their children about their husbands' situations. What they did depended, in large measure, on how old the children were. Very young children recognized that their fathers were gone, but they were unsure what "arrest" or "jail" meant. It was therefore easier to conceal information from pre-school children. Most wives of pre-school children practiced some form of deception in doing this. Some told their children nothing about their fathers' arrest and imprisonment. Others simply avoided the issue by telling them that their fathers were somewhere other than prison, *e.g.*, in the hospital, away at work, or at school:[6]

> We lied to them and told them that he went away to work. They looked at his having a job away from home. When they went to visit him, when they left, or came into the place the door would be locked. They questioned this. I told them that it was a top secret job. Betsy was six and Ben only four when he went. If they asked point blank, I wouldn't lie to them. Ben has not really questioned where Charles is. I asked Betsy not to tell Ben and she agreed that he is too young.

Many women were aware that their children could pick up information through neighborhood gossip or by overhearing adults. These wives, therefore, attempted to design their chil-

dren's environments to maintain secrecy, although they were not
entirely certain as to how well this deception worked.

Children of school age were likely to have witnessed their
fathers' arrests or to have heard about them from adults. They
were therefore likely to ask questions about their fathers' situations. Under these circumstances, wives were not likely to conceal information:

> I don't lie to the kids and when they ask questions, I tell them up
> front and handle it as it comes. Jason has heard something bad
> about his father. He has heard many bad things, in fact. When he
> comes and mentions it to me, I say, "Yes" he did it and I tell them
> to wait for the court to make its verdict and then we can talk about
> it.

Mothers who told their children the truth, often found themselves walking a precarious tightrope. They hoped their children
would continue to ascribe the master status "father" to their
husbands, and assign less importance to their status as "criminal." Many old timers shared the details of their husbands' criminal behavior and arrests with their children regardless of age. In
doing this, some old timers were more likely than neophytes to
place great emphasis upon the temporary nature of their husbands' situations. The common message was that the men had
done some "bad" things, but that they would not always do
these activities:

> There aren't any problems. Sally knew he was in jail. I told her.
> She'd ask me "Where is Daddy?" and I said, "Daddy has been a
> bad boy and when he is a good boy, they will let him out." I won't
> lie to the kids. I don't believe in ever lying to them. My sister
> doesn't tell her child. I want to be honest with them.

The old timers also more or less assumed that their children
were aware of their fathers' criminal behavior and had already
devised their own accounts. According to these same old timers,
their children took their fathers' arrests in stride:

> Everyone knows where he is and I don't keep it back from anyone.
> I tell the kids that he's in jail too. Mary would say as we rode by
> the jail, "Daddy's in jail! There's his house!" I say to her that her
> Daddy got into a little trouble and he's in jail.

On the other hand, neophytes were more likely to flounder and feel uncertain about the kinds of explanations to give to children. Most were disoriented by the enormity of their husbands' crimes and the drama of arrest. In response to their own feelings of shock and bewilderment, they were likely to disclose some information but were anxious about the adequacy of these explanations.

Wives were also likely to take the kinds of crimes their husbands had committed into consideration in deciding the amount of information to disclose to their children. When the men had committed property crimes, wives were more likely to tell their children the circumstances of their husbands' arrests and to answer questions than they were under other circumstances. Wives of sexual offenders were more likely to be uncertain as to what to tell the children. Partial disclosure or covering up was used with the children of sex offenders. Wives did tell children where their fathers were, but they tended to conceal most details:

> I kept asking myself, what am I going to say to Sara. I don't know how you tell a-nine-year-old girl: "Your Dad raped two women." I just told her that her Daddy had hurt two women when he was all mixed up. Then I told her that "Dad was very sick in the head and hurt two people. He needs help and now he can get it." I left it at that.

A wife, whose husband was involved in a sexual offense, recalled telling her daughter that her father was in prison:

> People around here talk about me. They say, "Imagine her standing by that rapist." And they say terrible things about us. Betsy found out about Charles through some child. The child said, "Your daddy's in jail!" She told the child that he wasn't. Then she asked me about Charles. I won't lie to her. I said that he was in jail. She said, "What did he do?" I said, "Right now he broke the law and he has gone to jail to make good." She said, "What did he do?" I told her that I would tell her when she's older. She said that she was old enough to know now. She asked me to tell her what he had done. So I told here that "Daddy hurt a woman," but I didn't say how. She cried and cried. Then she said, "I have one more question to ask. Can I love him now?" I said, "I love him and you can love him, too." She then asked when he was coming home and

I told her that I didn't know. She started writing Charles every
night after that. She has accepted it as far as I know.

By contrast, those wives whose husbands had criminally
abused them were not reluctant to provide details. While informing the children about their fathers, these wives described their
behavior as socially unacceptable. Accordingly, these wives were
likely to describe their husbands as unredeemable, "bad," "no-
good bastards," "sickies," or "turkeys." Children often accepted
these definitions, since the children had sometimes, themselves,
been abused.

As a rule, wives did not take community reaction into consideration in deciding whether to tell children about their
fathers—although wives who resided in crime-familiar neighborhoods were likely to be more matter-of-fact.

STIGMATIZATION: THE CRIMINAL JUSTICE SYSTEM

Arrest is the first official step in the criminalization process. As
men pass through other stages, they undergo a series of status
transformations. When they are imprisoned, they assume social
identities of "prisoners." In some ways, wives share their husbands' status transformations: when husbands are officially labelled as criminals, their discredited and devalued statuses can
be transferred to their wives. Thus, police and prison personnel
play a part in women's perceptions of themselves as prisoners'
wives.

Police

Wives reported that they experienced not only anxiety, but stigmatization when witnessing their husbands' arrests. Some felt
that the police had treated them as "discreditable by association" while arrests were going on.

Arrests had a nightmarish quality for the wives. This became
even more true if the police treated wives as discreditable by association. Those wives whose husbands were dealing in drugs
and/or stolen goods were most likely to experience their husbands' arrests as not only sudden and disturbing, but as stigma-

tizing. In many cases, this resulted from the police having devastated their possessions while searching for drugs or stolen goods.

Their sense of degradation was compounded when they were informed by the police—as they often were—that they had to go to the station for questioning. Being interrogated by police officers often was both discrediting and disorienting. Neophytes were more likely than old timers to react with shame, bewilderment, and fear to the experience since they usually had little information about how they ought to deal with police. For example, one neophyte whose husband was arrested for armed robbery, related how disoriented she felt at the time of the arrest:

> The next morning, we walked out to the car. I was in the car while Tim was shoveling off the snow from the car. I looked up and there was a cop staring at me through the window. He told me to get out as my boyfriend had just been arrested. They took me to the police station and wanted to interview me to see if I knew anything about it. They told me that they had some eyewitnesses and I should cooperate with them as they knew everything. They filled me up with a lot of garbage like that. They told me that they had him with all the goods so I should tell them. They had me in one room and he in another. We could see each other through a window. He had this terrible look on his face and I am sure that he saw fear on mine. We couldn't talk. We could only look at each other.
>
> At the police station I was terribly confused. I was awed because I never experienced anything like this. I had a peaceful childhood. I lived up north in the country. We had done drugs but we had no contact with the police. I was wondering about my rights. I told them in fact that I knew nothing. I refused to sign any statements and I told them that I wanted a lawyer before I signed anything.

However, in the majority of cases—where arrests were treated as routine and undramatic—wives were unlikely to report that the police treated them as discreditable and devalued. Instead, wives whose husbands were arrested in this fashion tended to perceive themselves as most vulnerable to stigmatization of some form or another whenever they encountered the various prison systems.

Wives' Contacts With Prison Systems

> The guards are very hostile. They aren't friendly and they don't seem to be glad you're coming visiting. I got the real feeling that we're no different than those on the inside. We're just one more wing that they have to let in and out.

Although shame and stigmatization are not central issues in wives' everyday lives, many wives recalled that these issues were important whenever they visited their husbands at various prisons. There are, of course, differences between wives' and husbands' statuses. Prisoners experience stigmatization as ongoing. The women's sense of shame and/or perceptions of stigmatization is not central to their lives. However, since they cannot avoid being associated with their husbands in these contexts, wives' encounters with the prison system persistently open them up to feelings of shame, humiliation, and degradation.

Vermont's Prisons

At the door of every center in Vermont is a list of regulations that pertain to visiting. Each prison has its own rules which specify visiting days, length of visiting, degree of physical contact allowed between prisoners and visitors, and goods that can be brought into the facility. While these "house rules" do vary from one facility to another, they have one characteristic in common: an emphasis on security.

In Vermont, facilities range from the most to the least restrictive. In the "closed" Londonderry facility, known for handling "intransigent" prisoners, security is the tightest. Rules and regulations for visiting are detailed and intended to control all aspects of prisoner and visitor behavior strictly. There are written rules, for instance, about when prisoners and visitors may embrace or kiss, where visitors may sit, how children are to behave, how loudly prisoners and visitors may argue, and so forth. Londonderry's house rules are also designed to prevent contraband from being smuggled into the facility.[7] All visitors are frisked and checked by guards standing at the entrance. All visitors then go through a metal detector, and all handbags, shopping bags, and packages are searched. If the institution suspects that a visitor is holding contraband, the guards may demand that the visitor be strip searched. Strip searches are done in private areas within the prison facility, and female staff members strip search female visitors. Ordinarily, a visitor undresses and then permits staff members to examine all her body cavities.

Security is also emphasized in the more "open" correctional facilities, such as the Newport and the St. James Community Correctional Centers. The house rules are similar, but are less stringently enforced. Unlike Londonderry, children are generally allowed to walk around, but adults must remain seated. As at Londonderry, the Newport and St. James facilities also have rules on decorum which prohibit loud conversations, physical violence, or disruptive behavior. In contrast, at Walden Farms—the most "open" part of the Vermont prison system—the house rules only relate to physical contact, to the kinds of clothes visitors must wear (*e.g.,* men must wear trousers, shirts and shoes, and women must wear dresses or slacks and blouses and shoes) and to the requirement that visitors leave all packages, gifts, money—and anything that can contain contraband—with the prison guards on duty. At Newport and St. James, guards generally frisk visitors, utilize metal detectors, and search packages on a regular and predictable basis. At Walden Farms, there is only occasional frisking or searches of packages.[8] None of these "open" facilities seem to employ strip searches, but officially reserves the right to do so.

Visiting

Vermont's prisons are not populated by conventionally-oriented people who subscribe to conforming behavior and not all friends and family members who visit prisoners are likely to be committed to a law-abiding lifestyle. In the past, some of these visitors have violated conventional norms of behavior. Over the years, these incidents helped shape prison rules and procedures for dealing with every aspect of visitor control. The bureaucratic style used in enforcing these rules is probably the only effective way to cope with the problems of control: the process thus takes precedence over the individual.[9]

Through the enforcement of prison rules and regulations, wives felt they received the message that they did not share the same status as prison personnel. They also claimed that these rules and regulations set them up for experiences in which they were degraded and humiliated. For example, one wife recalled her reactions to visiting:

> I hated and dreaded it. I hated going to prison. You see a lot of assholes there. I didn't like getting checked over. They treat every-body like they're going to sneak knives and guns in. I wouldn't do it. It's such a sick scene. I knew that I didn't belong there.

The requirements that wives only walk in certain areas, ask guards' permission to use the bathrooms, remain seated in visiting rooms, and obey guards' orders were a major part of the humiliation process:

> The way they watch me I begin to feel that I'm a little kid who sneaks behind the barn to see him. If I kiss him good-bye, I always know a guard is staring at me. There should be more privacy there. The kids must sit quietly in their seats from 1–4 o'clock and the kids go wild. They go wild over Reggie and over other people who are visiting. And they tell me to keep them quiet. And you can't smoke cigarettes nor can you drink any soda. There are so many don't do this and don't do that. We don't do much but talk. I feel I'm in jail myself.

Self-respect was further threatened by ever-present reminders that the prison staff appeared not to trust them, that their every act and word were viewed with suspicion, and that guards' words and actions were beyond reproach. One old timer related this conversation with the superintendent of Londonderry about the strip searching policy:

> He won't strip search the guards. I asked him why. He said, "They're public citizens." They were stripping the men at the time. Frank would voluntarily ask to be stripped in the hopes that then I wouldn't have to be. But they kept stripping me regardless of Frank. Doesn't make any sense! I told Cranshaw, "Fred," I said, "I'm a public citizen too." He said, "You're not a public citizen when you're visiting here. You're incarcerated all the time that you're visiting here. You're an inmate's wife and when you come here you lose your rights. You don't have any rights!"

Another wife recalled how she reacted to the guards' behavior:

I really resented the whole situation. I hate visiting at the jails. Most of the correctional officials make you feel that you belonged in jail, too. I felt that they saw you as worthless in their eyes. It comes through the way they treat you. They act rude and suspicious. They assume that you are up to no good because you're coming to visit there.

Contamination

According to their own accounts, prisoners' wives perceive visitation procedures as a source of contamination which leads them to believe they share their husbands' low and discredited status. Goffman (1961) observes that, in total institutions, territories of the inmate's self—his body, thoughts, actions, and his possessions—are violated. "The boundary that the inmate places between his being and the environment is invaded and thus the self profaned" (1961:23). Sources of contamination assume several forms: searches and confiscation of personal property, forced interpersonal contact with undesirable inmates, forced obedience to picayune orders, enforced public character of visits between prisoners and visitors. Given this, many wives in the study also related a sense of contamination through forced interaction with other prisoners' wives.

Prison policy, which demands that visitors wait to be processed by the guards before seeing their husbands, conveyed to these women the message that they had a special low status. All wives reported that, at one time or another, they shared the prison entryway with other wives and visitors while waiting to be searched for contraband. The majority of women reported that this herding together made them acutely aware of a common discredited status with other prisoners' wives.

Half of the women felt contaminated by these contacts with other prisoners' wives, although this reaction was more common among neophytes than with old timers. Twelve neophytes had unfavorable opinions about the other wives whereas only two old timers expressed such feelings. During the earliest stage of their husbands' imprisonment the neophytes came to visit with the assumption that *other* wives must be suspicious, inherently discreditable, and as committed to criminal activities as their husbands. Neophytes tended to believe that other wives were "old cons" since they appeared adjusted to prison life and to have made the prison culture the focus of their lives. A college-educated neophyte (who majored in sociology) said:

> It depresses me to see the other people come in to visit. Everyone knows everyone else. They took the visiting and the men's incarceration nonchalantly and there I was with my heart in my mouth the whole time. The visitors would sit around before visiting and gossip about the guards and the jails. It was like a subculture of visitors. They would associate with each other on the outside and they would get very friendly with one another. I didn't want anything to do with it. I never identified myself with it.

And a few wives expressed a distaste for the old timers who made derogatory remarks about the prison system:

> I've tried to make friends with the women who go up there. But the ones that I've encountered are just not in my league. Everything they talk about is jail-oriented. They say that they're going to fight this thing, they're against the Establishment and everything they talk about is against the system. They don't have any insight so that their men can be helped. They're down on the whole establishment and see the people up there as "pricks" and "pigs." I don't look down on it and I'm proud. When I tell them how proud I feel about Jim, most of them turn their backs on me.

Another reason some wives gave for rejecting other prisoners' wives was their fast-living lifestyles (partying, bar-hopping, and having sexual liaisons while their husbands were in jail):

> I talk to them but I won't make friends with them. Most of them are sleazy. They have guys in jail and they're partying it up and bar hopping and they have three or four guys that they're running with while their men are in jail.

A few wives observed that other prisoners' wives seemed to be slow-witted, passive, meek, or dependent. A neophyte commented:

> Most of them had a lot of kids for their age; they were too young to have so many kids. I felt bad because I don't think that they realize that they didn't have to stay with their husbands. I got the impression that they didn't know what else to do. They all seem to be amazingly patient with their husbands and what they do, and what they put them through. They are always adapting to their

husbands and the situations that they create. They seem to adapt very well. I made no lasting relationships with them.

Wives tended to use two strategies to deal with the sense of contamination they felt when associating with other prisoners' wives: dissociation and association. In dissociating, wives attempted to isolate themselves from contacts, situations, and involvements in which disavowal is difficult. They avoided associating socially with other wives by remaining at the periphery of the group of visitors, minimized interaction with them, and gave rides to other wives only when asked.

All the square jane neophytes found prison especially repugnant. They isolated themselves as much as possible from other wives, resisted forming any ties to them, and believed that isolating themselves maximized their ability to maintain a conventional identity. According to one square jane neophyte:

> Occasionally I gave lifts to women after a visit to downtown St. Albert and then I'd go on my way. I never struck up a relationship with the women other than giving them rides home. I didn't have the desire to know them. It appeared to me that prison was a part of their lives and I didn't want to acknowledge that it was part of mine. I didn't want to be part of it.

Association also occurred. As more conventional working-class neophytes became acclimated to the prison world, they were less likely to attempt to dissociate themselves from others. Instead, they came to perceive prisoners' wives as a varied group and to become acquainted with other conventionally-oriented women, while continuing to avoid the "fast livers."

Contact was usually made in the waiting area. As one wife related:

> I did get to know Judy and Charlie's mother and Rocky's girlfriend and Jimmy's girlfriend who was pregnant and bringing in dope. They were all occupied with their men and when I'd get there, they usually were with their men. I'd usually be a little bit late for visiting. At Newport I talked to Mrs. Garrows whose son was there and Diane and Lester's girlfriend, Beth, and Red's wife. We usually talked about the guys and the kids because the kids were right there playing. We also talked about what the men were in for and how long they had and how we were doing. Red's wife seemed to

be doing real good by being on her own. Rocky's girlfriend was engaged to him. Mrs. Garrows I found out was discouraged because her son was in jail.

Relationships formed in this way were usually short-term and terminated with the husband's release from a particular prison. By contrast, old timers—especially prison-wise old cons—made a point of contacting and associating with other prisoners' wives as much as possible, especially if they are also committed to fast living.

Wives' Perceptions of the Guards as Stigmatizing Agents

The enforcement of prison policies is usually left to the discretion of prison guards. How visiting takes place is, therefore, primarily their concern. Since guards will be held responsible for problems that occur they are likely to treat all visitors as suspicious or untrustworthy. In the course of this, prisoners' wives reported that the prison staff appeared to stigmatize wives and other visitors.

The guards at the entrance and in the visiting room actually represent the prison to the streams of wives who enter. Wives reported that they sometimes had superficial contacts with other prison staff, but most of their interactions take place with the guards. On busy days guards must work quickly and efficiently to process the large number of people waiting to get into the visiting room. Many visitors bring packages, gifts, and laundry for prisoners. Ideally, each person should be as thoroughly searched as the rules demand. To do a thorough job the guards must search all the visitors, their packages, books, shopping bags, etc. Given the time restrictions for visiting, this cannot be done. Therefore, the guards must exercise discretion as to which visitors to search and how thoroughly.[10]

On the basis of their encounters with prison guards, most of the women drew conclusions about how the guards categorized prisoners' wives. Many come to believe that guards collect information and conjectures about them—especially derogatory information—which serve to mortify the wives:

They are always making judgments about the women who visit. They take a look at everybody and see how the men act with their families and how the wives act toward their men. Then I think that they write some of their impressions down. Over a period of time they get some kind of impression of you. I don't do anything to make a good or bad impression. I just kept saying to myself that it's their job to do this.

Many of the wives agreed that guards' decisions as to whom to search appeared not to be based on any strong suspicions about which visitors were bringing in contraband. Instead, guards appeared to base their decisions on pre-suppositions about wives' characters: (1) whether they were "good" or "bad" wives; (2) their demeanor; (3) the other visitors with whom they associated; (4) as well as their husbands' prison behavior and; (5) their own criminal records.

Many wives thought that most guards categorized them as either "whores" or "good wives." A "whore" would be a wife who liked bar-hopping or partying, or had short-term sexual affairs while her husband was in jail. A "good wife" would be a conventionally-oriented wife who guards viewed as suffering from her husband's criminal activities:

> The guards look at you and classify you in two ways. You're either a cheat or a super-wife or superwoman. When the women play the super-wife role, it sometimes becomes a farce. They try not to show their anger and it eats them up. It's the role that is forced on them. For example, the guards treated me with respect because they saw me as a super-wife. I stood with Frank right or wrong. If the guards see you as a whore, they treat you that way.

According to the wives, if they acted deferentially and respectfully to guards, if their children were well-mannered and neatly dressed, if they obeyed all rules and regulations, did not swear, and were blatantly supportive of their husbands, they were more likely to be thought of as "good wives." If wives were fractious or obdurate, acted tough or uncooperative, were obviously "stoned on some drug," did their own thing, or acted "as if they did not give a damn" whether their men were in or out, they were categorized as "whores." The wives believed that once they were categorized, they were consistently treated accordingly. For example, those labelled "good wives" were less likely to be searched:

The guards were all right; they treated me all right. I couldn't understand it. They knew that Al had pot but they never stripped me. And I was the only one who visited him. They caught him with an ounce once, too. Maybe it's because I looked so sweet and innocent. They must see me as "Miss Innocent Looking." They gave him no hassles.

Many women also observed that prison guards appeared to make judgments based on whether or not they associated with other wives whose conduct they perceived as "suspicious." If wives were friendly toward these women, then they, too, could acquire this reputation by association. The prison guards would then treat these wives in ways they thought were appropriate for "whores."

A woman that I know, Lola, was one of these women who have four or five guys on a string. I tried to be friendly with her even though she's not my kind of person. She lived in town when I lived in St. Albert and so we began to see each other. Automatically the guards' attitude began to change towards me. They began to get a little fresh with me because I was coming with Lola. They thought that I had crossed the line and was starting to go to local bar joints because that was her game.

Some wives mentioned that guards seemed to use wives' behavior toward their husbands in forming judgments about them. Many of these wives reported that prison guards made a point of observing how men acted toward their families and how wives acted towards their men: some wives also reported that guards appeared to enforce the rules on the basis of their husbands' in-prison performance or reputation:

It's supposed to be no more than three visitors for each prisoner, but I've seen sixteen or seventeen people come in to visit with one prisoner. It depends on who you are. I get guards who treat me pretty decent because Frank's a pretty big man. It's absurd!

Finally, according to four wives' accounts, prison guards searched and supervised them carefully as a result of their past criminal records.

Most wives reported that they found the process of searching for contraband, in itself, stigmatizing. These wives noted that many guards made derogatory statements toward them or acted in an inconsiderate and disrespectful manner while it was going on. These wives felt that they, too, were being treated as "criminals":[11]

> I didn't like going to Newport. The guards treat you like you're an inmate. They're so snotty to you and they give out smart remarks. If you bring stuff in, they go through the stuff. When they look at you, they look like they think we're beneath them.
>
> At Londonderry, they make you feel like you are dirt. We have to go through this detector. Sometimes they like to ridicule you by making the buzzer ring for any object so that you have to go back and forth through the detector. They think it is funny.

Strip Searching

Strip searching only took place at Londonderry, the most "closed" prison. All wives who visited this facility considered this security measure to be thoroughly humiliating and degrading. Twenty-six wives had husbands who had been incarcerated in Londonderry at one time or another, so that the threat of being humiliated in this way was real to them. Nine of the wives in the study readily admitted that they had smuggled contraband into Londonderry and three other centers. However, when wives talked about strip searches, they usually presented themselves as innocent when these occurred. Strip searches were almost universally described as indignities performed on innocent wives.[12]

Not all wives whose husbands had been imprisoned at Londonderry had, of course, been strip searched. A few wives suggested that women labelled as "good wives," those who appeared to be of the middle class or living settled and conventional lifestyles, were seldom strip searched while fast-living women frequently were. One woman who pursued a fast-living lifestyle recalled:

> I felt degraded. It was especially degrading when I had my period because you have to remove your Tampax in front of them. One time when I was being strip searched, a man looked into the window. Now they assured us that no men could witness the searches. They consider me the ringleader because I know my rights and I fight them all the way.
>
> It's degrading. When I was strip searched, I signed the paper under protest. I signed my name and would write "under protest."

Lieutenant Barr has made some nasty comments to me like, "Women like you should be strip searched." I put grievances in on this harassment and on the man who looked in through the window at me. I know their games and it pisses them off.

The other criterion used by guards most frequently mentioned by prisoners' wives was the kind of visitors with whom the women associated. Some wives believed that guards were also likely to strip search women who associated with "fast-livers." For instance one wife provided her reasons for not associating with fast-living wives:

> My husband and I play cards and talk during visiting. We talk about the inmates and visitors that walk in. We talk about the way they act. One woman kept yelling at people in the bubble. She was stoned and being real loud. We hid in the corner to get away from her. I don't want to be associated with people like her or go through a strip search. Every time they mention strip search, I turn white and shake and can't stop. It's humiliating to go through that and I haven't done a crime.

According to wives' reports, then, guards are likely to utilize similar criteria to determine which visitors to go through routine search procedures and which visitors to strip search.

Many wives hesitated to give rides to, converse with, or even stand in the prison entry with any woman who had been strip searched:

> I became freaked out if the woman who had been strip searched asked me for a ride to St. Albert. I didn't want them to see me associating with women who they thought might be bringing in contraband. I'd be panic stricken.

Some wives reported that they, themselves, had been strip searched as a result of associating with women who had. If, for any reason, a wife came to be known as one who had smuggled contraband, she was *always* strip searched at Londonderry:

> They treat me like an inmate. I was accused of bringing in pot. They know Mark smokes pot and they think that I am always bringing it in. They have stripped me, his little sister who is 7 years old, and the baby too.
>
> I brought up a box with pot hidden in it and they found it. They have caught Mark smoking it and now think that it is I who

brings it in. I only tried to bring it in that one time. They have been strip searching me since December 25th. Cranshaw says that they'll continue to do it every visit.

Some wives—particularly those who had been stripped many times—reported that they felt a mixture of anger and hopelessness:

> When I went there I had to walk through that metal detector and then wait until I could sign this paper giving them permission to strip search me. I had to sign the paper if I was to see Jerry. Then I had to take everything off and they'd have me spread my cheeks of my ass and they'd look up it. They look up my armpits and at my whole body. Why put up with this to just get to see our husbands? If you wore a bra and the detector didn't go off at the place where the metal is on your bra, the guard would make some remark like, "I see you're one of these liberated women who doesn't wear bras." I didn't want this. I was being downgraded for giving someone an enjoyable four hours of his stay in the joint.

The ordering of events was completely out of their control. Over and over again, they reported that nothing they did could alter the impression of them as "suspicious." The wives' accounts suggest that they were treated as incorrigible sinners and the guards demonstrated in this unforgettable process just how low a prisoner is in the institution's estimation. Many wives observed that they were to be treated as prisoners until they were released.[13]

How the prison staff (always women) performed the search had an impact on wives' reactions to this procedure. Most wives maintained that, in some real sense, the guards performing strip searches had done something improper or unjust. At the same time, they felt the guards had to do it: it was their job. What provoked their anger—and feelings that they were being stigmatized—were the spiteful or derogatory comments guards made to them. This is when wives felt that they had been personally diminished. When guards performed this procedure in a neutral and impartial manner, the women generally expressed less immediate dislike for it. Yet underlying all their reactions was a feeling of righteous indignation, at having to undergo this procedure in the first place.

Well, you walk into a room and there are two women in the room with you. They ask you to remove all your clothes and place them on the floor. Then they take a flashlight and shine it in your eyes, up your nose, and in your opened mouth. I don't know why they do that. Then they ask you to let your hair hang loose and then you're supposed to hold it up so they can shine the flashlight into the hair around your neck. Then they shine the flashlight under your armpits. Then they ask you to lift one breast, one at a time, and they shine the flashlight under your breast. Then they ask you to run your fingers around your belly button in such a way that you place pressure on the skin in that area. Do they really think you're going to be carrying something in your belly button? Then they run the flashlight through your pubic hair. After that they ask you to bend over with your hands touching the ground. They ask you to "crack a smile," and they bend over with the flashlight, and examine your asshole, and then they look at your vagina with the flashlight. Sometimes when I'm like this, I'm tempted to fart. After this, they make you stand for fifteen to twenty minutes while they check your clothes. The two female officers like to make a lot of sarcastic comments like "It's time to buy a new bra don't you think?" or "This underwear is certainly soiled." If you have your period, then you have to stand there with the blood flowing down your legs. It's gross! They don't care.

As this quote illustrates so vividly, those women who had been strip searched experienced a common underlying injury: the violation of self. Some wives even reported that they experienced a sense of having been attacked in a sacred, inner place. They feel violated and contaminated by being strip searched. Strip searches crystallized a sense of injustice among those who knew women who had been searched and those who had actually been searched themselves.

COPING STRATEGIES

Putting on a Performance

Most wives reported that they became aware of the criteria guards used in judging whether or not they were "suspicious." Thirteen wives "put on a performance" in order to attempt to shape or alter guards' perceptions: they attempted to hide any visible signs that they were prisoners' wives, tried to appear "conventional" in their clothing, acted extraordinarily polite and self-effacing, and spoke in a respectful and respectable way. A square jane described how she successfully "performed" for the prison guards:

> I was horrified at the idea of being strip searched and I tried to make it obvious that I was not smuggling in drugs. I dressed like I was going to my office to work. Most of the guards there were a lot nicer to me than they were to others. I guess it's because of the way I acted. A lot of the visitors were very aggressive. I just acted as though they were any other worker in a public place. I talked to the guards about the weather and some of them would be nice to me.

Many wives who "put on performances" deliberately exaggerated their feminine characteristics whenever they were smuggling contraband to their husbands or when they intended to be sexually intimate with their husbands. The more prison-wise wives seemed to have developed skills needed in handling the guards. Most neophytes had not. Yet the younger, more naive and middle-class-looking wives learned to use their physical appearance to get away with rule infractions.

Dissociation

Since strip searching is an especially anxiety-laden and distasteful procedure, many wives deliberately attempted to disassociate themselves from other wives so as to avoid being stripped. Many wives hesitated to give rides to, converse with, or even stand in the prison entry with any woman who had been strip searched. Some wives reported that they, themselves, had been strip searched as a result of associating with women who had. This wife, for instance, recalled how she tried to avoid other wives of prisoners:

> And time had an effect on our relationship. The novelty of our blossoming relationship began to wear off. Even the novelty of the trauma of his being in prison wore off. I dreaded going there [to Londonderry]. They made these visits as hard on the visitors as possible. The other jails made you feel that the visits were constructive for both the inmate and the visitor. I became freaked out if the women who had been strip searched asked me for a ride to

Londonderry. I didn't want them to see me associating with women who they thought might be bringing in contraband. I'd be panic stricken.

It is clear from wives' accounts that prison visiting itself can be a grim experience insofar as wives come to perceive themselves as subjected to a series of abasements, humiliations, and degradations of their "selves." Upon admission to the prisons, wives are subjected to mortification by such contaminative exposure as forced interpersonal contact with other prisoners' wives, searching of their possessions, strip searches, closely supervised visits, and so forth. Wives' accounts furthermore agree that their self-respect is assaulted whenever they interact with prison guards who tend to type wives as "the good wife" or as "the whore," and who discriminate among them on this basis, making derogatory statements, or treating them in a disrespectful manner. House rules for visiting and the treatment by prison staff are perceived as ever-present reminders that wives share their husbands' stigmatized status.

Given the difficulties involved in visiting, the extent to which a hard core of wives visited their husbands was startling. The next chapter will provide some factors that motivate wives to continue formal visits with their husbands in spite of the stigmatization that they encounter.

CHAPTER VII

Marital Relationships: Visiting at the Prison

The visits affected my whole life. After a visit, I was affected the day after and maybe into the week, I felt affected. Then I would begin to look forward to the next visit. It affected my whole life and my moods depended on when I was going to visit him and then on dealing with the visits.

Prison visiting can be paradoxical. For wives, it is on the one hand, a reminder of the permanence of marital ties.[1] But, simultaneously, visiting can be a reminder of fractured lives, a source of unsettling anxiety, and a degrading and cruel experience. The ways in which prison systems structure visits can either strengthen or undermine marital ties.

Yet no matter how paradoxical it is for them, prisoners' wives tend to remain strongly committed to visiting. In many cases, it becomes a central aspect of their lives. Within the constraints of prison life, relationships can be strengthened or undermined as prisoners and their wives attempt to resume remnants of their pre-prison marital patterns and their roles as husbands and wives.[2]

Interactions between wives and their incarcerated husbands are complex, but in general, are characterized by three primary interaction patterns: (1) renewed courtship; (2) sharing household decisions; and (3) wives' arrangements made to supply husbands with both approved goods and contraband. The nature of communications between incarcerated husbands and their wives must also be seen in relation to the structure of the prison system, opportunities provided for and constraints upon visiting.[3]

THE WOMEN SPEAK FOR THEMSELVES

Most of the prisoners' wives interviewed felt that responsibility for sustaining marital relationships falls on the female partner. The following excerpts from two different accounts describe visits to Londonderry Correctional Facility.

Mildred, a neophyte, has two school-aged boys from a previous marriage. She occasionally takes them to visit her husband, Sam, who was sentenced for breaking and entering, a drug- related charge. At the time of the interview, he had served two years of his sentence.

> My first visit was all right. We'd have a good visit. We didn't get into sex. There were too many cameras and doors. When I got off the bus, everybody knew why we were getting off—to go to the prison. The first time, I had to ask where to go and so the people knew what I was doing. I took his clothes in a bag and that was embarrassing.
>
> When I go to see Sam now, I don't feel that people know. It's my business. I really don't know if people know. It's like going down to college to see a friend. When people know very little about Sam, I say he's in college learning his times. When someone asks where is my husband, I usually tell them. I don't announce it to them. But I won't lie. But it is his and my business.
>
> When I go to visit him, we sit in the corner and a lot goes on in that corner and they can't see us. Sam blocks their view of me because he is so big. We constantly look to see who's watching. He always tells me to get to the corner when I come to visit and sometimes other people beat me to the corner. But when Sam wants something accomplished, he gets what he wants. When we do get the corner and he manages to get it, we hope that not too many people are watching. We don't do too much talking. We had sex in the visiting rooms. We had some nice visits. I know that people who were visiting saw us having sex. Some of them get embarrassed. One guy would keep looking. He said, "Sam, what are you doing?"
>
> On the phone and in our letters, we have so much to say. We write and phone a lot. When I get down to visit, we have nothing to say. We just say "hi!" We've talked too much on the phone and so we have nothing to say. He does all the talking during the visit and then we end up necking and having sex.
>
> Sometimes we talk for half an hour. I don't really have anything to talk about. And he hasn't done anything to talk about. But when we do talk, we talked about the kids. We also talk about what we're going to do when he gets out. We want to resume our sex life. That's what interested us the most.

He likes to say that when he gets out, he wants to hang some signs on the door to my house saying, "Do not disturb." I wish I could go into his room and sit up there for the three hours. They could lock me in with him. I wouldn't do any harm. I don't understand why they won't let us go into his room. This separation has delayed one thing. I wanted to have another baby but his being there delays it.

He says that we're going to spend a lot of time in bed when he gets out. He likes to say that we're going to start right off and have ten kids. He must be joking. I hope he's joking!

Sam was doing 90 percent of the dealing in Londonderry. He usually sells the pot and I bring it in for him.

The guards were all right; they treated me all right. I couldn't understand it. They knew Sam had pot but they never stripped me. And I was the only one who visited him. They caught him with an ounce once, too. Maybe it's because I looked so sweet and innocent. I told Sam that I didn't like to do it, I didn't do it very often. Once when he was down at the Newport he got mad 'cause I wouldn't bring it in. It's worse down there—more scary. It's harder to pass it to him.

I really don't like doing it. I don't mind when I go through the machine. I don't feel nervous then. It's when I hand it to him that I feel scared that I'm going to get caught. I usually put it in my waist band or pants and I don't wear anything that the machine can pick up. I bring in about an ounce. I don't like doing it. If they strip searched me, I can't see him then because I would have to walk away. I couldn't let them strip search me or it'd be all over. But I have never been strip searched. I can't believe it. Those guys don't even make any money out of these deals. I guess it's just something for them to do.

I get it from someone I know. Sam tells me where to get it and I do it. I get it on my way up there. Somebody gives him the money up there and then I go get it and then he gets a cut of the pot that he can sell. But they never get ahead. I don't understand why they never seem to make any money off it. They go round in circles like I do with my welfare checks. For instance, Sam makes a deal for this small amount of pot. The friend borrows money. Then he gives it to Sam who then gets a cut. They get it and sell it, and then because they smoke some of it most of the remaining money goes to pay off loans, and reinvest so that they can begin all over.

At visiting time, I just give it to him in the visitors' room. He takes it, and puts it in his pants, and then he goes to the bathroom and puts it up his ass. They strip search him after the visit. They don't ask me for a strip search. I get nervous about doing it and picking it up and sneaking it in. I do it because he wants it done.

Lucille is also a neophyte. She had recently married her husband, Matt, who was serving a sentence for possession of stolen goods. She had five children by a former marriage and gave birth to a baby girl during Matt's incarceration.

I'm in a real good mood. I'm getting to see him. I put on my dress slacks. I'm in a real good mood. I'm feeling okay until the visit is over and I'm outside. When I'm outside the gates, I feel bothered. On Saturdays, I have to wait the whole week until I see him again. When I get home, I call him and he's so depressed. I wish he could walk out of the door with me.

I talk to a few of the girls when I go in. Such crazy rules about what you can do and can't do. The women complain that visiting is supposed to be 1–4 on Saturday and they don't let you in at 1. They only let you in after the boys leave their recreation. Why can't the boys leave the recreation earlier so they can have a full visit? On Friday visiting is from 6–8 and they don't check you in until 6. They won't give you extra time. In Newport, if they are late checking you in, they give you extra time to visit to make up for their lateness. Here they don't do that.

We talk about what is allowed in. I had an argument with the supervisor. I brought some coffee in a container. They let it in. Another time, I brought a jar of coffee down. He said, "You're not to bring that in." I said, "I brought it in a couple of times before." He said that the guards can be jumped on for letting me bring it in. And then I noticed that someone else was allowed to bring it in and I couldn't. I can't bring a glass jar in there and so I usually bring it in a container. They go through the diaper bag and they check the coffee. Sometimes they say something and sometimes they don't. How come other women can bring it in? I asked him that. He kept saying that Matt has to go through classification and said I'd have to send the coffee through the mail. You can't win with them. They have the craziest rules and they don't go by them.

I usually bring him down cigarettes, shampoo, soap, deodorant and $2 in change for phone calls and sometimes I bring him more money. I bring down what he needs. I've brought him a bedspread, books to read, and a typewriter. I brought him a clock radio for his birthday. It cuts me down. He smokes cigarettes like you wouldn't believe. He runs out of cartons every week. I have to send him money for more. It hurts. I only get $170 for food stamps and it has to go for the family and for him. Giving to him always cuts me short.

In a way I feel comfortable visiting him. In another way it bothers me. I find it's hard to talk with him when there is a guard walking back and forth and there are so many people there. There isn't any privacy. In Londonderry, when he was in D-Wing, we saw each other in a little room. We could sit and talk quietly and feel that we had some privacy. In Newport, the guards watch you like a hawk. I don't feel that I am able to open up and talk the way that I want to. I would like a few moments alone.

Our visiting goes pretty good. My just getting to see him means a lot to both of us. We talk about what's happening around the house. I talk to him during the visit about how the kids are doing. We talk about the same things, more or less that we talk about during our phone calls. He shows me the stuff he's made in ceramics. We also talk about things we're going to do. We want to move and get out of St. Albert. We're thinking of going to Texas. I've always wanted to go to Texas and Matt does. I don't know when but we're going. He says that the kids need another brother. I'd love to have another boy. I want at least two children like Matt.

Matt wants to make a new life and go somewhere where no one knows us. Get a different job and start all over.

He says he's going to change. He always says he's going to try his best when he gets out. He doesn't make any promises. They can be broken. He's going to try to make a better life for me and the kids. We both want a log cabin in the country. He says he will try his best. We like being in the country and that's where we want to be.

He talks about when he is going to get to a different level and talks about when he's going to get his passes. We complain about the coffee there. The coffee tastes like mud or colored water. We pick on a guard together. We ask him who makes the coffee! We sit and visit with each other.

At Londonderry we argued a lot about what goes on in the correctional center. I have a wicked temper too. I feel pretty bad. I should change the subject when he argues with me. These arguments could hurt him inside. He takes it out on other people. He argues with them. He's not good with them. He's got enough problems to worry about than to worry about what happens here. I shouldn't argue with him. But I tell him what I think.

I try to explain what goes on here but he really doesn't understand. I then get mad and give him more details. And then when he get's angry, I get angrier.

I'd like to tell them my suggestion. I'd like to tell the guards to let the wives be ALONE with their husbands once a month. It's a killer to go this long and not be able to touch him. I can't hold him and touch him. If you sit too close at visiting, they make you separate. We sit and play cards and talk and that gets pretty boring. Matt had problems because he was passing blood in his urine. His doctor told him that he had trouble with his prostate gland. He was told that the problem was that he was getting a lot of intercourse and now he wasn't getting any. That caused the blood. If they had their wives once a month, not so many guys would turn homosexual.

This wouldn't go on—homosexuality. It wouldn't go on. If they had their wives once a month, it would give the guys something to look forward to. Locking up men causes homosexuality. The correctional centers are going about it wrong.

Because of this, Matt worries about me leaving. Those of us who don't go running around, go up against the wall. All this tension is taken out on the kids. The Correctional Center has screwed up a lot of people. A lot of women go to men for comfort when their men are in.

When it's time to leave and I know that I have to leave alone— that bothers me. When I take the kids to visit, he's entirely different. He's not able to share their growing up. He becomes very quiet around them and seems like he's in a daze. He just sits there and looks at them. He just remembers what it was like when he was home. All I can do is look at him because he doesn't hear me. He spends his time just looking at them. I can understand what he's going through.

We're so close, the kids and I and Matt during our visits. He gets to see us and talk to us, and then we go our way, and he goes another. He can't sit there and play with the kids. He can only see them. We leave and we go out one door and he goes out another. He's really close but not as close as he wants to be.

CONSTRAINTS ON PRISON VISITING

As it is structured, visiting benefits both the correctional system and inmates' families. The Vermont Department of Corrections assumes that visits preserve, strengthen, and stabilize prisoners' marital ties. Administrators usually assume that visits allow prisoners to maintain contacts with their wives and families and that such contacts have a positive effect on prisoners' performance both inside correctional facilities and while on parole.

Although maximizing prisoners' contacts with their families is a formal goal of Vermont's prison system, each unit limits visiting to some degree through rules and regulations that determine visitng days, length of visiting time, degree of physical contact allowed, conduct of prisoners and visitors, and what provisions can be brought into prisons. While such "house rules" vary, they are all intended to ensure security and sometimes appear to conflict with the stated goal of encouraging prisoners to maintain domestic ties.

Although there is some variation in days and hours, all facilities in Vermont arrange for visiting at least two days a week.[4] In all facilities, except Walden Farms, this includes a maximum of one day during the work week, and two days on the weekend. At Walden Farms, visiting is restricted to Saturdays, Sundays, and holidays. Limits are also placed on the length of visits and these do not vary a great deal from prison to prison: in all Vermont prisons, except at Walden Farms, visiting hours range from one to three hours. At Walden Farms visiting hours are sometimes extended to four hours.

Visiting is considered a privilege that prisoners earn and, as such, it can be revoked. In the Vermont correctional facilities, the number of visits each prisoner is permitted is based on his security classification. For instance, at Londonderry, a prisoner who has been classified as needing minimum security is allowed four visits per week up to three hours at a time. A prisoner confined to the special adjustment unit, by contrast, is permitted one visit per week for one hour.[5]

Prison facilities range from the most to the least restrictive, especially in the most "closed" facility, Londonderry, where the rules and regulations governing visiting are designed to provide strict control over the behavior of both prisoners and visitors.

Physical Facilities and Atmosphere

Physical facilities for visiting also vary. At Londonderry, visits are conducted in a light, airy, and rather pleasant cafeteria. Couples may sit wherever they choose, although prisoners and their visitors are not permitted to leave their chairs except to use the coffee urn or the bathrooms. In contrast, St. James and Newport provide large, barren and dismal rooms where chairs are placed helter-skelter around the room. There are no coffee urns, but there are vending machines that are accessible with guards' permission. At Woodlawn, visiting takes place in the library, which tends to be drab and uninviting. There are very uncomfortable chairs and a few tables. Neither coffee urns nor vending machines are accessible. In all these facilities, visiting is conducted under the watchful eyes of at least one guard.

Even the more "open" correctional facilities, such as Newport and St. James, emphasize security. The two facilities have "house rules" similar to those at more "closed" centers, but these are less stringently enforced. At Newport, unlike Londonderry, children are generally allowed to walk around, though the adults must remain seated. As at Londonderry, Newport also lists rules of decorum which prohibit loud conversations, physical violence, or disruptive behavior.[6] According to wives' reports, Walden Farms treats visiting in an entirely different way: it encourages men to have more access to the grounds and, to some extent, the community. Therefore, in order to maximize prisoners' sense of freedom, visiting is less physically structured. For instance, during the spring and summer months, wives and husbands may stay indoors or go out at will. The husbands can choose to talk and play games with their children on the picnic grounds, families can choose to have barbecues outdoors, and most important, they can find places to be alone in somewhat unsupervised privacy. All wives reported that even though visiting rules are similar to those in other prisons, at Walden Farms there is greater opportunity for physical and verbal intimacy with their husbands.[7]

The wives interviewed felt that visiting is not an easy event.[8] Twenty-seven of them referred to three important constraints on their visits: lack of privacy, time restrictions, and lack of freedom of movement.[9] All reported that prisons appeared more concerned with fulfilling custodial goals than with maximizing interactions between spouses. Since time and privacy are prerequisites for authentic emotional communication, the encounters were perceived as somewhat artificial.

Visiting rooms are usually crowded with adults and children, and all wives reported that they could not help overhearing others' conversations and arguments. Crying children who could not move around freely also raised the noise level. Neophytes, in particular, found themselves distracted by the noise, arguments, and other goings-on. As one such wife reported:

> During visiting, I got the feeling that people were aware of each other constantly. They were always watching each other. There was a lot more going on there than I could imagine. It was all so paranoid. For many of the inmates, it was the only time that they saw other inmates that they knew. Visiting became a vehicle for sending messages, for doing battle with one another. I was so busy trying to figure out what was going on that it was hard for me to pay attention to Buddy. And I saw how they were watching me to see what I was doing. I really felt uncomfortable. I felt that people were tuning into what we said so I didn't want to talk to Buddy there. I began to hide things. Thinking of visiting still gives me goose bumps.

Sixteen of the wives reported that privacy was further undermined and communication inhibited by the presence and surveillance of prison guards, who are present to control communication and sexual intimacy, and to prevent the passing of contraband. Needless to say, many wives felt inhibited and unable to communicate freely or spontaneously with their men.

Given the lack of privacy, ten wives reported that sexually intimate couples distracted as well as upset them. They found it particularly difficult to be forced to observe other wives and girlfriends attempting to go beyond the permitted levels of sexual intimacy. Those wives who did not want to participate in sexual activities in public were most likely to complain about them. An old timer, whose husband had repeatedly been in prison, summed up many wives' reactions:

> Then I have to sit there and see the wives crying throughout the visiting time or if they're not crying, they are fighting with their men 'til we leave. The little children are running around and they can't understand why they are there.... You're so close to your man and you're only allowed to kiss and hold hands. But some of them go beyond that and it's disgusting with so many kids around to see them. It's very sad to go there and get locked in that room.

Another wife noted:

I'm not a very moral person but I hate to go to visiting. The people are doing all knds of things that I wouldn't like the children to see. Women's dresses are pulled up and some of them look like they're having the final sexual act right there in the visiting room and they don't care that there are children running around. I believe that a lot of babies have been conceived during these visits. I stopped bringing my children as I felt that they were seeing too much for their ages. What goes on there is not fit to be seen. And I'm not a moral person! I want to have sex and I miss my husband but I wouldn't carry on like that.

Time and Freedom to Interact

Almost all wives reported that the time specified for visiting also placed unnecessary constraints on communication. Thirteen wives specifically noted that visiting took place within a "painfully" short period of time, and no allowances were made for their needs for more extensive time with their mates. Many of these wives also mentioned that no additional time was granted even though they had had to travel great distances to get there. One wife put it well: "What can be said when one is limited to two hours at a time, sometimes a little more?"

Finally, wives wanted to utilize visiting as a time for families to be together—including children. Yet, at all Vermont prisons, except Walden Farms, visiting was not structured so as to allow children freedom of movement. Children's behavior was supposed to be regulated by their parents, i.e., children were not to play, run, scream, or cry, but sit quietly. If they did not, guards could terminate the visit. Thus, wives complained that visiting tended to center on controlling their children:

The kids want to see him and it's hard to keep the kids down and quiet when we're visiting. It's hard to visit with the two kids. I have to chase them around and at the same time try to see him. The guards tell me to keep the kids quiet. They can't be kept quiet. They've taken a long trip and have a lot of energy to get off. There's nothing for them to do but run around aimlessly.

And finally, another wife sums up the reasons why visiting is not an easy event:

I don't feel very comfortable. The guards breathe down your neck. It's hard to talk there because there are all these people yelling around you. And you can't do nothing when you're there. You can't get close to one another. If you do, the guards break it up immediately. And it's a long way for me to get there. I have to walk to the bus stop and catch a bus and then walk to Newport. I have to leave Newport at precisely the right time and if I don't then I miss the bus and I have to wait for another bus for an hour. If I have the kids then it's a pain in the ass. I have even a harder time of it. When the kids are there, they can't do anything but sit quietly. You can't expect the kids to sit for hours in one place. But if they don't the guards come over and tell the kids to sit. It's a hassle for them. I try to bring them something to occupy them. I'll bring books, little cars, paper and crayons. But how much drawing and playing with cars are they going to do. When it gets toward the last twenty minutes, they get restless. We try to get them to sit and talk. Reggie and I can get into a discussion and they interrupt us constantly and we get distracted. And then they start running around and there are a lot of interruptions. Sometimes when I visit Reggie, we just sit there and look at each other for one or two hours without having a thing to say. Sometimes there isn't much to say and we just look at each other. You see, I also talk to him on the phone and there's only so much to talk about.

The wives in the study population agreed that visiting was easier at Walden Farms and St. James because guards tended to be less obtrusive. Hence, there was greater opportunity for both verbal and physical intimacy.

Given these constraints, wives reported that they primarily spent visiting times conversing with their men. However, since visits were structured so that they had a defined beginning and end, all the components of wife-husband interaction had to be tightly packed in. Consequently, anxieties and tensions tended to build up. Both spouses came to face each other with their own anxieties, doubts, and fears. Pressures had built up since last they had seen each other.

Eight neophytes and four old timers reported that conversing with their husbands was fraught with difficulties and that they would experience, in rapid succession, anger and attachment, quarrels and remorse, vicious fighting and passionate reconciliation.

An old timer described the differences in how she and her husband interacted in the prison visiting room and in the privacy of their home.

> This time we fought all the time when he was in jail. He'd say something and I'd take it all wrong and I'd say something and he'd take it all wrong. We tried to cram so much in an hour and we never got a chance to talk things out. Then I'd go home and write a letter about the subject we were fighting about and he'd receive the letter and he'd get uptight. Then he wrote back and Big Mouth Bea takes it out.
>
> When we were home together, we have heavy discussions. We don't fight. We have the time. It's easier to talk. We have forever to talk and there you only have an hour and the kids are trying to talk with him and we're trying to have a conversation.

Regardless of the visiting structure, a small minority of women related that, for the first time, they began to communicate with their husbands. Six neophytes reported that they were able to get closer to their men than they had before incarceration. Relationships appeared to strengthen for these women during visiting, especially for the newlyweds. A newlywed enthusiastically describes how she feels closer to her husband during visiting:

> Our relationship was blossoming. It wasn't like it was on the outside. We had all these tensions because we constantly talked about what was going to happen. Now we talked about literature, politics, and things like that for hours. What had happened had happened. All this sorta proved that our relationship could be maintained and go on regardless of serious obstacles that were in our way. There was no way that I could break off the relationship.

This intensity of interaction is paradoxical in that it could contribute to both strengthening and undermining marital ties. The paradoxical nature of visiting is observed in Londonderry, Woodlawn, and Newport where more constraints are placed on couples. Even though wives can have time to speak with their husbands and to renew faith in their marriages, they also reported conversations to be restrained and arguments likely to erupt in these facilities.

In contrast, wives were more likely to report that they felt closer to their husbands, were able to communicate in a less restrained manner, and were less argumentative and hostile in the more "open" visiting sites offered by St. James and Walden Farms.

COURTSHIP AND INTIMACY

Remember when you told me that Rudi had told you everything was going to be sweet like roses when he got back? They promise anything when they're in jail.

—A Prisoner's Wife

A theme that recurs throughout the wives' reports is that visiting allowed them and their husbands to experience a sense of renewed courtship.[10] Even with the obvious constraints placed on prison visits, most couples appear to have achieved a degree of closeness and reaffirmed marital ties. Prior to the husbands' incarceration, couples had been free to express their sexuality with one another by holding hands, embracing, fondling, and intercourse. In contrast, the prison system only allowed them to interact sexually under very restricted and controlled circumstances.

To fill the void, twenty-three wives reported that they and their spouses tended to court one another. Courtship allowed them to acknowledge a romantic and sexual attachment to each other. What was unique here was that courting took place under the surveillance of prison guards who acted as adult chaperones. Almost all the wives reported that, during visiting, both they and their husbands tended to be in good moods, to try to be on their best behavior, and to dress in attractive clothes. They were likely to select topics which would make the best impression on each other. Courting also assumed the form of pleas for and declarations of love, flirting and jealousy, and mutual support. There was a feeling of closeness and rapport that made them enjoy each other's company and want to explore and deepen their relationships. Courting also provided the substance for everyday social conversations. For varying lengths of time, the realities of their former relationships could disappear and they could enjoy the "present."

Because visiting was constrained, nineteen wives reported that they found talking and flirting with their husbands enjoyable. They began to look forward to visiting time as a kind of "date." To some extent, courting could soothe the "pains" of enforced separation, and yet it could also intensify these "pains" since in-prison courting often cannot involve full sexual intimacy.

Sexual Contact

Within the context of courting, couples could participate in various forms of sexual contact. Sixteen wives reported that they did no more than hold hands, hug, or kiss their husbands. Eight wives reported that they had managed to cuddle and fondle their husbands, while five said that they had had intercourse. From these wives' accounts, it is clear that the degree of sexual intimacy achieved depended upon the guards' willingness to ignore it. The kind of contact varied with the tolerance of different guards. Moreover, wives reported that guards at some prisons are more lenient than at others. At Newport guards were willing to keep their eyes closed. For the most part this was not true at Londonderry. However, even at Londonderry, some wives managed to have intercourse:

> The guard closed his eyes and didn't bother us. I would send the kids to someone else to visit and we'd get together. We had sex in the visiting room. I know that the people who were visiting saw us having sex. We'd sit in the corner—way in the corner. I'd get there very early so I'd get the furthest away seat in the visiting room. The guards are nice there.

When the structure of visiting was relatively "open," sexual intimacy could occur more easily. Whenever supervision was reduced, many prisoners and their wives were likely to fondle one another sexually or to have intercourse. According to wives, this sometimes made visiting more enjoyable and exciting, since it involved risk:

> I was all keyed up. I was always glad to be there. To see him meant a lot to me and then I thought about what we could get away with—like touching and kissing. We had sex there too. We just got into a quiet place and did it.

Another wife notes:

> I got pregnant when he was in St. James. Well, I wore these gauchos with the crotch that opens up. I wore them wheneveer I visited. There was a little room off to the side of the visiting area where people would go and ball. We'd all cover for one another. The guards were never in the room. They left us alone to do what we wanted to do. We'd smoke pot and drink and have a ball whenever I could visit. Anyway, I got pregnant as a result. I liked St. James. We had a good time on my visits.

A little over half of the wives did not feel that "nice girls" had sexual relations in public. Sex, they felt, was a private matter. They did not alter these beliefs in order to relieve the tensions generated by sexual deprivation:

> In the visiting room, everyone sits on their men's laps and they would be mauling each other. I felt that this was pretty gross behavior. I got very cold there and it shook up Phil. I didn't want to conceal orgasms like the people are doing on each side of us. And sometimes if you normally embrace, then the guard comes over and separates you. That's completely bizarre.

A few wives were, however, willing to fondle their men sexually, or to be fully intimate with them. Six wives reported that they had only engaged in sexual play in response to pressure from their husbands. For example, one wife explains her reluctance to participate in sexual foreplay with her husband:

> During visiting at Newport, Charles saw everyone having sex. He wanted to play the game. He started petting, feeling me up, and sticking his hand in my pants. I did it a couple of times. But then I said, "No more!" Charles got mad then. He'd egg me on after that—like a game—like a child wanting something and the parent saying "No!" I threatened not come any more, and he'd cry and say he was sorry. After that we kissed but there was no more petting. I felt so conspicuous with all the people in the room. It's the way I was.

A few others reported that they wanted to test the threshold for sexual intimacy—to put one "over on the enemy." Like lovers courting, couples found all kinds of ways to achieve greater sexual intimacy during visiting. However, regardless of the degree of sexual intimacy achieved, wives reported that they got

little direct satisfaction since they had to be continually alert to
the attention of the guards and other visitors. One young woman
recalled how the constraints of visiting undermined her achieving full satisfaction from sexual play with her husband:

> I sometimes get him undressed and I'm very unravelled when I
> leave. I sometimes feel embarrassed. I don't like the guards to see
> us. I just don't want people watching us. I get embarrassed there. I
> don't usually do that stuff. Some people know what's going on. I
> don't understand why they take sex away from him. They take so
> much—like he can't drink after dinner, he can't do what he wants.

Since the majority of couples had to cut off the expressive
emotional sides of themselves, they could only express this side
by communicating their sexual feelings verbally. But they were
continually frustrated by this.

For many couples, sexual intimacy became problematic at
every visit—with each kiss, with each hug, or with each attempt
at sexual play. Many wives related how aware they were that
their husbands, more than ever, needed to reassert their identities as men who were important to their wives. This need was
undermined by the visiting situation. In turn, wives were frustrated in that they wanted sexual intimacy for their men's sakes
as well as their own: they wanted to demonstrate to their husbands that they still perceived them as attractive and capable of
validating them as women.

Effects of Courting

Courting does benefit wives. Renewed courtship can serve to
mitigate sexual frustration, reinforce couples' faith in their marriages, and reinforce wives' beliefs that visiting their husbands is
worth while. At the same time, nineteen women reported that
stresses and strains derived from enforced separation surfaced
during courtship. These often centered around husbands' anxieties about whether or not their wives were being faithful. Wives
reported that the question of sexual fidelity tended to provoke
arguments during visiting. Their men, to a greater or lesser extent, realized the temptations, conflicts, and anguish to which
their wives were subject. They seldom believed that their wives
could be absolutely faithful. Enforced separation created insecu-

rity among the men: insecurity which was continually reinforced when other prisoners received "Dear John" letters. No matter how "open" or "closed" a prison system, men are sufficiently isolated from their homes for sexual fidelity to become a major issue in their eyes.

When prisoners heard rumors about their wives' sexual infidelities, most men waited until visiting day to confront them. And wives who had had sexual liaisons, also waited until they could see their husbands to inform them. For men in prison, learning about their wives' infidelity is equivalent to learning about the loss of an attachment figure. Infidelity is seen as abandonment, and prison compounds this feeling. Many men feel that they are in jeopardy of losing their only satisfying connection to the outside world. As one newly married wife related:

> It was very hard to understand what was happening to him. At times, Matt was jealous of anything. He was afraid I was going out on him and seeing someone else. His accusations hurt because I wasn't. I was very defensive of anything he said. I began to feel like I couldn't move without his thinking that I was going out on him, I was afraid that he'd call and I'd not be there and then he would get all freaked out with jealousy. I think he was afraid that I'd meet someone else and he's in there and there was nothing he could do about it. He was afraid that I'd leave him if I met someone else.

Those wives whose husbands had correctly guessed or discovered evidence of sexual infidelities were amazed at the intensity of their fury. Most men reacted by threatening their wives and some actually attempted to strike them. One old timer, who reluctantly and infrequently visited her husband, recounted his reaction to her unfaithfulness:

> I guess he sits in jail and sees other guys' wives doing it. I guess he sat around and thought about it. Who wants to be locked in a room and asked if it's true that you're running around? I told him the truth and he almost strangled me. That was almost the last time I saw him. I told him I was seeing this guy and he first threw a chair across the room and then he tried to strangle me. I can't remember if I pushed him away or if I stepped on his foot to try to stop him. He told me to leave before he tried to kill me. I understand his hurt feelings. I'd have them too. It scared the hell out of me. I didn't want to see him again. I was the only thing he had

on the outside world and he finally understood that he didn't have it.

However, the structure of prison visiting generally placed limitations on the kinds of arguments that could arise. Prison guards do not, as a rule, tolerate any kind of disruptive behavior: either loud arguments or physical abuse. Thus the prison structure allowed spouses to vent their anger knowing that arguments usually could not escalate into physical violence.

Plans for the Future

Renewed courting not only heightens sexual and emotional intensity among couples, but it also provides them with a belief in the permanence of their relationships. One major component of courtship was the chance for couples to build a "partnership for life." Prison visiting became central to many wives' lives since it offered them a chance to begin doing this. During visiting, twenty-seven couples made plans of this kind. Release, and renewal of their lives on the outside, became primary topics of conversation.[11]

Plans for the future were typically made at the beginning and end of husbands' sentences. At these times, the men were psychologically close to "the outside." One old timer, whose husband had been sentenced to a minimum of two years, illustrated how plans were a major topic of conversation at the beginning of her husband's sentence:

> Q. You mentioned that your relationship has changed. How else is it in the process of changing?
> A. First of all, the first few weeks we discussed all our plans for the future. In the meantime, my life became pretty much the same thing day in and day out. I find it hard to find things to say to him and he wasn't having any new things happening to him. We laid our plans early in the game and we both found it repetitious to keep discussing them. Both of our lives were stagnating.

The "outside world" was prominent in the minds of wives and husbands when the men first began their sentences. As couples reached the middle stage, wives were more focused on their own independent lives and the everyday business of survival. For many men, the outside world began to fade and prison events took on more importance. Looking to the future continued, wives reported, but with less intensity. As release became imminent, both wives and husbands were drawn back to their future plans, and these were placed within the context of the parole program. According to wives, twenty-five husbands made promises to them about future behavior.

Through this process of courtship wives got a glimpse of their original dreams about what their married lives would be like. Many men made promises similar to those they had made prior to their weddings. Twenty-four incarcerated men assured their wives that they were now ready to "settle down." All these men promised to become steadily and gainfully employed, to provide a satisfying standard of living for their families, and to stay out of trouble. However, most of the men did not specify the kinds of work they intended to do. Thus it may well be that wives only needed to hear that their men wanted to work in order to remain committed to them. Or perhaps, prior to prison, many of these men had been reluctant to submit to a regular work routine. The promise to work would then, in itself, have functioned to provide reassurance that the men intended to be the kinds of husbands their wives had always wanted:

> Sam said that when he got out, we'd get along better and he'd work. It was what I wanted for us. I wanted him to have a job and straighten out. That's not too much to ask. I know he likes to work but he had to be led by the hand to get a job.

Another wife describes her husband's plans to move to Texas and find work there:

> We want to move and get out of St. Albert. Maybe we'll first move to the lower part of Vermont and then later to Texas where we don't know anybody. He loves farming and I'd like him to have a farm. He gets tired out. . . . Here in Vermont, the wages are terrible and with a large family, it's hard to get all we need with these wages. Down in Texas, there are all kinds of jobs. We might be able to do something down there. He'd like to work on a farm or on a ranch. I imagine he'd look for a farm job.

From the wives' accounts, a second theme emerged. This theme was the family-oriented dream: to settle down and work hard in order to build a home in the country,[12] obtain a new car,

and provide a warm and emotionally nurturing environment
for their soon-to-be-blissful children and wives. Men's promises
also included plans for greater sexual intimacy with the wives.
As a consequence of being denied a multitude of small plea-
sures and several major ones, including sex, the couples tended
to give a great deal of thought to planning how they were going
to catch up:

> He wants a home. He wants to build one. We want to get a lot of
> room. He wants a new car. He wants me to get a clinker now so
> that he can ride around with me when he gets passes. He wants
> eventually to get a truck. We want children. Only two children.
> We won't be able to afford more. We're just making plans to go
> places—like to go dancing.

According to the wives' accounts, some men emphasized
their willingness to "settle down," but only with the stipulation
that they be able to continue to participate in such "controlled"
deviant activities as occasional marijuana use, accepting only
those stolen goods needed by their households, or occasionally
gambling and sharing winnings with their wives.

Most wives were more interested in their husbands' willingness to get jobs than they were in plans for controlled deviance.
But most important to the women was hearing that their husbands did not intend to get into trouble with the law. Husbands
expended considerable time and energy during visiting reassur-
ing their wives that they were going to avoid any acts associated
with a high probability of detection and re-arrest. One wife,
whose husband had attempted to escape from various prisons,
recalled:

> He told me he'd have a job and we'd have children when he got
> out. He's promised me that he'd never escape and that we'd have a
> house and a car and live comfortably. . . . He promised me that he
> will never do anymore [breaking and entering] and that he'd make a
> life for us and a home. He's told me all this the last time and he
> told me that he'd never escape again. He realized now that he has a
> good wife and a home and he now knows that I wouldn't wait all
> my life for him to grow up.

And a common-law wife explained to the author how her
husband's determination not to commit any more crimes pro-

vided her the opportunity to dream of a happier life in the future:

> He didn't make any explicit promises. He inferred them by saying
> what a bad trip this was and he wasn't going to do this again.
> That's all I needed to fantasize on my own. We were going to get
> married and he wasn't going to get into crime and we'd build a life
> together. We'd get financially together and buy a house and land
> and then have kids. We'd both have our careers. I took it just from
> his inferences and I assumed he had the same desires. All he said
> was that he wouldn't commit any crimes. I took it the rest of the
> way. I assumed he was cured of everything. He never really made
> any promises. We each had our own fantasies.

In planning to shun their old ways, many men stated that
they would avoid old criminal associates or criminally-involved
family members. Some of these men discussed plans to leave the
state or, at least, to move to rural areas far from their criminal
associates. These plans were based on the notion that they could
only build "new lives" for themselves and their families by leaving their old haunts:

> We plan to move out West because he has a brother who lives in
> Wyoming. We could stay with him until we settled down. Willie
> wants to get into heavy construction work. There is a company
> that he wants to get into. And it's warm out West! And there are a
> lot of people in Vermont who don't care about Willie. They don't
> like what he did so it's kinda dangerous for him to live here any-
> more. What he did only came out in the courtrooms. There are
> people who are really after Willie. These are the people who are
> associated with some of the people who were busted because of
> Willie. They have hard feelings for Willie.

Prison visiting, then, also was a time for repentance. Many
prisoners felt that they must put on a public front of reform in
the presence of conventional people. Husbands were likely to
show their wives that they had reflected on the "errors of their
ways," and were committed to righting these "errors." The men
made these future plans to demonstrate convincingly that they
had sincerely repented and that imprisonment had lastingly altered their conduct. Many wives, moreover, expected their husbands to repent and wanted reassurance that they would not

experience enforced separation again. Over and over again wives reported that their husbands assured them that, if they had not had such faithful wives, they would not be so motivated to get out on "good behavior."

It seems reasonable to expect that prisons would encourage inmates to want to settle down, lead a normal life, and stay out of trouble. Prisoners have found prison to be so unpleasant that they sincerely and adamantly do not want to return. The mere fact that the men's movements are restricted, however, is far less painful than the fact that they are cut off from their wives and/or children. It is not difficult to see this as painfully depriving or frustrating for them in terms of lost emotional relationships, loneliness, and boredom. Prisoners, therefore, tend to look to the outside community and will promise those things that can ensure their place in their homes with their wives and/or children.

Repentance also served as an effective strategy to motivate wives to remain committed to their marriages. Seventeen wives asserted that this time their husbands had learned a lesson and that going to prison had helped them to make the transition from boyhood to manhood. It had encouraged them to want to settle down to conventional lifestyles:

> He never gave me any reasons for why he did these things. He told me that he had the little kid in him. But since jail, he's learned a lot and he's grown up now. He felt that jail has changed him. All he wanted to do was get out and settle down and lead a life like anyone else. He told me that he's learned his lessons the hard way.

And another wife said: "I wanted my marriage to work. I loved him. He promised me that he'd never do it again. He'd be a good boy."

Neophytes, of course, were more likely to accept these promises than old timers: out of eighteen neophytes, twelve believed that their husbands were sincere, while only seven old timers did.

Wives who did accept their husbands' promises gave two types of reasons for doing so. First, none of the wives placed much faith in these dreams without other indications that their husbands' behavior had changed. Most wives reported that they came to the visiting room searching for clues that this was so.

Since prisoners' wives frequently accepted the notion that rehabilitation could transform prisoners' behavior from criminally
oriented to conventionally oriented, they often expected that
their husbands were going to change. Second, the wives also frequently used visiting as a time to acquire information about
their husbands' in-prison performance, *e.g.,* the extent to which
they participated in prison work and leisure activities, stayed out
of trouble with prison personnel, and the kinds of friends they
had made. In turn, the men cooperated by providing the appropriate cues to convince their wives that they had reformed. They
would inform their wives about how they were going to prison
counselors and AA meetings, how they were working on their
high school diplomas, or even how they were making their own
beds in the morning:

> Charles has made a lot of accomplishments. He's going to school
> for water treatment plant maintenance. He has made a break-
> through with Dr. Stoneburner and he now feels that he has enough
> insight into his problems that he would make it. They consider
> Charles an alcoholic because he has blackouts in which he remem-
> bers little or nothing of what happened. He was chairman of AA
> but he's too busy now to be chairman. I think he tries to do too
> much. I feel he's done his time good! I'm proud of him! He does
> not like to hear me say that because he says he should have done
> right all along.

And an old timer spoke about her husband's change in attitude:

> He feels that Londonderry is good for him. For the first time he
> has more responsibility and he feels that he is learning how to act
> more responsibly. At Newport he learned nothing. Now he has to
> have a certain number of points to get a pass. He's trying to accu-
> mulate these points. He feels that he's working for something now.
> I think it's done him a lot of good. I see a change in him now. His
> attitude has changed. He didn't care about anything before except
> his drugs and now he cares. He cares about his family and our
> well-being. He stays to himself there and tries to help the other
> guys when they need help. He hasn't fought up here as he did in
> Newport. He has learned that there are responsibilities in this life
> and he didn't learn that at Newport.

The promises, the contrite and loving behavior, and the participation in prison activities make visiting worth while. Many wives said their husbands were men of their words: they never broke promises. And the wives frequently believed that this time their men would get the kind of help they needed.

Several wives did not believe in their husbands' promises and future plans. Each arrest, conviction, and imprisonment had brought the same promises and plans for the future. This made old timers increasingly reluctant to listen to them with feelings of good will:

> Everybody gets these promises. The men will say, "I'll straighten out. I'll never get into trouble again!" I never believe these promises. I know how he is. I feel sorry for him.

And another old timer whose husband has been incarcerated numerous times said of her husband's promises:

> None of them he kept. Before he went to jail, we were not a family. He did what he wanted. He now tells me that he is going to be a real father, cut down on pot, and be a real husband, and stay home. All our bills are paid. We'd start buying new stuff for the house and all that garbage.

Old timers offered a number of reasons for reacting this way. Some were reluctant to believe their husbands were sincere in their expressions of love and repentance, because they reported that this kind of behavior only emerged during incarceration. One old timer, whose husband was then incarcerated for the second time since their marriage, stressed this point:

> He was much sweeter when he was in jail. He was sweet because that was the only way to get the things he wanted. He couldn't treat me mean because I was the only one to come in to see him. It was the only way he was going to get his smokes. When he was outside, he didn't treat me sweet. In jail, he needed me and I felt helpful. I didn't feel totally shut out of his life. He needed me more when he was inside than outside. When he was outside, he could be mean because he could take care of these things he needed for himself.

A second reason was the belief that prison guards made judgments about the manner in which their husbands interacted with them. These judgments could influence future decisions concerning their husbands' early release. An old timer recalled how skeptical she was about her husband's behavior during visiting:

> He never talked about life after jail. He just talked about moving to New Hampshire. We haven't made any plans. I was worried about what it was going to be like, when he got released. I didn't know how we'd get along or what he'd be like. I felt that he was acting for the guards when he was being nice and kind.

And another old timer questions her husband's sincerity during visiting:

> When I went up to visit him, I couldn't ask for anything better. I got a notion that he was just acting so that he could get out of there. His counselors were there to watch that he treated me differently. They knew how his temper was. I thought he was putting on an act. When he'd phone home and ask me for something and if I didn't bring it, he'd holler and scream and call me every name in the book. If I didn't have the money for cigarettes, junk food, or dope so he could sell it, he just hollered. I felt I was being used. All he wanted was stuff for himself and the hell with me.

These old timers reported that their husbands were skilled at fulfilling the expectations of both their wives and the prison staff. Thus, the men went about acting contrite and being loving and attentive to their wives. Arguments were avoided and wives placated. On the basis of their husbands' past behavior, these wives believed that their husbands were running a con. The men appeared to be more interested in a short stay and maintaining relationships with their wives than with positive adjustments. Promises and plans for the future, therefore, were not to be taken seriously.

What keeps wives returning to the prisons, then, is the chance to court their husbands and thus reaffirm themselves as women who are loved by their men. This promise of renewed courtship, with its focus on building a permanent relationship, reties most wives to their husbands, and allows them to wait for their release. Wives themselves want to believe that promises will be fulfilled this time. Thus, promises function to motivate wives to overcome the difficulties of prison visiting and to manage alone during their husbands' confinement.[13] The difficulties of enforced separation, therefore, became worth while because wives could continue to believe that their husbands were eventually going to provide them with the kinds of conventional marriages to which they aspired.

DECISION MAKING

Courting is not the only way that husbands and wives interact during prison visits. Many couples resume some elements of their marital patterns; in particular, making joint household decisions becomes satisfying for both spouses.[14]

Many wives envisioned a family structure in which men were still symbolic heads of the households and therefore should be involved in every important decision. These decisions were usually similar to those they would have brought to their husbands' attention prior to enforced separation: (1) household finances; (2) child-related issues; and (3) major household purchases. Some wives discussed every aspect of their lives with their husbands, made absolutely no decisions, and encouraged their children to ask their fathers for everything they wanted. Explaining why she did this, one woman reported:

> Whenever the kids want something, I say to them, "Ask Daddy!" I make them ask him for permission for this and that. Truthfully, this makes me feel funny. It reminds me of being home again and asking my own mother and daddy. I feel the same way with Matt. I had to ask for everything from my parents. I had no choice. But with Matt, I do it because I want to. It makes me feel better. I want him to tell me what to do and then I go ahead and don't do it. For instance, this dryer. I wanted to know what he thought about it but I wanted it to be my decision. I'm the one who is going to use it. I wanted his opinion and yet I didn't. I don't want to be helpless and yet I don't want to be without him.

By involving their husbands in the decision-making process, some women were able to resume, temporarily, their roles as deferential wives. They recognized their husbands' continuing position of power and authority within the family unit. By assuming domestic responsibilities, the husbands could, to some extent, neutralize their roles as prisoners. Thus, visiting provided the men with the chance to relieve some of the "pains" that stem from the loss of decision making within the prison environment. For example, a neophyte stressed how bringing these decisions to her husband's attention underlined his importance to her and the children:

> I put responsibilities on him. One problem of his is his facing realities. I'm trying to get the kids into parochial school and I have made up my mind that this is where I'd like them to be. But I more or less let him make these kinds of decisions. I gave him the pros and cons of parochial school and he then said that they should go to one. I brought Jenny a bike for her birthday and some kids broke it. I told Randy about it and asked him what should be done. Randy said to go and have it fixed so long as it doesn't cost more than $40. . . . I feel that I have to talk to him and confide in him. He is a part of our household. He agrees and wants to know what is going on and he doesn't want me to hide anything from him. He says that he wants to help and feels terrible that he can't. I say that he does help. He listens to me and helps me make these decisions.

However, some aspects of this pattern of interaction are illusory. Not every household decision was referred to the men. Wives generally imparted information and concerns to remind their husbands of their identities as husbands and fathers. Many wives reported that, before visits, they decided the kinds of household decisions they were going to reveal to their husbands. Their foremost thought was their men's position of helplessness. Many wives deliberately hid those decisions that were beyond the men's capabilities. For instance, it did not help the men to hear about how children had done something naughty at some time in the past, or that the plumbing had needed to be fixed, etc., when they could not do anything about these problems:

> We'd talk about what we did. But the conversation was not very much. I usually just bitched about my work, about the dishes, and things like that. There was no sense in telling him about my problems with the kids. There would be a gap in between what happened to them and my seeing him. It could be a gap of five days and the issue would be all over and would have dropped out of the kids' minds.

Some wives withheld information about financial problems. Knowledge of financial crises might confront the men with the painful reality that they were not sending money home to stabilize their families or to provide comforts.

A few of the women reported that their husbands' requests to share in household decisions were unexpected. Prior to imprisonment, these men had rejected this kind of household responsibility. Because of this, these wives came to believe that some of their husbands' best qualities had finally emerged.

By sharing decision making, the women could resume their wifely roles by referring matters of concern to their husbands, and the men could resume some aspects of their former position of power or authority. What the wives gained was some temporary relief from having to make a multitude of decisions alone. Therefore, involuntary separation and imprisonment encouraged the men to assume this decision-making role and in turn, encouraged the wives to see their husbands as the men they had expected to marry.

TRANSACTING BUSINESS

Visiting also was a time when arrangements could be made to conduct various kinds of "business," usually related to acquiring legitimate and illegitimate goods. Two ways to "soothe" these "pains of imprisonment" appeared to be: (1) acquiring material goods and services to alleviate material deprivation; and (2) consuming drugs in order to "cool out," *i.e.,* relieve boredom and monotony and make time pass as quickly as possible.

Approved Material Goods

Following the precepts of community corrections, Vermont correctional centers have been designed so as to minimize the extent to which prisoners experience material deprivation. Prisoners can acquire some or all of the following goods depending on their security classification: their own clothes, items for body care, reading material, certain electrical appliances (stereos, radios, televisions, etc.), and other such items for recreational purposes, arts and crafts, decorative items for their rooms, coffee, tea, snack foods which do not require cooking, and cigarettes. In the more "open" correctional centers such as the Newport facility, prisoners classified as minimum risks can, for instance, acquire the full range of these items. Thus Vermont prisons are structured in such a way that inmates are likely to make additional demands on their wives. The more "open" a prison, the longer what many wives call "the grocery list."

Inmates usually must rely on their wives to obtain items on this list. Twenty-six wives reported that they had provided their husbands with at least some clothing, snacks, cigarettes, and body care items. Eleven also assumed responsibility for their husbands' laundry, washing, ironing, and mending their clothes. Nine wives reported that they assisted their husbands in acquiring stereos, radios, televisions, musical instruments, reading material, as well as new clothing, cigarettes, snacks, and so forth. Seventeen other women reported that they only provided their husbands with the minimum necessary for survival.

Taxpayers save a good deal of money as a result of wives' efforts. During the field research phase of this study, the Vermont Department of Corrections spent an average of about $12,000 a year to keep each prisoner incarcerated. A few wives spent up to $2,000 to make their husbands more comfortable during the period when they were imprisoned. Assuming this responsibility can, however, become a burden for many wives. There are, ultimately, both satisfactions and drawbacks to be derived from providing their men with some of the amenities of living. Wives frequently reported that they derived satisfaction from continuing to nurture their husbands. Many indicated how acting as nurturers provided them with a sense of purpose and pride: even with limited financial resources, they could fulfill their husbands' requests. One wife who was receiving welfare described, with pride, the kinds of material goods she provided for her husband at some sacrifice to herself and her children:

> I brought everything—Ringos, lollipops, cans of Tang, Kool-Aid, bouillon cubes, hot cereals, munchies. I brought pot in. I stuck it down the baby's Pampers.... I used to give him money and clothes, and at Christmas time, I'd have two garbage bags of gifts. I brought him a stereo, albums, and tapes. He had his own pillow, lights, rug, sheets, and fan. I went without for him but he had all

that he wanted. I'd pay the rent and had my food stamps and I'd save $20 for myself and I'd buy three cartons of cigarettes and give him the $20. He always got $40 a month from me. I never had any spending money and he never went without. He was inside and he couldn't have nothing and there was no reason for him to go without. I'd always give to Randy and the girls before I had anything for myself.

Under these circumstances, providing for the husband simply meant that the rest of the family had to go without. Only a few wives had little financial difficulty providing for their husbands. As in this case, providing material goods was not difficult for this woman:

> All the time I brought him stuff. I brought him food, cigarettes, drugs, clothes. Everything he asked for. I paid for it through welfare. It wasn't hard to do.

Visiting day became the time when the men either placed or received their orders for approved goods. By accepting these orders, wives reported, they were able to legitimate their husbands' roles as heads of their households. As a result, the men were still able to tell their wives what to do, how to do it, and when—at least in some areas. For instance, one wife treats her husband's grocery list as part of her job and comes to visit prepared to take his orders:

> He gave me a kiss and the rest of the time he spent with the kids. He'd horse around with the kids and all he'd tell me was what he wanted me to bring him. I always knew he'd ask. He always wanted something. The day I'd visit, I'd check to make sure I had paper and pen with me in order to get down what he wanted. It was a normal occurrence. I got used to it after awhile.

By accepting their husbands' orders for material goods and services, most wives derived considerable satisfaction. Most hoped to alleviate their husbands' discomfort or their diminished sense of autonomy. A few, however, felt great pressure to meet their men's needs because of their guilt over imprisonment and realistic worries about their husbands' present situations.

Enforced separation placed the wives in a position where they were more apt to support than be supported, nurture rather than be nurtured. Love and service became intertwined. Services symbolized love. In the main, twenty-six wives accepted this as an outcome of enforced separation. As wives they had already been trained for caring and service. Consequently, they often treated fulfilling their husbands' needs not only as an obligation, but as a desirable activity—something they wished to do.

The fact of imprisonment placed the men in a situation in which they were unable to reciprocate in very significant ways. It is rare that the men were able to give their wives money for their provisions—much less money to ease their families' financial burdens—from their institutional earnings. Resources typically flowed to the men. Some wives mentioned that, occasionally, their husbands' demands became excessive or resulted in arguments. Couples often spent a considerable part of their time together dealing with these issues:

> I don't have money to bring him clothes and food. He gets his coffee and cigarettes. I pay it. That's all he gets, It's all I can afford. For our anniversary, I'll get him a shirt and some other things. I take clothes for him when I can find them at rummage sales or friends give them to me. Not being able to give him some nice clothes makes me feel extremely low. I'm out of money. He keeps asking me for money for cigarettes. I have to pay for the transportation to see him. That costs $6 and when I visit him it depletes my finances. I try to first pay my bills and my doctor bills. He doesn't realize that I have to pay bills. He's been in so long that he doesn't realize that since he's been gone the price of everything has gone up.

Most women eventually gave in to their husbands' demands, at considerable cost to themselves. Usually wives were exhausted and worried about finding enough money on which to live, much less support their husbands. Only a few flatly refused to exceed their already tightly stretched budgets. Many other wives found that filling their husbands' grocery lists placed a strain on them—but for a different reason. They described visiting as a one-way process, and the grocery lists symbolized this process. The normal give and take of marriage became so difficult when men were in prison that, by the second or third time, many of these wives came to wonder whether their husbands only valued them as emissaries to the outside world:

I used to bring him cookies, coffee, cigarettes, and sometimes I'd surprise him and write a letter and stick that in. I brought him the TV Guide. I did his laundry. I brought him clothes when he needed them. He got the stuff for his own room through trading this and that. It didn't bother me to bring them in. At times, I felt used. Every woman wonders about being used at different times. Sometimes the relationship seemed more of a taking than a giving from on person to another. I used to get depressed and feel sorry for myself.

Those wives who felt used by their husbands, and those whose incomes could barely sustain them and their children, eventually became resistant to their husbands' demands. These wives generally used visiting days as an opportunity to confront their husbands with the fact that they could no longer place their needs first:

That was all he wanted from me. He wanted his smoke. When I first went to visit him, I'd bring him in books, cigarettes, toothpaste, cookies. Then it got to costing more to put food on the table at home and the kids needed things and I didn't have the money. I told him that I didn't have the money to supply him with goodies. It was like telling a child that I didn't have it. I was dealing with a temperamental child and he fought the only way he knew. He fought very defensively. He was using self protection. Most of the time he threatened me. Then I'd say one thing and he'd say another. The magic was gone from us and only bad feelings were left.

Such arguments frequently escalated over the course of a series of visits. Differences were usually resolved in the wives' favor since the men were only symbolic heads of their households. Wives could still choose whether or not to follow their men's decisions and demands. Most of the wives realized that they actually had the final say in these matters and used this fact.

Smuggling Contraband

Visiting was also the time when wives smuggled contraband into prisons for their husbands' personal consumption or when future arrangements could be made to continue smuggling activities and transfer money for drug purchases.[15] The extent to which smuggling contraband was possible depended on the structure of various prisons and the extent to which wives were willing to assume the risks.

There are two ways that men can obtain recreational drugs within a prison system: (1) they can purchase the drugs from fellow prisoners and/or guard; or (2) they can obtain drugs from visitors who are willing to risk bringing them into the facilities. The wives in the study reported that men would frequently add marijuana or mood-altering drugs to their grocery lists. Of twenty-seven women who visited their husbands, twelve had smuggled drugs into various prisons. Among these, eight were old timers and four neophytes.

As a rule, wives learned how to smuggle drugs into prisons from their husbands, who in turn, often learned from fellow inmates. Their techniques were astonishingly simple. The most common technique was to carry contraband on their bodies: inside their pants, inside their bras, secured between their breasts, on their hips, in their socks, or, less frequently, in their vaginas. For example, one wife described how she placed the marijuana inside her pants:

> I did it in Newport. I passed pot to Jerry. I would put it in my pants. I'd put it in a plastic bag and then make it very flat. I'd place it around the belt area of my pants and the belt would keep it from slipping down.

Another woman recalled observing some mothers smuggle drugs to their sons at Londonderry:

> I know there are women bringing in contraband, and these are the women who aren't being searched, because I know the women who are bringing it in. You can see it in the visiting rooms if you watch! Usually it's the mothers; the mothers bring it in their suit jackets, or if they wear a pants suit, they bring it in their pants pockets, or their jacket, and they don't hassle the mothers. They just hand it to the men!

Only a few wives reported having placed contraband on their children. An old timer described a favorite technique:

> I've brought it in for Randy. I usually put it into a plastic bag and then flatten it out and tape it onto the kid's Pampers. I put it in the back of the kid's diaper. He then just holds the baby and puts his

hand inside the diaper and gets it out. It's hard on him being locked up and not being able to do anything.

Once these wives had successfully smuggled contraband into the waiting room, they then had to transfer it to their husbands. Transfers usually took place at the beginning of a visit. Wives would go to the bathroom, remove the drugs or other contraband, return to the visiting room, and then inconspicuously pass the drugs to their men. Another wife described this procedure:

> They would go to the bathroom and remove the stuff from where it was hiding and then bring it in to their boyfriends in the visiting room. You can't miss seeing what's going on. The boyfriend would then shove the stuff up his rear end right in full view of everyone. They would shove it up so far that you can't find it when they are searched.

Husbands were usually able to avoid detection by hiding the drugs in the vicinity of their genitals. If the men wanted to be especially secure, they placed the drugs up their rectums. Many wives, out of pure nervousness immediately passed the contraband to their husbands who placed the drugs on their bodies:

> I just looked around to see if anyone was looking at me. I was always looking around. I was very uptight about it. I had to go through the metal detector and I felt afraid that it would beep. There was a lot of guards there and when I went into the visiting room, Gary hugged me. As he hugged me, I slipped it under his shirt and he grabbed it. I felt such relief once I knew he had it. He sat in his seat and put it up his rear.
>
> We had the rest of the visit to talk about what we usually talk about. Then he went back to his block. I was afraid that he was going to get caught.

Most wives reported considerable anxiety about smuggling based on the likelihood of detection. Wives were more likely to be anxious about being detected during strip searching than going through metal detectors. Many of these wives reported that at Walden Farms security goals were de-emphasized and therefore they did not believe that smuggling was a high-risk activity:

> At visiting hours, I have seen these girls bringing in pot to their men. They don't care who sees them give it over to their men. . . .

They have no difficulty in pulling up their skirts in front of everyone and taking the pot out of their vaginas in front of everyone, no less!

Eight wives assessed the risks involved by observing the extent to which other visitors smuggled contraband. When asked to explain why they risked detection and arrest, twelve wives said it was to help their husbands do "their own time." These wives believed that drugs would help their men pass through prison with the least amount of suffering. They could therefore soothe the "pains" of imprisonment. Smoking marijuana appeared to give men something to do and helped break the monotony of prison life. These wives also reasoned that, as long as their men consumed drugs, they were more likely to be "mellow," to "cool out," and therefore adjust to the prison environment better. As one woman said:

> I usually do it. If it calms him down, then I bring it in. Every time he's stoned, he sits in his room and listens to the stereo and relaxes. He hasn't had it for a while. That's why he's freaking out.
>
> Also Mark made me feel so guilty about his being in jail and I being on the outside. He was always telling me that he needed the pot to cool him out. I felt so guilty that I brought him his pot.

A secondary reason was that the wives, themselves, derived some satisfaction from smuggling. It allowed them to resume another component of their role as nurturer. Providing their husbands with marijuana, therefore, could become a commitment to "help" their husbands do "good time."

Short-Term Criminal Partnerships

Some wives and husbands established short-term criminal partnerships, usually centered on distributing drugs for profit within the prison system. Small quantities of drugs were smuggled into the visiting site and given to their husbands who would then sell them for a profit within the prison's *sub rosa* economic system. For these couples, visiting became focused on transacting their "business": drugs and money were transferred and new plans were formulated for obtaining more drugs. Six old timers and three neophytes reported that they did not smuggle drugs during every visit. Only three women smuggled contraband into the prison on a weekly basis. Both the wives and husbands involved willingly placed themselves in jeopardy since they felt that the stakes were high enough to warrant the risks.

This kind of criminal partnership could be highly profitable for both spouses. One old timer described dealing in drugs within a prison:

> I cared for him and I knew if he had it the time would pass away quicker for him. Plus he was making money because he was selling it. So he gave me most of the money he made. I brought the drugs to him when he was at Newport. I brought them when I visited. I brought it in about fifty times. I'd bring in half an ounce at a time and I paid $20 for it and then he made $60 off it. I made $120 a week and he was trading things for it. He got this beautiful ring for five joints and he lost it.
>
> He gave me most of [the money] and I then bought more drugs with it and I'd pay my bills and get things for the kids.

As a result of the high volume of prison business, this wife managed to save over $2,000, as well as contribute to supporting her household. However, most women reported that their profits were considerably lower: from $20–$75 dollars per unit of drugs smuggled into prison.

These short-term business relationships between spouses appeared to be primarily a response to the economic pressures that both were experiencing. Although the bulk of the money they earned was spent to cover wives' household expenses, a large portion of it went back to their husbands in the form of material goods needed to make their time "easier" in prison.

These transactions were also socially satisfying for the men and their wives. The men could, in effect, reactivate another aspect of their role as husbands: they could resume their role as breadwinners and make financial contributions to their households. Wives who received the money could also take up their earlier roles as consuming agents for their husbands and children. In this way, these criminal partnerships strengthened the couples' marriages.

Ironically, illicit partnerships were more prevalent in the "closed" prison, Londonderry, than in more "open" facilities.[16] This was probably largely attributable to market factors: with tighter security, scarcity would occur, prices rise and profits become commensurately greater. Therefore potential benefits would tend to outstrip potential risks:

> When he was in Newport, before he went to Walden Farms, I'd buy it, clean it, and get it to one of the inmates who then passed it to Rex and sold it. We had quite a business. I paid $40 for it on the streets and he'd make $200 on it there. We made money on it. A lot of money. We did it probably for about four months. It didn't bother me or scare me. If I was strip searched, I'd be legal because I didn't have it on me.
>
> When he went to Walden Farms, there was no reason to get it to him. It's so easy to get it into the farm. No one checks the guys or the visitors and what they bring in. The guys get it on their own there. There's no market there.

And still another woman discussed the pros and cons of smuggling contraband into Londonderry and Newport:

> All I brought him was cigarettes and money. They give you clothing. It's more risky to bring drugs into Londonderry. At Newport, you get lost in a bunch of people and hide giving it to him. At Londonderry, you sit at a table and the guard is sitting right there. I refused to bring it in and he got mad at me.

Criminal partnerships between husbands and wives, however, had a tendency to disintegrate over time. Partnerships usually were dissolved once wives became unwilling partners. Eight women reported that they decided to stop smuggling. A few of the women reported that this was because they eventually became disillusioned or disenchanted with the activity. The novelty and excitement wore off and they found that they no longer derived sufficient satisfactions from it. For some of them, visiting had come to be centered primarily around drug-related issues, *i.e.*, the quality of the drugs they brought in, future deals to be made, the kinds of drugs the men wanted their wives to deliver, etc. This wife recalled her disillusionment with the process of smuggling drugs:

> I was dealing with people I didn't like. And sometimes the smoke wasn't good enough for him and he'd get angry at me. Then I had to return to these people and say that the last batch of smoke wasn't good enough for him and I had to buy better. Once I

brought an ounce and for a change I cleaned it so I could carry it in easier. I caught hell from him because he couldn't make more sticks out of it. To him, it wasn't worth much when it was cleaned. I didn't like it that I went out of my way to get it for him, took my chances in bringing it in and then he continually bitched about what I did wrong.

Two other wives refused to continue once they realized that providing drugs drained essential money from their own meager funds. Two other wives decided to stop when their husbands were transferred to Londonderry where they thought the chances of being caught were too high:

We talked mostly about what happened, the kids, and about going to court, and about drugs. He wanted me to bring stuff in. I said that I wouldn't take the chance and lose the kids if I got caught. And I was pregnant and didn't want to have the kid in jail. He would holler and fight with me about it. He'd say, "You never done anything for me." He never thought about when he was in jail the last time and all the things I brought him then.

And finally, another wife refused because she was being strip searched at Londonderry:

He wasn't seeing his son and he wasn't getting things brought in to him. He wanted me to bring in smoke for him. I told him that they were stripping me and I wasn't about to get caught. I had done it before. I did it when it was easy. I'd tuck the stuff into my jeans. But this wasn't my thing to do. There is more to life and to a relationship than how much smoke I could smuggle in. There is a whole lot more. I was depriving myself.

He had no one to bring it in other than me. He was in top security and only certain people could come in. He rarely asked me to bring in any money. At the beginning I took the smoke in every time I visited. I'd buy it and he'd sell some of it and then he'd give me the money that I paid for the smoke.

THE RESULTS OF VISITING

On the basis of wives' accounts, visiting does appear to strengthen marital ties since many wives and husbands come to share a common interest: the procurement and distribution of contraband, either for profit or recreational purposes. Also by smuggling drugs, the wives can soothe their own "pains" of enforced separation by resuming three satisfying components of their roles as wives: consuming agents, nurturers, and procurers of personal services. In resuming components of these roles, wives were fully aware of their husbands' dependency upon them. They were their husbands' major connection to drug sources, and furthermore, they also knew that they could act independently: they could stop bringing drugs into the prison whenever they decided. In turn, the men could resume their roles as husbands by making demands for drugs and/or providing some income for their families. But the extent to which the husbands could activate these aspects of their identities as husbands was, once again, dependent upon their wives' willingness to acquiesce to these demands. As long as the wives acquiesce to these demands, visiting becomes a time in which a sense of shared partnership can develop which soothes "pains" and reinforces marital ties.

CHAPTER VIII

Living Alone

I guess you've noticed that we smoke a lot. Prisoners' wives smoke a lot of cigarettes. We live on cigarettes, coffee and nerves.
—A Prisoner's Wife

This chapter explores one facet of the impact of men's imprisonment on their families: the consequences for the lives their wives lead. Wives managed to pursue their own lives yet continued to be involved with their imprisoned husbands on a daily basis. However, prisoners' wives often believed that they, like their husbands, had been deserted by society and deprived of the relationships most important to them.[1]

Prisoners and their wives were not cut off from one another as much as might be supposed. To the extent that prison systems permitted inmates access to telephone or home visits, incarcerated husbands continued to participate in their households and to influence the ways that wives structured their lives and organized their homes.

WIVES SPEAK FOR THEMSELVES

Nancy and Vicki are both neophytes. However, Nancy's husband, a sexual offender, was just beginning to serve an 8–10 year sentence, while Vicki's husband was preparing to re-enter the community.

The other two women, Arlene and Tammy, were both old timers whose husbands were repeaters, arrested for crimes related to drug and/or alcohol abuse. Arlene's husband, Frank, was incarcerated in the Federal Penitentiary in Kansas and had served 16 months of his sentence. In turn, Tammy's husband, Mark, has two more years to serve of his 6 year sentence. Tammy has been a full-time mother, receiving a welfare grant.

190

Arlene has been intermittently employed with additional income supplied from a welfare grant. At the time of this meeting, she has a part-time semi-skilled factory job to help support herself and her daughter, Lilly, 11 years of age.

NANCY. I'm not keeping on top of things like doing the laundry. I'm not even getting drunk or going to a lot of parties. I'm not sleeping well and I've been staying up to 4 o'clock in the morning. I'm hating my job. Everybody at work is just bitching. I get so weird out at night. It's like an inertia that has hit me. I know that I have things to do. I know I'd feel better if I painted the shutters, got the basement cleaned and did things like that. I've made lists of everything that I have to do and then I'd lose these lists. I write letters to Kevin and lose them. I'm not comfortable being this way. I'm in a rut. I feel like getting drunk. I have been getting stoned every night and I think it's a combination of everything—inertia and getting stoned all the time.

And I've been sleeping on the floor! I hate to go to bed. I feel so alone when I go upstairs and sleep in the bed.

VICKI. The last year that Charles was in jail, I went through it very badly. I'd watch the kids go to school and I'd change Justin's baby pants and I'd sleep until it was time to take Pete out of kindergarten. I'd get lunch for the kids and then sleep until Betsy got home. I felt that the house looked like shit and what kind of mother was I?

NANCY. I'm making sure that I have a lot to do during the daytime so I don't sit around feeling that I have nothing to do. I write things to do on a paper and I have a little book that I carry around and write out what I should be doing. I set up my chores by the day. Every week, I list the same things to do.

One thing that upsets me is the feeling that I don't have time for myself and yet the time I have, I fritter away.

I know that there is no reason for this except for stress. I know that if I come home and take a shower, I would feel refreshed enough to stay up. I'm feeding myself negative things. I feel that I have to suffer because Kevin is suffering. And Kevin is suffering because he's in jail. And since he's in jail, I'm in jail. Emotionally it's hard for me to realize that I'm not in jail. I feel so tied into the whole thing. I have some good days in which I go out with friends. When I go out with them then I have a good time but when I come home, I find myself getting into these feelings of "I miss Kevin," "Is he OK?" I've been trying to deal with this as Kevin's trip and it's not mine. If I could change my attitude it would be good for my self.

VICKI. I don't think that life could go on without Charles. I'm now finding that life can go on and go on for my advantage.

NANCY. I keep thinking to myself that a certain night would be his night to do the dinner or this would be his time to do the laundry and here I am having to do all these things by myself. I don't want to work.

VICKI. Go on welfare. You can own your own house and be on welfare.

NANCY. I'd do anything to stay home from work. It would be so nice just to stay home.

VICKI. I envy you. I want to work.

NANCY This job takes so much out of me. People are always dumping their problems on me. I'm drained by the end of the day. I just blitz out. I don't want to go to work. But it takes energy to look for a job.

When Kevin went to jail, I didn't feel sorry for myself. I thought that I could be strong and in control. Now it has hit me. Before I was keeping everyone together. I was so busy keeping Sara and Kevin together. Now Sara is trying to keep me together. My friends say that all I do is give, give, give. When am I going to start getting for myself? I need some support for myself I guess.

I need people to be more responsive. I need people to say that they will come over and take care of Sara so that I can go out. My mother does it but I feel obligated to her. My friend, Molly, is babysitting tonight. She offered.

VICKI. I know what you're going through. When Charles first went to jail, my girlfriend lived with me. It was pretty good when she lived with me. When she moved out, I still will always say, "Thank God, she's not with me." But when she left, I fell apart. I looked at the four kids and I was all alone. I'd get sick of talking to these kids.

NANCY. I'm scared about dumping all this shit on Sara. Who needs this—not a nine-year-old. It's not fair to talk to her like a grown-up. She said that she gets sick of being treated like a grown-up. She told me that I needed to talk to some adult.

VICKI. I was pregnant when Charles was in. But I didn't feel angry about being pregnant alone because I have been alone throughout all my pregnancies. My first husband could not tolerate my being pregnant. When I began to really show around the eighth month, he would leave. I never had a man around.

TAMMY. I felt so lonely. Here I was all alone and no one to be supportive with about the pregnancy. A lot of anger came out of me then. Here was the time when I needed him the most and he wasn't there.

ARLENE. The hardest time for me was after the labor. Here I was holding this little baby in my arms and he wasn't there. I could see all the husbands coming in to see their babies and their wives and I was all alone. And then they placed me at the other end of the ward. I was placed away from the other women and they all had their husbands around. Frank didn't know that I was pregnant because we had broken up. He found out when I showed up at court when I was seven months' pregnant. He looked astonished.

TAMMY. Mark has been going through his changes about me again. He's afraid that I'm going out on him and he's been acting terrible. All he thinks about, it seems, is what I am doing.

ARLENE. I know what you mean. Lots of the women I've talked to have had the same problem. When I was up at St. Albert, I had an open house for the women. Remember Tammy? I told you that you could stay any time at my house whenever you wanted to. And there you were pregnant and making those long trips to St. Albert. When I asked you to stay at my house, you shuddered because you were afraid what Mark would think.

TAMMY. Yeh. And it's not different now. I went out, and I just went out with my sister and some girl friends, and Mark gets all upset. He said, "How could I trust you now?" But when he was home he was going out with who knows who. He ran around all the time and was seldom home.

ARLENE. You're supposed to sit home all the time and take care of the house and the kids while they run around. But Frank just wrote me that I should go out and do things for myself. I have been going out. A year ago Frank would have been very upset if I had gone to this meeting. Now he's supportive. And I feel as though I've come into my own and he knows that.

TAMMY. I'm getting to the point that I'd like to say, "Screw it all!" He's going through the same old routine and I feel disgusted. He's afraid that I'm going to leave him. He's afraid that if I go into nursing, I'll meet a doctor or an intern and that's the end of him. So he doesn't want me to go through with it. But I am, regardless of him.

ARLENE. The best thing that happened to Frank and me is that he went Fed. I got my act together this time. I'm off complete welfare and I'm now on partial welfare. I have a good job at a furniture factory and I love going to work. I feel good now. I'll never go back and surprisingly Frank is supportive.

PROBLEMS OF ENFORCED SEPARATION

Sentencing and its aftermath means that wives must immediately reorganize their households. Changes in family structure must be immediately initiated, and decisions made about whether to work or remain at home, whether to change residences or remain living where they are, whether or not to apply for a welfare grant. At the same time, most wives have to find time to deal with their own sense of loss and anxiety. Under these circumstances, prisoners' wives make a deliberate attempt to weather the crisis and begin to pull their families together. As wives attend to their most pressing concerns, their sense of crisis generally subsides. This allows them to reorganize their lives, their households, and their relationships with significant others.

For the wives in the study, reorganization involved attempts to establish conventionally-oriented lives. Once their men were incarcerated, all but two described themselves as pursuing conventional lifestyles. Even those women who had previously lived fast claimed that they had resumed a more conventional style of living. Six "fast-living" old timers, for instance, reported that they had, over the years, acquired the necessary skills to shift from "fast" to conventional living and back again when the occasion demanded.

Twenty-one women with children organized their lives around their children *and* their absent husbands; they visited, telephoned, wrote letters, worried about their husbands, and performed as many wifely duties as the prison system would allow.

The everyday lives of the working wives were similar to those of the others, centering around absent husbands and a settled, conventional lifestyle. Most women in the study did not consider taking a job; five women with, and five without, children were employed outside their homes. Of these, only two found jobs after their husbands' arrests. One wife was a full-time student at a college. Nineteen wives with children said they chiefly relied on Aid to Dependent Children for their support.

The majority of wives experienced at least one important hardship during their husbands' confinement. No single hardship, however, runs through the histories. Even the basic deprivation of having to do without their husbands was not universal: in some cases husbands have been so abusive and irresponsible that their absence is considered a blessing.

The women reported many of the difficulties commonly associated with enforced separation: loneliness, deprivation of their husbands, financial difficulties, child care and child discipline problems. A further hardship mentioned by these wives, but scarcely noted in previous reports, was that of "waiting" or psychological adjustment to the prospective duration of their husbands' incarceration and absence. Overwhelmed at times by their problems and worries, these women also reported considerable illness, depression, anger, and resentment.

Waiting

After their husbands' imprisonment, many women reported that the most difficult problem that they confronted was coming to terms with the lengths of their husbands' sentences. Seventeen wives indicated that they felt as though they, themselves, were "doing time"; their lives were in limbo until their husbands returned. Only then did they feel they would resume active and meaningful roles as wives. What made waiting difficult for the women, therefore, was the suspension of their identities; they were their husbands' wives, with no other significant roles to play. Their backgrounds, as a rule, had not prepared them for the work world. Their families in many cases were estranged, and they were sometimes shunned by neighbors or were avoiding them. Thus, within this phase of imprisonment, the wives found themselves serving time with their husbands. Time was not a resource for them, but was used by others to control their lives. Like their husbands, they served rather than used it. Under these circumstances, it is not surprising that prisoners' wives often lived for the present. As one wife explained it:

One day at a time. All I think about is getting through the day. The hell with tomorrow, yesterday is already gone. I don't think about "X" number of days or "X" number of years. I think about today. I get through the night and then instead of saying one day longer apart, I think that we are one day closer together.

Loneliness and Deprivation

Twenty-five prisoners' wives mentioned deprivation of their husbands, and the attendant loneliness, as an important hardship they experienced. They missed their husbands as companions, fathers, bill payers or income providers, and as handymen around their homes.[2] This form of felt deprivation primarily stemmed from their husbands' physical absence.[3]

This sense of loss could be exacerbated by the types of communities in which the wives lived. In many towns in Vermont women are expected to be married. By not having a visible husband, women beyond a certain age become socially marginal. Many wives reported feeling like "fifth wheels" at social gatherings, especially when these gatherings largely consisted of couples their own ages.

This sense of loneliness and disorientation was often compounded by sexual frustration resulting from their husbands' prolonged confinement. Two wives, determined to remain faithful to their husbands, talked about how they dealt with sexual deprivation:

> The time is getting closer to his release. But where is my sex life? I do know that I must have done it once because I have Lilly to show for it. I feel that the first few months is when you feel the horniest. Then you get used to it.
>
> When Rudi comes home, that's when he loses weight. I just wear him out. But when the men are in, the women just try to shut off their sexual feelings. You can use Rosemary and her five sisters—that means masturbating.

Loneliness also was magnified by the fact that wives had to endure critical events alone. For instance, thirteen women reported that they had been pregnant during at least one of their husbands' imprisonments. It is up to prison personnel to decide whether married prisoners can have supervised or unsupervised passes in order to be present at deliveries and/or to visit their wives and their babies. Their husbands' presence at births can be both joyous and soothing but it can also be both tension-producing and stigmatizing. Usually men appear with arms and legs chained, closely followed by guards:

> I feel lonesome and deserted. He's missed almost every pregnancy except Sally. He missed John because he was in jail. They did bring him up to see Jesse. They brought him up in handcuffs and shackles. I was shocked to see him that way. They wouldn't even take the handcuffs off so that he could hold the baby. He couldn't hold the baby with them on. And everybody was looking at him and saying, "Look at that criminal!" Some people even pointed at him. I felt terrible. I didn't want him there like that. They brought him there like that because he was an escaped criminal. I felt terrible.

Child Care and Discipline

Child-management problems, here a function of the women's status as prisoners' wives, can also be viewed within the larger context of problems experienced by single mothers. Of the twenty-one wives with children, seventeen reported that having full responsibility for raising their children—together with the special strains created by children's responses to their fathers' imprisonment—was a severe hardship. Prisoners' wives readily admitted that their children had problems dealing with separation and loss.

It appears that imprisonment functions as a precipitating factor, rather than a cause, of these children's problems since imprisonment was only the most recent of a series of crisis producing events they had experienced. In most homes, family life had been marked by frequent upheavals, alcohol and drug consumption, violence, and prior separations. All wives claimed that involuntary separation had adverse effects on their children. Many reported that children went through periods of insomnia, nightmares, and bedwetting:

> To this day I have to hold her when she goes to sleep. I guess it started when her father went to jail. She started sleeping with me. I wanted her in bed with me. When she got older she'd have these nightmares and she'd be up all night crying for her daddy. She really missed him.

Others reported that children experienced loss of appetite—or overeating—temporary withdrawal, fretting, clinging, etc.[4]

About half of the children who attended school had problems: temporary falls in grades, truancy, or dropping out of school.[5] One child, whose father had been home for fourteen months out of her seven years, became suicidal:

> I don't trust Lilly. If it goes through a six-year-old's head that she wants to commit suicide, I'm really scared for her. Frank was home for 14 months and she really became attached to him. Now she's having a lot of problems at school. They told me her hyperactivity could be emotional. She's been kicking the teacher, disrupting the class, and won't follow through on her book work.

Only two children, both adolescents, had become involved in delinquent behavior since their fathers' imprisonments.[6] Both children had experimented with stealing. In general, prisoners' wives reported that fathers were missed. The children talked about them and usually remembered the good things that their fathers did with them. Often discussions centered around their fathers' return.

An important source of problems for wives was the restrictions placed on their freedom as a result of having sole care of their children. Many wives reported that their tolerance was reduced. When their energies were absorbed by their own concerns or daily tasks, children's demands seemed to drain already reduced reserves. They often reacted by yelling at, shoving, shaking, or slapping their children. When stress became overwhelming, children became targets of wives' anger and frustration. One mother of two preschool children described her experiences:

> I yelled at the kids, hit them too much, and I felt like killing them. One time, instead of killing them, I broke a popcorn bag and threw it all over the house. Instead of killing them, I threw pictures of them all over and broke pictures. While I threw these pictures all over, they never moved an inch. After that, Randy called and I was crying. That was all I could do on the phone. He kept asking me if I can handle them. I said that I wanted to go somewhere and do something besides be with them. I just wanted them to stop doing disastrous things.

Most women with children complained about the task overload. Two parents are hardly enough to deal with many of the demands of child care. Prisoners' wives often encountered a succession of days filled with too much to do. Unrelieved responsibilities can be especially depleting if there is no one to attend to the wives' needs, *i.e.*, no one with whom to talk, share household responsibilities, etc. Many wives reported that this often led them to despair.

Finances

Twenty wives experienced extreme financial pressures.[7] Even when finances had not been a major concern before their husbands' imprisonment, it became one later.

Women whose husbands had been steadily employed indicated that the problems arising from loss of income far outweighed any benefits from increased control:

> I chain smoke now. That's new since October. I have been eating badly and sleeping badly. I feel there's no time to do anything but exist. I have to find out if I'm eligible for Medicaid and food stamps. I have to make out on a very small amount of money and I keep saying to myself there's no way I can do it. I have to find a way to make extra money. I know I can make $200 a month extra. I don't want to work nights and do this to Sara. His parents will help me. It's hard to say to them that I need $200 a month for three months. But I'm going to have to. It's easier for me to ask them for a hug and support, but not for money.

Seventeen women reported that they were "just scraping by," living at or below the poverty level. Of these, most had collected welfare before their husbands' imprisonment. They had adjusted to having low incomes and little cash at their disposal. One new source of financial strain, however, was that before imprisonment they had been accustomed to having their husbands provide some cash for "extras." After imprisonment, these extras stopped.

Four wives who received welfare, however, claimed that their financial situation had improved. All these women built their incomes by combining a number of sources, including part-time work, welfare assistance, help from relatives, profits from smuggling drugs into prison, and rent from boarders.[8] While these income packages were better, in some sense, than those they had before their husbands were imprisoned, they were frequently still not sufficient.

Women said that they had a sense of having more after their husbands were in prison, even though their incomes were actually reduced. Having control over their money made them feel "better off." This control made a great deal of difference to them since they had had little say in these matters before their husbands were imprisoned.

Only six women reported that the family income had not changed significantly as a result of the enforced separation.In most of these families, the husbands had not held regular jobs, whereas the wives were gainfully employed and had been the primary breadwinners before enforced separation. After their husbands' incarceration, these women continued working and providing for their families. A few women reported that, since their husbands were unemployed prior to imprisonment, they qualified for welfare assistance and continued receiving their welfare grants after their husbands' imprisonment.

Illness, Depression, Anger, and Resentment

Wives' responses to the husbands' absences varied considerably over time. These fluctuations were not apparently a function of the length of separation, although there was a tendency for certain responses to increase as prison terms stretched into months. Generally, changes in the wives' response-sets depended on the kinds of daily events with which they were coping. For example, if a child were severely ill, a wife might feel very resentful about being left alone by her husband. On another day, when the same wife had just given birth to a baby, she might well feel proud about how well she was coping with separation.

Four common response patterns were reported by wives: illness, depression, anger, and resentment. Twelve wives indicated that they experienced a higher rate of "attacks of nerves," headaches, indigestion, ulcers, shortness of breath, etc., after their husbands were imprisoned. Most of these obtained prescriptions for some form of tranquilizer. Depression tended to occur when wives were overwhelmed with tasks and conflicting demands by their children, husbands, and kin.[9] For instance, an old timer described the kinds of conflicting demands that wives could experience:

> Some women can't hack the game. Their sex lives go down the drain. They can't take the pressures, the loneliness, the feeling of isolation, and trying to communicate with their men through letters. And the prison set up these rules for visiting. It's wrong to kiss your man. They tell you that when you have the legal and moral right to be intimate with your man. And then your old man is continually saying that he doesn't want you to do this or that. You're continually pulled a thousand ways. A lot of women just bail out!

Several wives thought their marked increase in smoking was attributable to depression. Some wives also mentioned that they smoked marijuana more frequently during their husbands' absences. However, none of the wives reported that they drank alcohol more frequently, or that alcohol and/or drugs had presented a serious problem.

A few wives described problems of depression so severe that they had become almost incapacitated as family heads.[10]

> Six months ago, I started getting very depressed and despondent. The kids irritated me and anything they did I would yell at them. It's called situational depression. The house started getting the best of me. I didn't neglect the kids. I fed them! I'd get up in the morning and get the kids their breakfast and get them off to school. See that high chair over there? I'd put Justin in his playpen and sit. I didn't answer the phone. My mother and my mother-in-law could call and I'd tell them I didn't want company if they wanted to come and visit. The house was a mess and I didn't want them to see it like that. So I sat until the kids came home and I'd feed them dinner and put them in bed and sit in that high chair until it was time for me to go to bed.

Other women coped with stress by eating inordinate amounts of food or sleeping most of the day, and a few reported thinking about suicide. As this woman said:

> I have not felt rested from the day that Kevin was arrested. I feel drained and tired all the time. And yet I sleep all the time. When I

come home from work, I don't want to make supper. I feel as
though I have climbed a mountain. I just get through the day. My
job is a high tension job and when the day is over I am drained
from it. I never know what to expect when I get to work. There is
always some crisis to manage. When I get home, I sleep off and on.
I somehow make supper. When Sara goes to bed, I lay down on the
couch here and I fall asleep. I wake up in the middle of the night
and drag myself off to bed. When I do manage to stay up after
Sara has gone to bed, then I eat continuously from nine to eleven
at night and then I conk out on the couch. I know that there is no
reason for this except stress.

Many wives reported that they sometimes experienced anger
and resentment when they believed that their men's lives in
prison were better than theirs on the outside. Looked at from
the outside, the prison system sometimes seemed preferable to
being overloaded with stresses and strains. These wives came to
believe that their men were both well cared for and free from
responsibility:

He's up there and he gets three good meals a day. He's eating food
like steak and roast beef and I'm eating hot dogs and hamburgers.
What worries does he have up there? I used to tell him that I
would like to trade places with him. I'll go up there for five days
and he comes here and he would have all the burdens. And I'd
have a much needed rest. He can pinch the pennies and worry
about the kids, and wonder if the bills are being paid. Those guys
have the best of everything. They have their own rooms, color TV,
and wall-to-wall carpets. I get very hostile. I don't have these
things. Let me take a vacation. Then I hear their gripes. They are
in there locked up and they can't go any place. But they go places.
They get passes for work release. And when they get the work release passes, they don't really look for work. They go out and pass
the day. But none of the men have any worries. They don't face the
bill collectors, wonder where the food is coming from, go to the
hospital and really face the responsibilities of their families.

In many cases, these wives reached the conclusion that prison
was a more positive experience than it is. When their husbands
participated in prison programs—such as group counseling, education, Bible study, and arts and crafts—their anger and resentment intensified. These contrasted markedly with what they
perceived to be a dearth of services that they could draw upon:

All I hear about are all these support groups for these "poor men in prison." Then the bleeding liberal hearts come in and fight for the men so that they can have color TV and nice food and all the comforts of home. No one cared about the families on the outside. We're hurting. We're resentful. We're trying to feed our kids and all these bleeding liberals are crying for the men and no one cares for us. I feel resentful.

BENEFITS OF ENFORCED SEPARATION

There is a paradoxical aspect to the ways in which prison extends into the lives of prisoners' wives. Although the "pains" of separation can be extreme, real benefits can accrue to wives from enforced separation.[11] These "benefits" can soothe some of the pains, as well as strengthen marital bonds. Separation can, for instance, provide freedom from domestic routines, peace and quiet, personal autonomy, a new sense of competence, and a "Queen for A Day" syndrome.

Freedom From Domestic Routines

Fourteen of the wives found that they gained freedom from restrictive domestic routines—revolving, in many cases, around their husbands' needs—as a result of separation. After imprisonment, these wives no longer had to consult or please their men unless they chose to do so. Consequently, many began to enjoy the opportunities for personal control that "living alone" offered:

> I don't enjoy being alone, but I like living alone. I like to have dinner when I want it, and when you have a man around you have to cook certain things that he wants. I'm not picking up after any man and my boys pick up after themselves—they're pretty good about that. A man is a lot of work though. When he's not around, then I can say "Good, he's not as much work." I do my own washing and ironing. When I was with Burton, I'd stay up nights and wait for [him] to come home. If he was out, I'd stay up and wait and wait. Now that is all ended. Now I can go when I want to go. There is a certain amount of peace and tranquility about going to bed by myself. There is no more anticipation about whether he's coming home or not.

Many wives noted that, without their husbands, it was often easier to organize their lives. They could cook simpler meals, did not have to pick up after their husbands, ran their own errands, etc. A number of wives found that, without their men around, it was easier to maintain their standards of household cleanliness as well as to develop their own schedules for child care and domestic duties.

Peace and Quiet

Twelve wives noted that they had more "peace and quiet," as well as freedom from their husbands' drinking and/or drug use, after they had been separated. Their husbands' imprisonment allowed these women to remain married, but without the domestic problems their men created. All these women felt that their husbands' alcoholism, drug use, and absences from home had disrupted or nearly destroyed their lives. Once their husbands were in prison, they knew "where [they] were" and this reduced anxiety and tension:

> I just became more independent. When Duke was around I was always at home and it was hard to get me out. I'd sit here and worry about him. I'd sit and wait for him to come back. When he was gone, it was more relaxed. I knew where he was exactly. I was content with my life when he was gone.

As a result of their husbands' repeated imprisonments, three old timers established what they considered to be satisfying marital relationships similar to those of service wives. They reported that they enjoyed being in control of their own lives and free from worry about their husbands' comings and goings. As this old timer said:

> Once he's gone, there's no pressure about whether he's going to drink and the guys stop coming around. I feel more relaxed. I don't have to deal with his problems. It's hard to explain. I'm comfortable living alone and living with Frank. I'm comfortable with both. Frank has learned my ways and I've gotten so set in my ways that I don't want to live with anyone else. We are conditioned to react a certain way.

Under these circumstances, they could pursue a conventional

style of living, free from anxieties about drug or alcohol problems, etc. At the same time, they could enjoy the status of being legally married.

Personal Autonomy

Although their responsibilities might be burdensome, these prisoners' wives also benefitted from the increased personal autonomy that came with greater responsibility. They exercised greater control over their children, their households, and their resources. Many women reported that even with reduced income, they often felt better off. They also said that they could exercise more control of "social time"; select friends and sexual partners, determine where to go, select their own social activities. As one young woman said:

> I like coming and going when I want to. I have ties with Tom but I like coming and going as I want to. I have my own money and I can do with it as I want to. All my bills get paid and I'm well organized now. I think that I cared for Tom too much and I didn't care for anything else. Before he was arrested, I was buying him all his clothes and buying a lot of pot for him. Anything he wanted, he got. I didn't think of anyone else. Just Tom's needs. I didn't give a shit about the bills. I didn't care if they got paid or not.
>
> Well, now I'm on my own and I know I have to make it. I'm on my own and I feel as though I am making it. It's easier now. I don't have him to support.

New Competence

As single-but-married women, ten wives reported that, by dealing with new areas of responsibility, they developed a greater sense of competence and self-worth. This self confidence, they reported, emerged not only from the process of redefining their roles and opportunities within their households, but from changing their patterns of social interaction outside their homes. Four wives had made decisions about the kinds of work or education they wanted for themselves. Two had decided to enter the job market and establish careers. One returned to school in order to "better" herself. Another was reinstated as a student at a college near her home.

The "Queen for A Day" Syndrome

Another benefit derived from enforced separation has been characterized by Holt and Miller (1972) as the "Queen for A Day"
syndrome. Five wives cited their husbands' convictions and imprisonment as proof positive that their husbands were responsible for any problems in their marriages. By placing blame
squarely on their husbands, it was possible for wives to assume
roles as silent sufferers who stuck by their husbands when they
were "down":

> Another payoff might have been that, because Tim was in jail, I
> had an excuse for being paralyzed, inactive, and not doing things. I
> had an excuse to make people so that they felt sorry for me and in
> a way it was an attention-getting device. You're getting a payoff
> from this. You can feel bad about yourself. You can say, "I was
> doing well before this and now look where I'm at and it is all be-
> cause of him. He has done this to me."

By staying with their husbands as loyal and long-suffering
wives, they obtained some measure of respect based on how well
they bore the pains of separation:

> On the inside I got to play the martyr and so did Slim, and I could
> convince myself that we were such martyrs and therefore that we
> were good people. I was valuable since I played it well. The payoff
> for staying in the relationship was that. I guess that's it. The mar-
> tyr role was the big payoff. I think all the women get this payoff.
> They suffer with strength.

ACCOMMODATIONS TO ENFORCED SEPARATION

To make their lives more bearable and to maintain their marital
commitments, the prisoners' wives primarily employed two accommodative strategies: (1) making time pass; and (2) perceiving their homes as prisons.

Making Time Pass

The most common strategy employed by seventeen wives was
"doing time": finding those activities that made the time spent
waiting for their husbands as easy as possible.

"Doing time" in most cases consisted of little more than attempting to forget about the past and future, and to concentrate on making each day pass as quickly as possible. Thus, wives tended to live their lives from day to day, from one small event to the next: watching their children develop, making special treats for them, going to birthday parties, or family gatherings, and so on. Time became a series of days to be marked out and "gotten through." They might choose to "lose themselves in their jobs" or to "retreat into their families." More commonly, wives managed time by "keeping busy": involving themselves in domestic chores, planning and carrying out activities, and taking on work-related activities that fill time. Those who were employed frequently rushed from work to home and—when the last household chores were done in the evening—fell into bed exhausted. When work and domestic activities could not fill up the hours, these wives generally turned to television for distraction.

A few wives reported that they "did time" by absorbing themselves in domestic activity during the days and partying at the bars at night, which sometimes led them into sexual liaisons:

> It's so boring sitting home and having nothing to do so I go out with my friends. It's just boring being around the house all day. I go to the Zodiac and to the Outpost and I have a good time. All I have is a good time, that's it. When I go, I dance and drink a little. That's as far as it goes. I don't have affairs with these men. I love Butch and I'm waiting for him. I tried to have an affair and it didn't work. Butch is always on my mind all the time. But I can't see staying home seven days a week. Butch doesn't mind my going out but he doesn't want me involved with guys. I see his point.

Perceiving Homes As Prisons

Whenever prisoners' wives mentioned that they, too, were serving time, they also were likely to remark that they, like their husbands, were in prison.[12] Although their prisons had neither walls nor guards, the wives felt that their homes had become prisons. All these wives reported feeling this way when they were confined in their homes. Like men in prison, they experienced a sense of isolation, lack of stimulation, continuous pressure from other people, boredom, and monotony. As do prisoners, these wives had a sense of the sameness of their days, with little variation in their day-to-day domestic chores:

> When the men are in jail, you only have yourself to lean on. When you have kids, you have to worry about them alone. It's like a prison. You can't say that you're fed up and that you won't worry and you can't walk out. In jail you don't have to worry about anything. They tell you what to do every minute. Outside it's harder because I have to do it. I'd wake up and I didn't want to clean the house but I had to clean because I didn't want it to be dirty. If you have a dirty house, then you don't respect yourself. When Spike was in jail, I was in jail in my own home. I could go as I wanted but I had to come back all the time.

During enforced separation, most wives pursued few outside social activities. These women's involvements in their homes and/or jobs intensified along with a concomitant reduction in social activities such as visiting friends and relatives, going to bars and movies, and so forth. Instead, there was a marked increase in home-centered activities such as knitting, looking at television, and having friends and relatives visit them. Some wives frequently visited with relatives and friends in their homes. Only a few wives said they occasionally played bingo, went bowling, or went to the movies. Those wives who did not participate in informal or organized social activities were the most likely to experience the structure of the prison in their everyday worlds.

The reasons given for adopting this situation varied. Many wives mentioned that their child care responsibilities tended to keep them at home. Some of these emphasized that they regarded confining themselves as proof of their love, loyalty, and faithfulness to their husbands.

> This is a route you choose though. You choose to be with these men. I know that I choose to wait for Tim and I wanted to wait for him. You don't have to lock yourself up and I have realized that I did just that. I created my own prison.
>
> I felt as though I was in prison, too. I wanted to show him that I loved him. I wanted to show him that I could wait for him. I never went out with other men. I feel that I've already proven that I can wait and now I can do what I want to do. I don't need to prove anything to him.

Some wives said that they avoided possible confrontations with new stimuli which might induce them to change either themselves or their commitments to their husbands. Therefore, confinement, these wives believed, was the best way to place their images of themselves, their husbands, and their marital relationships in cold storage for the duration of their husbands' sentences.

> At the time, I had this philosophy that I shouldn't do anything at all and I should keep to myself. I should try to stay the exact way I was so that when Grant got out there wouldn't be any changes. I wouldn't go to bars and I kept away from any kind of wild things that might be going on. I didn't want to be the life of the party because I didn't want to give myself any opportunity to meet anyone. So I decided to lock myself away from the world and I would stay the same way so that two years later I'd emerge just the way I was when he went to jail. I wanted to settle down and get a job and I didn't want to avoid the realities of our situation. I got the job and initially used it as a mechanism to keep myself the same. I'm not sure what I was escaping from but the job and my home life became my prison.

Plans to Terminate Marriages

In many cases, the couples were unable to support each other in coping with feelings of loneliness, isolation, anger, depression, etc., and the stresses that produced them. During their husbands' incarceration, eight of the wives made plans to obtain a divorce. Not one woman cited imprisonment as the sole reason for seeking a divorce. In all cases, however, wives saw their husbands' imprisonment as the "straw that broke the camel's back." The other reasons for divorce which wives reported centered around their husbands' "fast living."[13]

All of these wives reported that conditions related to separation exacerbated those marital conflicts that had existed prior to their men's imprisonment. Such factors as wives' infidelity, their financial difficulties, and their problems as heads of households drove couples further apart. Also, confinement to their homes caused some wives to attempt to widen their social activites against their husbands' specific wishes. For some, waiting, and what it entails, simply became too difficult to endure. As one woman said:

> His going to jail made the relationship foolish. Having a relationship with someone in jail is not my idea of a relationship. I want someone who can support me and he's not a support for me. He's not able to help me. I want a family. It's like having a ghost in your life when he's in jail. You can't get anything back from them when they're in jail. I'd be putting into a relationship and receiving nothing. A relationship also has to do with paying bills and with how much you can put into it. All you have when they're in jail is seeing him on visiting days and writing letters. I knew that there was no more that I could do for him. It's a waste of time. I have very high expectations of relationships. There has to be communication and if there isn't, why sell yourself for second best. I don't know how else to say it.

A few women whose husbands had been in and out of prisons reported that "doing time" had dried up their reservoir of good will toward them. This time they found themselves unwilling to continue waiting because of disappointment over their husbands' past failures to reform:

> You're by yourself and no woman should be in jail like that. He had a choice and his choice is to be there instead of here. It wasn't my choice. He knows that I don't like the corrections and I don't like visiting there. He has known this all along. I feel as though I've paid my dues and maybe a few more. I want to have something that is my own now. I want to take the chance of living and not be dead from waiting and waiting. And he's done it all over again.

Finally, a couple of the wives reported that, during separation, they and their husbands had developed different interests. Both spouses were unwilling to resume pre-prison patterns. However, only three of the eight women who filed for divorce actually obtained them. The other five temporarily separated from, but were subsequently reconciled with, their husbands.

MARITAL RELATIONSHIPS ON THE OUTSIDE

By allowing inmates the use of the telephone and mails, prison personnel hope to increase the likelihood that prisoners will maintain close ties with their families. However, there is little empirical evidence as to the actual impact of this kind of access on prisoners' wives.

According to wives' accounts, the Vermont correctional system is not a traditional closed system. In fact, all Vermont prisons make at least minimal arrangements for visitation, correspondence, and telephone conversations between prisoners and their families. Arrangements vary among institutions, but some allow extensive contacts with the outside and, in some cases, appear to promote prisoners' interactions with families and friends. All inmates have access to public pay phones for receiving unlimited calls at specified times of the day. Calls are rarely monitored and prisoners are informed in advance when this is to be done. Two patterns of telephone use emerge in the present study. When men were transferred from one prison to another, the frequency of contact by telephone with their wives varied. Most women whose husbands were incarcerated close to home reported that they had spoken to their husbands at least once, and often as many as three or more times a day. These women were defined as having "regular contact" with their husbands. In contrast, women whose husbands were incarcerated far from home reported unpredictable and infrequent telephone contact. Since long-distance calls are expensive, they were generally not maintained on a daily, or even bi-weekly, basis. Most of these couples corresponded by mail. These women were defined as having "infrequent contact" with their husbands.

Use of Telephone and Marital Relationships

Regardless of whether contact was frequent or not, in most cases, conversations appeared to reinforce marital ties and to mitigate the pain of separation for wives and of imprisonment for the husbands.[14] Moreover, reaffirmation of marital ties appeared unrelated to frequency of contacts. Although conversations included such topics as child care and discipline matters, and prison life in general, wives reported that they and their husbands used telephone calls primarily in order to communicate about intimate matters—emotions and sex—that are difficult to put into writing. Telephone conversations therefore helped couples to maintain or rekindle their relationships. Also, through these conversations, spouses restated their plans for the future, provided information about their lives, and shared concerns about their children and homes. One wife recalled that her telephone calls with her husband were about,

> Oh, stupid things: how much we missed each other, how lonely we were. We pulled each other's hearts out! We'd listen to each other breathe. It was sort of a continuation of the talk during the visit: what the kids were doing; what did he do that day; how we both were trying to change. It was the same old shit constantly.

Through communicating with their husbands, "waiting" became worthwhile for many wives, and most came to believe that marital ties had been strengthened by it—a belief probably arising from their husbands' renewed interest in family well-being and plans for a conventional life. In effect, use of the telephone allowed wives to place their men in the role of understanding-but-distant observers in their lives. This helped them to sustain their beliefs that their relationships were worthwhile and that their husbands were worth waiting for. Regardless of the type of prison, none of the wives reported having sufficient opportunity to interact with her husband in a realistic way. This meant that wives had to form judgments about the likelihood that their spouses were prepared for conventional life after release on the basis of very little—and often distorted—information.

In most instances, wives reported that telephone calls were like visits; they were planned for, looked forward to during the day, and thought about after they were over. These conversations, therefore, created a diversion from wives' domestic and work-related chores and the tedium of prisoners' lives inside.

It is also clear from the wives' reports that telephone communication enabled the men to retain their roles as husbands and fathers. Fourteen of the nineteen wives who had regular telephone contact with their husbands said that their husbands used these opportunities to maintain their positions as head of the household. For instance, some demanded that their wives stay more or less confined to their homes, presumably thereby demonstrating love, loyalty, and faithfulness. Working class men were most likely to want wives at home minding the children;

they also frequently demanded that their wives have minimal interaction with friends and relations, and report to them, by telephone, the minute details of their daily lives. If these wives left the house for any reason, accusations of infidelity and arguments would invariably follow. To ensure that their wives stayed at home, some husbands called as frequently as possible to check up on them. One woman described how her husband controls her life:

> He was very bossy. I couldn't go to the movies or to concerts. When I would get my welfare checks, I had to go somewhere to cash the checks and pay bills. I had to do this. He more or less had to know where I was. When I went to my mother's house, I called to tell him where I was. Whenever he called, I was usually here. If I went shopping and took longer than I thought, I'd call to tell him where I was. This way, there would be no arguments that I was away longer than I was supposed to be. I have had him yell at me for not being there when he called. . . .
>
> He was worried about what I was doing. He asked what I did and at times he didn't believe it. He wasn't in the house and he didn't know. It was kind of hard to reassure him. It was hard because he'd say, "I'm here and you're not here with me."

Most wives were aware that they were their husbands' major contacts with and emissaries to the outside world. They were also mindful of their husbands' fears about the possibilities for illicit sexual affairs or commitments to other men. Some husbands became suspicious of social activities that might provide wives with opportunities to meet other men. For instance, one wife recounted how she had to check in by telephone with her husband after attending a dance:

> He won't let me go to dances. I can't even go with his sister or the guy who lives upstairs with his girlfriend. Once I did go to a dance and I had to call him when I got back. And he told me what time I was to be back. I did call him and I told him what I did at the dance. I told him exactly. I'm very honest with him. He doesn't want me to go out because he feels that I would look at other men. I don't drink and he felt that I did drink and that when I went to that dance, I danced with men. I told him that I didn't do either. He didn't believe me. After that, I decided not to go to any more dances.

On the surface, prisoners' wives generally seemed to accept their husbands' authority in these matters, but the cost of compliance was high. By putting aside their own needs, they were left dissatisfied and socially isolated. A great deal of ambivalence about this issue is also evident. Fifteen wives said that their husbands' attitudes contributed to their own sense of being in prison. The more "open" a prison system, of course, the better able men were to control—or attempt to control—wives' lives. By using the telephone as frequently as possible, men could assume roles as prison guards, constantly alert to any possible infraction of "the rules." Ten men used the technique of calling at "unpredictable" times—in effect, the prison strategy of spot-checking. As one wife elaborates,

> I never phoned him. He phoned me. He phoned maybe once or twice a week. If I wasn't home when he called, the next time he'd ask me where I had been and whom I saw. If he knew I'd planned to go somewhere and I wasn't there, he'd call later. Sometimes he reacted so violently if I wasn't home but if there was a legitimate reason, like I had to go to the doctor, then he was fine. He wanted me to do the things I had to do.

Another wife recalled:

> We usually talked once a day. He usually called me at work. Otis was checking up on me. He did that even when he wasn't in jail. He had nothing to do and he had to have something to relieve the pressure. He was wondering what would happen to me. Was I getting involved with another man worried him.

Of the nineteen women in frequent telephone contact with their husbands, only four reported that husbands seldom or never appeared to be checking up on their activities or whereabouts. All these wives were expected to act in the same manner as they had always done, that is, to pursue a middle class lifestyle, have their own interests, to be active in the community, and to pursue their own recreational interests. In effect, these husbands continued to be more egalitarian and less obsessively jealous in their relationships with their wives. According to two women, their spouses insisted that they "get out and have some fun."

Effects of Telephone Contacts on Family Role Structure

The extent to which wives were able to assume their absent husbands' domestic duties and responsibilities varied with the frequency of telephone contacts, since more frequent contacts enabled husbands to exercise more control over their households. Most women reported that their husbands were able to continue making major household decisions, in particular, those regarding household finances, child-related issues and major household purchases. Wives frequently deferred to their husbands in these matters thus relieving themselves of the burden of responsibility while allowing the husbands to preserve a sense of being the heads of their households. Eleven women also reported that their husbands reasserted their dominance by demanding that they reorganize their lives and households around their husbands' own needs—both material and emotional: relaying messages, handling their legal affairs, running errands for them, and filling their "grocery lists." One woman made this clear: "He'd ask me for things every time he'd call. I'd say to myself, 'What am I, a grocery store?' " When prisons permit, the most common means of communicating these demands is the telephone.

Since telephones promote communication, they can also undermine or weaken marital ties.[15] When couples regularly conversed over the phone, marital conflicts sometimes erupted about exactly the same issues which, in other cases, strengthened marital ties. Wives' accounts indicate that disagreements and verbal clashes generally centered around husbands' attempts to retain their dominance and authority and wives' resistance to this. For instance, twelve wives reported that, as they developed greater confidence in their own abilities to exercise judgments and make decisions, they became increasingly likely to challenge the legitimacy of their husbands' authority. Hence, they were less likely to seek their husbands' permission to do things, defer to them, or rely upon their judgments in handling household decisions. This led to clashes over household budgets—how far to go into debt, kinds of appliances to buy, etc.—child-rearing, wives' work, and the scheduling of visits to the prison. For instance, one of the women, who resisted her husband's demands for her to deliver what she considered an excessive amount of material goods, describes how their arguments affected her.

> I'd get hurt and I knew he was getting at me. His hollering upsets me and he'd say to me that he was the boss. I don't let it bother me as much now. I tell him that I'm a person and I have a life to lead, too. I've smartened up. In the past, when he hung up, I'd cry and be very mad and then I'd try to get back to him on the phone. And then I couldn't because the line would be busy and then I'd become madder. I'd get madder and madder the longer I waited to get through and then I'd cry even more. Then I'd be even madder when I finally got to talk to him. I felt used all the time by him and he got angry because I felt this way. I felt used because he kept wanting things. If I couldn't get hold of him on the phone that night, I'd wait until morning and then I wouldn't be mad by then.

Another wife recalled her reactions to her husband's demands for money:

> We'd argue about whether I was spending too much money or I couldn't give him as much as he wanted. He was afraid I'd be running the road. I kept it a secret that one time that I did run on him but then I told him on the phone. We argued for four-and-a-half hours. Then the time went out on him.

Finally, in a few cases, serious conflicts arose over wives' educational aspirations.

In the course of these disagreements, many of these wives began to adopt the position that they, too, were qualified to make decisions and should share equally in doing so. Recognizing that this was extremely threatening to their husbands, most wives compromised by establishing some areas of personal autonomy for themselves while deferring to their husbands on other issues, *e.g.*, the children. It is interesting that, whether or not couples were in frequent and regular contact by telephone, the lowest rate of marital stress was found among those whose decision making was jointly shared.

The nature of relationships between couples varied substantially depending on frequency of telephone contact. Among those with infrequent contact, fifteen wives reported that they were unable to predict when, and to what extent, they could depend on their husbands' companionship and support. Husbands were often not well informed about important household events and decisions, or the stresses experienced by their wives, and were less able to assess their wives' loyalty and fidelity. The wives, in turn, experienced considerable uncertainty regarding when their husbands might call (and thus, when they might leave the house), and which decisions should be referred to their husbands. In general, they were likely to consult with their husbands on broad policy issues, while making their own decisions in more trivial day-to-day matters. Wives in this position were less likely than the others to refer household decisions to their husbands and to consider them active heads of their families. They were also more likely to busy themselves with child-rearing and domestic activities. Social and emotional support from their husbands, while evident to some degree, was clearly limited and these wives learned not to depend on it.

Home Furloughs

Vermont correctional policy attempts to ease prisoners' reentry into the community through a series of gradual steps, based on a program of home visits. Such visits, which might or might not be supervised and which occur in the final months of confinement, are also intended to encourage prisoners' contacts with wives and families, solidify marital bonds, and provide a gradual reintroduction to the demands and responsibilities of freedom. However, wives reported that most home visits functioned primarily to provide both husbands and wives with a brief respite from the pains of separation or imprisonment.[16]

Eleven wives reported that their husbands had received at least one supervised pass during their confinement. Seventeen men had received more than two. Some husbands obtained these passes irregularly, while others received them at least twice a month. Only a few husbands had had weekend passes.

All the wives whose husbands were furloughed reported that they cleaned their homes, cooked special meals, and dressed up in anticipation of these visits. At the outset, home visits were often like honeymoons: both spouses tended to try to look their best and to be on best behavior. Couples were likely to seek the kind of intimacy that emerges only when everyday concerns are minimized and they can give each other undivided attention. As the following report shows, the novelty of the husband's visit and the presence of the guard made it difficult for normal interactions to occur:

> He's had three supervised passes. He's come with a good guard. He lets us go upstairs. The kids are gone for the day. One was for five hours and one was for three hours. We were very nervous at first. I feel uncomfortable with the guard watching us. It's my place. The guard stays in the kitchen. I feed the guard when he's here. When they come it's either been around lunch or supper time so I feed them. I try to fix something special. The first time it was steak. I went to the meat market for it. Then I had pie for dessert. The second time I had lasagna. I don't get over my nervousness. I haven't been with Jerry for a long enough time and the guard is in the house. Jerry's nervousness is because he's out and it's hard for him to go back there when he's been out.

As with honeymoons, home visits also became a period of rest and relaxation. Usually, wives reported, the couples relaxed at home—sometimes with their children. Eight reported that they and their partners smoked marijuana or drank alcohol during these visits. If guards were present, they often smoked marijuana or drank alcohol with the couples. One woman described a home visit in which her husband and his guard smoked marijuana:

> He only got one supervised pass. It was my kid's second birthday. They gave him four hours. The guard had supper with us. He told us to have our own fun and he'd do the dishes. He watched the kids and we went to the bedroom and had some sex. He even smoked with Randy. The guard had some pot and Randy didn't. He gave some to Randy. He was really good. It was comfortable to talk to him. He played with the kids. He was real good.

During these visits, prisoners' wives went out of their way to avoid placing any pressures or demands on their men. All the wives cooked meals, prepared their children for the event, planned activities, and attempted to create an atmosphere of cordiality. Wives did not ask their husbands to take on responsibilities within their homes. Although husbands frequently spent time with their children, wives assumed actual child care responsibilities. This allowed the men to enjoy their children without having to supervise or care for them. Describing one of the home visits, a wife concluded:

> Things are working out good now. He's getting passes home now. He's spending time with the kids and me. He never spent much time with the kids before. Like this weekend, we had a birthday party. Before he never went to the kids' parties. Now he was home for Josh's birthday. We had a cookout and then Sunday we all went to Smugglers' Notch and we went hiking and fishing. And he played with the kids. He's trying to make the marriage work.

Home visits became a time in which couples reaffirmed their faith in one another and achieved some degree of intimacy in a more private setting than prison visiting rooms. The resurgence of romantic feelings elicited by such visits is evident in the following reports from two different wives:

> Most of the time they were good. There would be the five of us and we either did something or sat around here. At first, he had to stay in the house. It was nice. It was nice to have someone to get the house clean for. I'd remember all the nice things that happened over the next week and I'd laugh about them. It was nice and like a new beginning.

Another wife said:

> It was hard to say good-by. I got so much out of it that I felt almost peaceful. It reinforced the relationship for me because the time we had together was good. We'd make it and everything would be OK. I'd go home and just be quiet. I'd put on an album or read a book and I'd be real mellow.

What all wives found most pleasurable, of course, was the opportunity to mitigate a major "pain" of separation: sexual deprivation.[17] It was only through home visits that couples could resume sexual relations under normal circumstances. Generally if men were visiting on a supervised pass, this could only occur if the guards or volunteers were willing to let the rules slide so that spouses could have some time alone:

> At Londonderry, when he first got them, they were supervised and they were for an afternoon. The guards took him where he wanted but he had to be at his mother's house. I'd go there and have din-

ner and the guard let us go into the bedroom for an hour and we'd
have sex and be intimate for a while. It was so strange. We knew
we only had a certain time. No one else was around and we were
ourselves. Then we'd come out and deal with the reality of the
guard. When we were in the room, we were just ourselves. We'd
talk about ourselves and not about jail.

However, as in this case, a few couples sneaked around
uncooperative guards or volunteers in order to have sexual
intimacy:

> Kevin got two passes. He got one in August. They wouldn't let
> him come home for these passes. They thought he'd try to escape
> because he had so much time left and it might be tempting. Scott,
> his counselor, Sara and I went for a picnic at the Sandbar. It was
> such a pleasant day. He was happy to be out. Scott really cares
> about Kevin. He's interested in him. This was a chance for me to
> talk with Kevin, and he let Kevin and I go off, and we made love
> in the ladies' bathroom. We locked the door and made it fast. We
> felt so mellow! It was a nice time. We went swimming and played
> frisbee.

In the privacy of their bedrooms or other secluded places, the
spouses were shielded from "real life" for a short while.

The wives' accounts also suggest that home visiting exacer-
bates the sense of unreality associated with marital relations during a husband's incarceration. At no point did husbands
confront the realities of everyday domestic life. Rather than providing "dress rehearsals" for later reintegration into the larger
community, home visits, because of their limited frequency and
duration, encouraged a kind of honeymoon atmosphere in
which couples sought to avoid sources of conflicts.[18] Moreover,
they allowed wives to sustain idealized notions of their husbands' abilities to assume roles as conventional husbands and
fathers.

It was also clear that, like in-prison visiting, home furloughs
facilitated the strengthening of marital ties. Home visits improved family morale by adding intensely pleasurable events to
the couples' collection of memories about their relationship and
helped them weather the difficulties involved in "waiting" for
their men's release date. According to thirteen women, family
morale was also heightened by the break in the monotony

of confinement to their homes and/or jobs that home visits provided.

Communicating with their husbands became a vital part of the lives of prisoners' wives for another reason: each chance to interact with their husbands, whether by telephone or during home visits, temporarily released the wives from the persistent illusion that they, too, were in prison. It enabled them to reaffirm their commitment to waiting for their husbands' release.

CHAPTER IX

Repeating The Cycle: Wives' Accommodations To Paroled Husbands' Re-Entry

> There are two things that you're not going to like about your man when he comes home from the joint. Accept it. I expected a story book ending. I expected that I would have a Prince Charming with a 9–5 job and he'd leave in the morning with his lunch box and then he'd come home every night. I expected he'd be like that once he left the joint. What a complete asshole I was. I'd do it again though.
>
> —An Old Timer

After months of planning and dreaming, many prisoners and their wives are reunited. Although such reunions can be joyful, the ensuing period of adjustment can be a difficult time. Of primary concern are the difficulties encountered by wives as they attempt to establish the kinds of marriages they had planned during their husbands' imprisonment and to support their husbands' reintegration into family life.

The problems and dilemmas of re-entry after imprisonment are similar to those following other types of enforced separation. For example, returning servicemen and repatriated war prisoners also disturb the ongoing flow of their families' lives.[1] What is unique in the cases described here is that husbands return to their families as officially convicted criminals who are still being supervised by the prison system.

There is, in the literature, virtually no discussion of the impact of parole on the wives of former prisoners.[2] However, released prisoners' perceptions of domestic and family life have been examined. These studies have consistently shown a strong positive relationship between parole success and the maintenance of family ties while in prison.[3]

Irwin (1970) specifically looked at how returning prisoners perceived domestic life, and his findings provide a possible explanation for the relationship between parole success and strong family ties. He points out that the types of support, both practical and relational, provided by families have implications for the kinds of adjustments prisoners make to their status as parolees.[4] Specifically, families can act to buffer newly released parolees from immediate problems by providing economic, material, and social support. With this help, parolees show a better chance of succeeding on parole.

The literature also suggests that factors operating in the family setting exacerbate parolees' problems. In his classic study, Glaser (1969) argues that "the absence of presence of conflict within the family, conflict between the parolee and his family, the compatibility of the parolee's and the family's commitments, the total character of the family's and parolee's past history together will have an important bearing on the solution of problems. In many instances, the family may be the major force driving the men back into systematic deviance." (Glaser, 1969: 245)

Specific evidence indicates that post-prison success is explicitly related to discord with wives. Oddly, there is no extensive description of how wives perceive their husbands' post-prison performance. This chapter suggests that whether or not released prisoners establish conventionally oriented lives, their wives have their own personal reactions to the necessity of continuing to play a supportive role in their husbands' reintegration into the family. One significant dimension of this process is the range of accommodative strategies that wives employ to support their husbands' settling down and to deter them from resuming fast-living patterns and criminal activities.

THE WOMEN SPEAK FOR THEMSELVES

Bea had been married for fourteen years. She noted that her husband, Rudi, had spent most of their married years incarcerated for alcohol-related crimes. After one year in prison, he was back on the streets for less than six months when he had gravitated back to his pre-prison patterns of heavy drinking, running with criminally inclined friends, and forging checks. In this account, Bea describes the circumstances leading to his arrest and her responses to his resumption of these pre-prison patterns of behavior and subsequent arrest.

> Dear Rudi has taken a drunk every month. In September, my son was in a cast, then I was in the hospital. He went on a drunk. When I came home, everybody threw everything on me and he went on a drunk. He couldn't stand the pressure. Next month, my son shot himself in the leg. He went on a drunk. Too much pressure. All these pressures increased. In December I went and found out that I needed an operation immediately. He doesn't come home. Rudi is on a drunk. The shopping wasn't done for Christmas. He wasn't in trouble then. I felt that if I could get him off the drunk, then everything would be all right. I bought some pills and I spent all my money on them. They cost $35. I wanted them to get him off the drunk but he didn't get them. I was so uptight and I had no money. He wasn't in trouble. I then got the pills to him. I put him on sleeping pills to try to calm him down. Then he decided to go to Danville to get a job. Two days later he ran out of money and he got in with his friends. I'm not blaming his friends. They knew what he would do. These friends told me that Rudi had checks. They gave them to him. Now they're saying that he broke into an apartment and stole the checks. It's no fun, I'll tell you.
>
> He's out having a good time. I sat home and prayed to God that he would get picked up and that he won't get into more trouble. My daughter calls me in the hospital and she's crying. He's in trouble. What can I do? I'm sitting in the hospital. I don't want him to come to the hospital. If he got arrested in the hospital, I couldn't take it.
>
> I didn't hear anything until he called and said that he was coming to the house and taking the car. What does he do but comes to my house and tells me he loves me. Fifteen minutes after he leaves, he's picked up.
>
> Barney [a police chief] calls to tell me that Rudi's been arrested. He says, "Bea, here we go again!" Rudi calls and says, "Bea, here we go again!" That's our private joke. Three times he calls to tell me he's all right and has been picked up. I said, "This is it!" I couldn't take it any more. I felt so confused and mixed up. If I talked to anyone, I felt like I'd break down. The man wasn't worth it.

I do know that he took off with these two guys when he was drinking. They wanted to go to Florida. They got him to cash these checks and then got the money. They ripped him off for $800 and then they went to Florida. They came here and apologized to me for what they did. And they wanted to leave their clothes at my house. Can you believe it! They then got Jill's husband to drive them to the bus depot. They cashed checks too but Rudi is taking the whole rap.

It's always been that way. Rudi doesn't get a cent and they went to Florida. They took the checks with them. Don't tell me they're not going to cash these checks.

You know, when he was picked up, he was drinking over two gallons of vodka a day. You'd think he was a god damn camel. He has to have someone. If my son was alone and in trouble, I couldn't live with myself if I didn't stick by him when I know he's alone. I feel the same way about Rudi. He has no family. He only has the kids and I. I can't have that on my conscience, that I deserted him. I'm very bitter. I pity him and I feel sorry for him. I don't know why. When I've needed him, he's never here. When I had the operation, he wasn't there. I need him now when I'm so sick and he's not here. I need him with Joyce and he's not here. My sister keeps telling me that I shouldn't let him see Joyce. He's no good! Joyce answers her aunt by saying that "He's my father, stay out of it." My family doesn't understand alcoholics and they don't understand what he's going through. I don't think anyone can judge him except myself and the kids. We know what alcoholics go through.

I know that they're thrilled to have him back at Newport. As soon as he was less shaky, they called him into the office. They said, "Rudi, as soon as you feel better, we want you to go and head the kitchen again." He then becomes an important person. Now he has no worries. He knows where his meals are coming from, people admire his cooking. He has his own room and can have privacy whenever he needs it. I resent it. I'm holding down the responsiblity and he enjoys himself. I resent him. I don't know what to do. When he's up there, he's happy as a pig shit. They give him everything there. They know that he won't run away. He never has.

I told the prosecutor that they weren't doing right by him. I'd give anything to be able to talk to the judge who sentences this time. I'd tell him that Vermont is doing wrong to this guy. If they had said, in his papers, that he couldn't drink then I could have

had him violated. I'd have turned him in right at the beginning
when he started drinking. Then he'd do his six months and get
sober and he wouldn't have gotten into trouble. He might have
resented me but in the end he'd see that I was right. There was no
way that I could have had him violated until he got into trouble. I
remember that they had picked him up for DWI and then they let
him go that same night. I had to come down to the police station
and pick up his car. When he's drunk, he knows nothing about
what is happening to him.

I miss him though. I miss our laughing and joking. I miss his
getting up in the morning and giving me a good morning kiss and
then kissing me when he comes home in the evening. He's given me
a lot of happiness even though he has also given me a lot of pain.
I can't stand to see him with a bottle. I said that he's like two
people. He's like a camel when it comes to drinking—there's no
bottom. He becomes obnoxious when he drinks.

We're always there for them but I told Rudi that I wouldn't be
around. This time I'm not going to be there for him. No way! I
don't want my kids to see him drunk.

Vicki has three children from a previous marriage and one
baby from her marriage with Charles, who served a sentence of
2-1/2 years in prison for attempted rape. Here, Vicki describes
the circumstances that led to her separation from her husband.

You know, I went out by myself on my birthday. I went out at nine
and didn't come back until four in the morning. I went with my
sister and we first went to Burger King to eat dinner. Then we
went to Friends and had four beers and then we went to Sambo's.
I danced the whole time we were at Friends.

He went out two nights before my birthday and he stayed out
until twenty after two. But when I came home he was waiting up
for me and he immediately said, "You must be fucking up a
storm." He then swatted me against my head. He told me to get
out of the house. I simply agreed with him because I knew that he
felt very threatened. I don't talk back when he's like that.

When he hit me, I didn't feel so bad. He didn't really hit.
He didn't use his fists. He was striking out at me like he would
strike out at a child. He can't handle what was going on so he hit.
If he had brought blood, I wouldn't feel so lightly about it. I
worded everything I said after that carefully. If I had said that
I went out and I danced up a storm then the deuce would have
happened.

I have an awful mouth. I know that. When I open it now, he tries to control himself. Now he usually stands there with his fists clenched but he won't hit. He hit me twice since he's been home. I provoked him to no end. We had a fight and he went off to bed. I said, as he was going upstairs, "I know what you're going to do. You're going upstairs to be all alone so that you can watch Channel 2." He said nothing. He went up to the bedroom and closed the door. I turned on Channel 2 to see what was happening. On the screen was a man and a woman completely undressed. The woman was fondling the man's parts. I hollered up the stairs, "You queer bastard!" I had the baby in my arms. Charles came down and hit me even though I was holding the baby. He said to me, "You son of a bitch, don't you ever call me queer." He then masturbated because he felt so angry.

That's his mechanism to shut me up. He knows I fear it. Charles is not good with his mouth. All my artillery is with my mouth. I'm good at it. I know that. And all he has are his fists.

Usually when Charles gets drunk, I baby him. I feel this is better than getting beaten. It's better so that the kids don't see any beatings. I witnessed a lot of them when I was a child. Now, I don't say a word to Charles. I grit my teeth and underneath I want to stab him. I baby him and treat him like King Tut.

Later that night he told me that he expected me to go to the store and get him a soda and some munchies. They had to be here by nine o'clock the next morning. He went to bed and I slept on the couch. I said to myself. "Fuck you! I'm getting nothing for you!"

The next morning he came down at nine and he didn't see his munchies and soda waiting for him. He was pissed. He said, "Where are the car keys? I'll get them myself." I said. "No! I'm not going to give them to you." I wasn't going to give him the car that I worked for and I wasn't going to have him mess it up. He then came over and grabbed me by the hair. He pulled my hair so that now I have a huge part down the back of my head. He then belted me so that he split my ear open. I told him that he wasn't going to do that again because I was going to call the police the next time and have him arrested.

Next morning, he went to St. Albert. While he was gone, I packed my clothes and the children's clothes and put the children and the dog in the car and drove over to my brother's house.

After I moved out, we had a long talk. We both felt that we weren't able to stay together. It just won't work. He'll always love me. But he wants kinky sex. He wants to have sex with a woman and have another man watching. He's so screwed up. I don't understand him. He said, "It's too late for me. I've gone too far. It's better to end it because there isn't anything that can help me."

I felt that if he could belt me like that when he's sober what could he do to me when he's drunk. I'm scared of him. I felt as though he could kill me and over something so trivial. What could he do to me when he's really fucked up? He's not motivated to do the right things to stay out of jail. Everything is back—the masturbating, the kinky sex, the porno books and fantasies. It throws me to have someone with a sex problem. I can deal with the alcohol problem. I dealt with it with my father and my former husband.

He doesn't seem to have any kinds of limitations. He's dialed the cops and Newport and told me to tell them that he pushed me around that day and that he was drunk. He said that I should rat on him. I can't turn him in. The family thinks I'm nuts. But my family are a bunch of cop callers. They told me that he's violated his parole and I should put him back in. I don't know why I don't call the cops. I'm afraid of Charles and I don't feel he's sane.

I don't care what he's going through. This is it. I want him out of here. I know what he's going through. He can't support all this responsibility. Now that he's facing real life situations, he can't face them. He can't face being the only supporter of the house and that we rely now totally on his pay check. I went off welfare when he got settled in this job. When I'm depressed, he's at his worst. He can't stand to see me crumble. Once I get depressed, he starts acting up or getting even more depressed than me. Comes home from jail and he immediately sees that he really has a wife and kids. But why knock me down? I'm not his enemy. I can't fight him like that.

He lives in a fantasy world where things should be perfect. When he was in jail he claimed that he wanted a job, any old job. He just wanted to be working and get out of there. Now he got this good job. Is he pleased? He comes home from work and whines, "I work eight hours in my job and I don't like it. I work to support you all in a job that I don't even like." He has told me that I have never earned any money. I just receive handouts. He feels that I haven't earned the money that I got from welfare but that it gets handed to me. I know that I worked for every cent of that money. But I just agree with him and let him call me a puke. I agreed with anything he had to say at that point.

I see this man as a person who doesn't want to be this way but he's not willing to change. He's set in his beliefs but he's not happy with these beliefs. I feel that Charles has three personalities. He wants the good things out of life—that's the first personality. The second is his fantasy and sex life and the third is the little boy who never grew up.

I feel like this was the ultimate irony. I put all this into the relationship and I wait for him so that he can leave me. This is the ultimate humiliation.

THE HONEYMOON

Prisoners' returns to their wives are often dramatic. Of twenty-nine men, fifteen left prison for their homes and families. The time had come for couples to put into practice the plans made during the months of enforced separation.

Anticipations About the Reunion

Prisoners' wives generally had mixed feelings about their husbands' release from prison. They looked forward to their husbands' return with eagerness and were initially optimistic about the chances that their husbands would stay out of trouble. Moreover, they believed that their husbands would fulfill their promises to establish law-abiding lifestyles so that the women could establish their roles as traditional wives. Most wives believed that their chances were better than average that they would be able to live this way.[5] At the same time, these wives had some misgivings. Some were anxious about whether or not they and their husbands would be "strangers" and, whether their husbands would disrupt the lives they had established for themselves. The source of their anxiety was the fear that incarceration and enforced separation had allowed them and their husbands to develop in very different directions. A neophyte expressed such anxieties:

> Recently, he called and told me that he's going to be released early. He has a job waiting for him in St. James in the museum. He works in their printing office and he likes it. He was so excited. It was finally over. I cried and cried. I felt that as soon as he got out then his release would be the answer to everything. I always felt that way. What surprised me about my reaction to his release was that all of a sudden I realized that for two years everything was

geared to building him up, to his progress and that my reward for these two years of centering on him, would be HIM! But I realized that this was not enough any more.

I know that I'm important to him, but I don't want to be that important. He's said that if he doesn't have me there is nothing. I don't like this kind of pressure and I don't like to think that I'd be the guiding light in his life. That I would spend my life guiding him through his own life. I don't want it.

Neophytes were more likely than old timers to report that they had no idea what to expect in the role of parolee and parolee's family. Wives had no sense of what their husbands would expect from them. Thus, they were likely to speculate about possible re-entry problems. Some wives worried that their husbands would simply resume the cycle of unemployment, fast living and criminal activity:

I don't want to be a police woman for the rest of my life. I seem always to be telling him that he shouldn't be doing this or that. And I know that whatever he does is going to reflect back on me.

I certainly have been quite adamant about his activities in the past. He couldn't do anything illegal around me now. I don't want him getting high around me now. But when he does get high, I hope he is discreet about it because I feel now that it's his problem. I've gotten completely paranoid about him and what he does. Like he's not supposed to drink and I worry when he does drink. I feel like his mother and I don't want to be in that position. Under no circumstances would I stay with him if he got arrested again. I'd leave. I told him that.

Another neophyte related her anxieties:

It scares me. The fact that he's been incarcerated for two years. When he get's out, time will tell the truth. Time will tell whether he gets himself together or goes back to the old things. I'm wondering if freedom is going to be so nice to him that he's going to be out chasing women. I wonder if all these things we've planned for are going to happen. After two years, I could find out that I waited for nothing because we can't live together any longer. For Christmas, he had a forty-eight hour furlough. We spent it at the Holiday Inn. We found that we couldn't sleep together in the same bed. He was in jail for so long that he wasn't used to sharing a bed. We wanted twin beds because we were not used to sleeping together. We went into separate beds that night. We laughed about that.

The Honeymoon Itself

With parole or extended furlough papers in hand,[6] fifteen prisoners returned home to what were usually joyful reunions. This initial period was similar, in certain ways, to a honeymoon. It was also a period of transition from "married-but-single" to "married," when the couples had the opportunity to resume or redefine their previous roles, establish new patterns, and explore new possibilities.

Of fifteen wives, eleven claimed that in the early days of their reunions, they experienced extreme elation, pleasure, and shock at having their men in their homes again. Reunion was a time of celebration in which most couples established a moratorium on dealing with everyday stresses and strains and on outside social activities. Like a honeymoon, couples sometimes took extended trips together, with or without their children. Others, who stayed at home, took a vacation from the routines of home life. Wives reported that they tried to extract as much relaxation and enjoyment from this period as possible.

> It was a real good week. I picked up the kids on Saturday night, and took them camping. Rudi and I played a lot of frisbee with the kids. Rudi pitched ball with Todd. He also went out to look for a job every day. Rudi was so relaxed and so different. We'd play cribbage at seven o'clock in the morning. We laughed and joked. It wasn't a strain that either of us would do something wrong. We didn't have to worry about that as we did when he was living at our house. It was like the "old " us when we were away from here and in Nebraska. It was terrific! It was like the old times, real good.

Given the "pains of imprisonment," wives—especially neophytes—expected that the euphoria of reunions would overshadow any initial difficulties, at least for the first few days. Instead, twelve wives reported that the honeymoon initiated a period of crisis in their lives.

All these wives reported that, although they were elated, they also reacted with shock, bewilderment, and disbelief at the behavioral patterns their husbands displayed. Many were disoriented and appeared to be ill-prepared to fulfill their wives' expectations, at least in the short term. This disorientation stemmed from a sense that they were "strangers" in the "free world." Thus, they were uncertain, anxious, and self-conscious. Wives also reported that the men sometimes experienced acute anxiety, trouble talking to people, difficulties in making decisions, and difficulties in adjusting to their own homes as well as their communities. One woman described her husband's difficulties in this way:

> He had trouble going to sleep at nights and he was paranoid. He didn't feel right being out and he was scared to go out. He was afraid that he was being watched to see if he would do anything wrong. That's why he stayed in for that month. If he couldn't sleep, I'd sit up with him. He was drinking but not too much. The baby had to go to the hospital for a week and we both were together with her during that time.

Another woman discussed her husband's initial behavior upon his re-entry:

> The first time he came home, I grabbed him one time when he was resting on the couch. He jumped up immediately and knocked me out! He thought that I might be a guard and he had forgotten that he was now home. It's like walking on shells because he's going through so many changes. When he came home and we lived in a trailer, he thought that tiny trailer was too big for him, the ceilings were too high and he would wait for me to open the doors for him. He thought they were locked.

Old timers expected that their husbands would be disoriented and temporarily suspended expectations that their husbands would resume their former roles. For instance, an old timer explains what to anticipate when husbands return from prison:

> When a guy goes to prison it's a dramatic change. He is told when he has to be out of bed in the morning and he's told that he has to be in bed at nine o'clock at night. He's told when to eat and he's told everything to do. All the things that we take for granted that we make decisions about is taken away from him. He has no control over his life. If he's sick, he can only go to the doctor when they say you can go. Everything you take for granted becomes more intense. It's taken away from you. The only outlet he has is his dreams and his memories. When he gets out, he says, "I want to walk in the fields, etc." But when he gets out, he can't decide

what to do first. He wants to cram it all in at once. And he says to himself, "No one is ever going to tell me what to do again. No one is ever going to have control over me. I'm not going to be treated like a child again." He rebels when he's told what to do. He does just the opposite.

Neophytes, on the other hand, who were unprepared for this kind of thing responded with bewilderment at their husbands' abrupt and sometimes dramatic changes:

He got this apartment in St. James. I went up there for a weekend when he first got out. It was a bad weekend. He acted real strange. I was so excited that we wouldn't have to sneak around to talk to each other. But he was completely freaked out. He was terrified to leave the apartment. So we hung around there for four or five hours. He tried all the locks on the door and the windows and he was completely edgy. He wanted to have a beer but he was afraid to go to the store to get some. I went and brought him a bottle of beer and then he had me sneak it into the house. Then he locked the door and closed the curtains and drank his beer. I wanted to go out and buy things for his apartment. The next day we went to Zayre's and he was so nervous. He was completely paranoid. I spent most of my time trying to find him. He at one point hurried to the bathroom and threw up. I didn't know what was wrong with him. I just went ahead and bought everything. I bought the store out—pots, pans, dishes—and he just stood next to me and watched me buy these things. We went home and he just sat there and looked at these things. He looked like he was from outer space. He kept staring at the things that I had bought. I didn't realize that he only saw plastic knives. And now he was looking at real knives. For two years, he hadn't seen real plates and things like that. Now I understand but then I felt that he had lost his mind.

Some women observed that their husbands tended to remain close to home during the early phase of the honeymoon period. The old timers were more likely to recognize that their men were not used to having freedom and found it disorienting to place themselves in unfamiliar surroundings. If nothing else, home is familiar territory. Neophytes were more likely to interpret this unfamiliar behavior as a sign that their men were really ready to settle down and enjoy the companionship of their wives and children.

In contrast, three old timers reported that, instead of being disoriented, their husbands spent little time at home and moved easily into their old familiar scenes with their peer group. These old timers suggested that imprisonment could reinforce husbands' inclinations to "make up for lost time":

> We talk a lot about what it's like when the men come out. I tell them that the men are going to want to go partying for a couple of nights and that this is normal. They can't keep their men home right off. I had a girlfriend who was going through this and we talked about it. I told her that he wasn't rejecting her, but he's going from no freedom to too much freedom and he's only trying to learn how to handle it.

Many wives noted that the correctional system prepares neither the men nor the women for re-entry. During imprisonment, men are socialized into roles which they must discard when they are released. Prison systems, no matter how opened or closed, are, in some sense, total institutions. Prisoners are socialized to behave as conforming members within the prison community. After release, the men experience a sharp discontinuity between their inmate status and those as husbands and fathers, which bear little relationship to it.[7]

All the wives functioned as heads of their households during their husbands' incarceration. As a consequence, all fifteen wives expected their spouses to settle down and resume at least some of their previous responsibilities: most wives desired some relief from economic as well as child care responsibilities. Their husbands, however, were often ill-prepared to deal with either of their wives' demands or the demands of community living.

> In jail, he didn't have any responsibilties and for the men who have wives and families, that's difficult for them. When he's released, she sees him coming and she wants him to take the responsibilities over now. And she then pushes these responsibilities on him and he's not ready. He's not had any responsibilities or made any decisions for a long time. How can he do it instantly just because he's released? He's had no preparation for it.

Although the honeymoon period eases the transition for all concerned, it is nevertheless a disruptive event in wives' lives. Eleven women reported that marital conflicts erupted. These problem areas emerge from forced separation and the fact that neither spouse found the other to be exactly as fantasized during involuntary separation. They therefore perceived the others as changed. Some wives reported that arguments erupted over their new-found independence and their husbands' demands that they return to the old familiar dependent role. Another issue which provoked marital conflict was the conventional working class square jane lifestyles that wives established during enforced separation. For instance, this woman has changed her lifestyle patterns from fast living to a square jane lifestyle. During a trip to the Bahamas, she attempted to inform him of these changes and their effect on their relationship:

> ... I thought that if we went to this tropical paradise everything would be OK. And if everything wasn't all right, at least he'd enjoy himself and we'd never see each other again. We started talking. I tried to explain what was wrong. He wasn't capable of understanding what I meant. I really didn't want to explain to him how I felt but I knew that it wasn't fair not to tell him. I was reluctant to tell him how I realized how much I had changed. For him, I realized, he felt that everything had changed back to the way we were before he went to jail. I had to try to impress upon him how much I had changed and things were not like they were before. He didn't want to hear it. I tried to explain that I was tied up with him. But now I realized that I was beginning to be happy again because I have developed new interests and I have become very involved in my job. I tried to explain that I was no longer willing to rush off on a fishing trip at the spur of the moment. I liked my independece and going out and doing things for myself. I was getting myself together and I was afraid of what would happen when he'd land on my scene with a whole new set of problems. I just cried instead of telling him these things. I cried for three hours and said nothing. He felt I was upset.

Only a few wives resumed their family life as if it had never been interrupted. In effect, both spouses seemed to give minimal evidence of disorientation in making the necessary re-entry transition. These wives reported that neither they nor their husbands had undergone any permanent changes. However, they did recognize modifications in their personalities and expectations for their marriages which had made re-entry relatively easy. Enforced separation, these wives claimed, had been beneficial for both spouses insofar as they had gained time to reflect on their marriages, to come to terms with their possessiveness and their jealousies, and to develop as separate people.

How abruptly husbands are released from prison affects wives' ability to handle these problems. When husbands were gradually reintegrated into their homes and communities through the home furlough and work release programs, they were able to observe some changes in their spouses and to cope with them. Release therefore can be both beneficial and crisis-provoking for both wives and husbands, depending on a variety of circumstances.

PATTERNS OF REORGANIZATION

Honeymoons, however, do not last forever. Afterwards, couples encounter the problems and dilemmas of reorganizing their families. Reorganization was seen by wives as essential for establishing conventionally oriented lives. After the honeymoon, couples either settled down or resumed fast living and criminal activities.

The wives' accounts revealed that enforced separation encouraged them to develop certain behavioral patterns that either increased or decreased their ability to establish satisfying marital relationships. Whether or not they resumed old patterns, negotiations with spouses were based on the expectation that shared dreams were to be finally realized.

Nine wives reported that they and their men had resumed some old marital patterns, but within the framework of a conventional and settled lifestyle. They further reported that their husbands actively attempted to transform their identities from ex-convicts to ordinary citizens, and to establish a more conventional lifestyle. These men frequently followed a very narrow and exacting path. For instance, they often adopted steady work patterns. When not working, they spent most of their time at home watching television, listening to their stereos, etc. If they drank or consumed drugs, they did it moderately. They looked to their wives and families for support, and avoided contacts with criminally-oriented friends and family members:

> I think that Barry has straightened out now. Barry used to think a lot about drinking. When he's with his friends, he drinks quite a

bit. When he's drunk he has this real shit attitude—he doesn't give a shit. His friends will say to him, "I know where you can make some easy money real fast." He'd fall for it. He's an alcoholic.

He's avoiding all his old friends because they are in trouble. He's made a good start. When he hangs with his friends, he drinks and then he's not coming home. Next thing we're fighting and then he's packing his clothes. I'm sick of it! Lately, he's doing nothing but hanging around the house.

Six of this group reported that their marital roles were based on traditional sex roles: their husbands continued to be the economic providers, with their wives primarily responsible for the domestic and child rearing chores. The women saw these kinds of marriages as conventional or "doing good." In all these cases, some mutually satisfying marital patterns were established. Whether or not wives had had intimate and satisfying marital relations before prison, they reported that they and their husbands discovered new values in family life and established a more cooperative relationship. Their husbands approved of their wives' management of the households and children during separation. In turn, these wives approved of their husbands' ability to handle the hardships of re-entry as well as their newly acquired commitment to a conventional lifestyle.

As the months went by, however, more wives were astonished, bewildered, and sometimes driven to despair when they learned that their husbands had resumed the old and all-too-familar marital patterns they had established before prison. Shortly after release, six women reported that their husbands were "not doing too good." Three more made this observation six months later. Their husbands' commitments to conventional style of living had apparently been short-lived: in particular, they were unemployed, associating with criminally inclined friends, staying out late, drinking and consuming drugs, or perhaps having short-term extra-marital affairs.

PROBLEMS OF RE-ENTRY

The major problem for paroled prisoners was getting and keeping steady jobs. Twelve men were steadily employed shortly after they were released from prison. However, most of these men had been released from prison with no training, and few, if any, employable skills which would qualify them for jobs that provide a steady income. Few prsioners actually received substantial job training inside Vermont's correctional facilities or through arrangements with outside agencies. Most work within the prisons, or on work release, was unskilled, or, at most, semi-skilled.

Three men had been released from prison with no jobs in hand, and remained unemployed. Their wives reported that they did not appear to be motivated to find work. The most frequent explanation given by the husbands for this was that they needed a "rest from prison" or that they were taking a "little vacation" before looking for work. In contrast, the three wives, who worked outside their homes during their husbands' imprisonment, continued to be employed. The wife who was a college student continued her studies. The remaining ten wives continued to be housewives and kept their welfare grants as supplements to their husbands' incomes. Three arranged to have their unemployed husbands included in these grants. None of the women who remained at home were totally dependent on their husbands' incomes. Most looked to their husbands to provide for their families' economic well-being, which they saw as necessary for a conventional lifestyle. Thus, all women felt that "settling down" did not simply mean spending time at home listening to the stereo, watching television, or providing them with companionship, but that it necessarily involved steady employment.

By the end of the field research, eight of fifteen men were unemployed. In three cases, the reason for this was that the men had been laid off since they had been hired as temporary workers for government-sponsored or seasonal jobs. Two men quit, saying they did not want low-paying, unskilled jobs under poor working conditions. The three men who were unemployed on release simply did not look for jobs.

Unemployment was a source of problems and stress for most women. Six said that their unemployed husbands would consider accepting jobs that offered them more status and prestige or that their physical ailments prevented them from searching for work. Often, they reported, the men simply avoided the subject by being home as little as possible. Contrary to what one might expect, most men did not find themselves stigmatized when seeking employment: only two women reported that their husbands' status as "ex-cons" interfered with their obtaining satisfactory employment.

For all these wives, unemployment meant a continuation of grinding poverty. These wives either continued their welfare grants or reapplied when their husbands became unemployed. One wife, who received public assistance when her husband was in prison, reported that when he was released her grant was automatically terminated. This was most acutely felt by her family, since her husband was not working.

> They stopped our welfare and Medicaid and everything. He didn't earn enough money in prison to qualify for Aid to the Unemployed Fathers . . . we're at rock bottom. I've been writing bad checks to eat. I still get a small amount of food stamps. I've been working myself sick. I have to go to work whether I'm sick or not. There is only my income to feed the three of us. I can't afford to take off a day from work or we'll starve to death. I'm working and I'm responsible for Frank now, but he's not working. It hurts me bad. I make $2.99 an hour. I'm the working head of the household and I support the family. General Assistance won't help.

It is interesting to note, however, that wives whose husbands were working were not significantly better off: even if husbands were employed, their families could continue to be extremely poor. Some wives reported that their husbands' incomes were far less than what they had previously received from welfare.

> Randy got laid off in December and we got behind in the rent. We were 2-1/2 months behind and so the landlord evicted us. I've been looking around for a place to live. We have no place to go and we're supposed to be out of this house on Monday.
>
> It all comes around to money. Mary is going to school, I have to get clothes for her for school. All Randy's teeth have to be taken out. My teeth are bad. We don't have the money for it.
>
> Randy finally got a part-time job. He's working on the rubbish route for his father. Welfare gives us $179 and we have $373 coming from what Randy makes. When Randy was in jail, I got $490 from welfare every month. We're all getting along but everything is coming at us at once. It's the bills and the money.

Moreover, wives were now not just maintaining themselves and their children, but also their husbands. However, almost all wives expected that their husbands would eventually obtain adequate employment.

In contrast, only a few women did not equate unemployment with poverty. They were employed, and provided the economic foundation for a middle class lifestyle, Hence, their husbands' incomes were not necessary. Another wife, whose husband had a highly skilled position in a water treatment plant, reported that her family is economically better off as a result of her husband's job and a welfare grant that covers her handicapped child.

The stresses and strains of poverty took an immediate toll on almost all the wives. Moreover, the long-held dreams which sustained them during enforced separation were rapidly disintegrating. Their husbands' inability to achieve one primary aspect of their dreams built old familiar resentments in these wives:[8]

> One of these days I'm going to be fed up. When I go back to work and he sits on his fat ass at home, I'm going to kick him out. I don't want to change him. I want the lazy bastard to work. I'm not supporting him—not any more. I see my mother's life all over again —supporting a lazy bastard. I'll go back to nursing until I can't work there any longer.

Repeating Fast-living Patterns

Within six months, nine of the unemployed men had resumed fast living. Eight wives observed that they were most disturbed by the fact that their husbands resumed their old patterns of alcohol and drug use. Six of these wives also noted that when their husbands reactivated old prison friendships it indicated to them that trouble was about to happen. As this woman noted:

> He drinks alcohol constantly. He's back to drinking since he left Newport. He's not drinking alcohol as much as before he went to jail. I don't know if it's lack of money or lack of interest.
>
> He's always thinking of stealing now. He sees my brother a lot, the one who put him in jail. My brother has done a lot of time in Newfane for breaking and entering. He's been straight now for quite a while. He's been out of jail for a good year or two years. Anyway, he likes to hang around my brother and listen to the types of crimes he's committed. They always talk about stealing together.

These wives emphasized that dissociation from friends or acquaintances who are criminally involved was an important component of "going straight."

Four wives provided an explanation for their husbands' resuming their old criminal ties. They indicated that their husbands gravitated back to these friends because they believed that other people could not appreciate their prison experiences. Thus, wives who dreamed, during enforced separation, about evenings spent in front of the television with husbands, now spent evenings alone waiting for their husbands. Husbands' "night out with the boys" all too frequently became "nights out with the boys." All these wives believed that their husbands were not only associating with questionable peers, but with women of questionable intentions. Six wives reported that their husbands physically abused them. No matter how severe the batterings, all wives were reluctant to inform either the police or their husbands' parole officers. They simply did not want to be responsible for sending them back to prison. This is clearly illustrated by the womens' accounts:

> Q. How did you react when he hit you?
> A. I felt terrible. I felt like having him arrested. I told him before that if he ever hit me again, I'd have him arrested. And he hit me again. I used that as a threat to stop him from hitting me and nothing more. I felt like I hated him. Later I sorted out my thoughts and realized that I wasn't going to turn him in. When he came back later, I apologized to him for what I said and he apologized. I then felt things would be all right. We live on apologies. All I do is apologize.

This fast living severely threatened the lifestyles wives had established, often at considerable cost to themselves. Yet, they continued to accommodate to their husbands' problems and to the marital conflicts related to these re-entry problems. They coped because they continued to believe that their husbands would eventually come around to a conventional lifestyle.

Repeating Cycles of Unemployment, Fast Living, and Crime

Within six months, nine women reported that their husbands were involved in crime again. Their husbands had violated at least one condition of parole—such as associating with known criminals, possessions of guns, drinking excessively, and drug consumption:

I wasn't off welfare when he came out and I still haven't been off
it. When he was unemployed, he went on welfare too. We were
barely making it. I had to pay for rent and electricity and the heat
cost $200 a month and that took almost the whole check. Then I
had food stamps and what little money was left went to Pampers.
We were barely making it. Gary didn't go back to stealing. He has
gone back to drugs. He's doing pot and acid. I don't know what
else he's taking. He's doing pot heavily. That scares me because I
don't like him on it. I'm afraid that he's going to be busted and I'll
lose him again.

Six had participated in chaotic, careless, unskilled and op-
portunistic crime—such as burglary, check forging, aggravated
assault, or shoplifting. In all cases, these crimes were alcohol- or
drug-related:

He went and got me some slacks, three pairs of shoes, and a jacket,
a digital clock, and he got himself dungarees and jackets. I broke
my sandal and he said, "I'll get you a pair of shoes." . . . That's
Frank's way of taking care of us. It's the only way he knows.

I went to the car and waited for him to come back. I told him
"You're crazy!" He said that this store is the easiest and I
shouldn't worry . . . That petrifies me. He sat Lilly on top of the
meat in the grocery store and wheeled her out on top of it. What
would happen to the kid if he had been caught?

Still another wife reported:

Harry said that he does things because he isn't working. Because
he doesn't have a job, he drinks. He refused jobs though. I think
it's his drinking that's the problem. He doesn't have to think about
anything when he drinks; he just does what he wants. When he
gets drunk he does his B & E's. He's already done a few.

I told him I'll not wait this time. He's nervous about them
coming and getting him. He's worried about being in jail again.
He says that if he goes to jail, he'd kill himself.

If he gets drunk like the last time, then I knew he will do another job. I was afraid he'd do it again. He knows that he does
them. Even though he's drunk, he knows what he's doing. He says
that he doesn't plan them, but just does them. He does them alone.

In another case, the husband resumed his sexual patterns,
e.g., masturbating while watching couples' sexual activities on
television, reading pornography and so forth:

It was dumb. We had had a good steak dinner. We had decided to watch a movie on the TV. When the movie was ready to come on, he changed his mind. He wanted to watch Juke Box. Here I am all ready to watch this movie and we're going to see Juke Box. He went to get a beer and I associated beer with sex and sex with watching something like Juke Box on the TV. I immediately felt that I was back in the same old spaces. I think that Juke Box is stimulating, like sex. He said that he'd go upstairs and watch it alone and I could watch my movie down here. I felt that he wanted me to get him angry so that he could go and masturbate.

All these women were afraid that their husbands were going to return to prison. Six had become reconciled to this eventuality. Within six months four husbands had had some type of encounter with the police which had not led to arrest, *e.g.*, they were searched, questioned, warned by police, or stopped for a traffic violation. It came as no surprise to most of these wives when they learned that their husbands had been picked up by the police. In some cases, wives reported that their husbands' status as ex-convicts was not an issue and that the police had some other basis for suspicion. In a few cases, old timers indicated that their husbands had been picked up by the police because of their extensive criminal records.

By contrast, six women whose husbands rigorously conformed to a conventional lifestyle, also encountered old and familiar problems. Once again, these were related to unemployment.

PROBLEMS DUE TO ENFORCED SEPARATION

Reunion is a period in which husbands can begin to move back into the family circle and resume familial responsibilites. In order for this to occur, the family unit itself must reallocate roles by realigning power and authority, reworking the division of labor, and sharing home and family activities.

REALLOCATION OF ROLES

According to wives' accounts, they, themselves, played the central role in this allocation. Twelve wives indicated that this involved negotiations with their husbands. Most reported that these were done consciously and carefully. Wives tried to remember to consult their husbands about household problems, children management, and to defer to their husbands' authority. In these cases, they reported that they initially forgot to do this: "I'm used to doing it all by myself," they said.

The eight couples that began to establish conventional working class lives reported that when husbands immediately resumed the role of economic provider it facilitated their assumption of other conventional roles. This made it easier for the women to accept their husbands as partners in family management.

Although husbands assumed some household responsibilities, they seldom fulfilled the entire range of expectations. Instead, as a young woman reported, they were likely to do just what was demanded of them:

> I told him to make out the bills at least every other month. If I died, he'd know nothing about how to run the house. I've been doing the bills. He agreed to do this. But then he told me that he didn't even know where I kept the bills. I told him to figure that out. I had him take the baby out for a walk a few times. He did and actually enjoyed it. He's trying!

Wives claimed that they encouraged "traditional" divisions of roles and responsibilities: children and home were the wives' domains and the occupational world was their husbands'. Wives reported that husbands accepted what they considered to be an old and familiar division of labor with a minimum of resistance.

This process was more problematic, however, when husbands were gravitating back into unemployment and fast living. Of the nine women involved, seven reported that their husbands had, to varying degrees, resisted participating in day-to-day household responsibilities. As one wife whose husband is unemployed, recalled:

> I'm sick of doing the housework by myself and he throws things around. He can't stand to live in a filthy house. I told him to help. He's not working and he's spending money like it's going out of style. I tell him that he's selfish and irresponsible. He spends money on what he likes. When we're in front of people, he asks for money and makes me feel like an asshole because I say "No!" He said that he was fucking me, wasn't he. I said I could get a stud

ported us. I threw him out and told him he wouldn't see Lilly until he supported her. I told Frank that he didn't know the first thing about being a husband.

Once again, these wives found themselves gradually encountering marital patterns similar to those they established before involuntary separation, together with the additional responsibilties they assumed during enforced separation:

He didn't want the responsibility of the bills and household decisions. He was scared. He never told me why. I asked him to help me pay the bills. He said he didn't want the responsibility. He still doesn't. I'm worried because I don't know what it's going to be like in the future and if he is ever going to want to take responsibility.

Two other wives discuss their husbands' escape from responsibilites:

JENNY. When I was pregnant, he was gone week after week.
ARLENE. I've always had to go through these things alone. He's seldom around. But if anything happens to them, your're supposed to be right there and rally with them around *their* problems. Whenever they're having a crisis, you're supposed to be there.
JENNY. When Harry comes home, he always wants dinner to be served promptly. I usually have it ready for him. I had to go to the hospital with Alex. When I got back home, the kitchen was covered with dishes and he's sitting there high. I expected different than that since he knew that Alex was sick.
ARLENE. When I was in the hospital, Frank was drinking and I worried constantly about Lilly. As soon as I came home from the hospital, he takes off and I said to him, "Hey, where are you going? I'm sicker that I've ever been. I need help!" He kept going.

All these wives eventually stopped trying to negotiate with their husbands about these issues.

Division of Authority

Questions of authority within family units were exacerbated by enforced separation. Husbands' failure to participate in household decisions was not the only issue raised by women whose men were gravitating toward fast living; it was part of a larger failure of husbands to assume authority within their families. Most wives found that, after the period of reorganization, they retained some authority they would have liked to hand over to their husbands. They reported that authority and involvement in family life were related. In order to get more power, their husbands would have had to get more involved; as long as they remained uninvolved, their husbands were "guests" in their own homes.

According to eight women, while their husbands wanted minimal household responsibility, they did want to resume control of household finances. Wives were reluctant to relinquish this for several reasons. First, as a consequence of "forced" separation, they had discovered how completely they could handle money. Secondly, money was a scarce resource. They felt that if their husbands controlled it they would absorb too much of it. However, if they did not relinquish control they were aware that it would only reinforce their husbands' positions on the fringes of family life. These two women put it well:

> JENNY. I have always controlled the money. He seems to want to take $20 whenever he wants to. And then he takes it and he goes out. I try to hide a little from him. I hide it for emergencies. When I got the last check, I paid my bills and I felt that we had enough money to go to the movies. I hollered at him that I wanted to go to the movies. He said that we'd go tomorrow. Every time that I ask, he'll have some excuse. He'll always have an excuse.
>
> I don't think that he cares about what's going on in the house. I don't know how you can feel like a part of the household when you don't care.
>
> ARLENE. Harry has told me that he gets so mad because you want him to do this and that. He said, "She makes me feel like I'm being a visitor" and then he has to retaliate. When Harry takes the key to the house, you ask him why is he doing that? When he goes out, you ask him where he's going. You're either playing Big Mama or the Correctional Center. It's the way you ask him.

These wives recognized that money could be a crucial factor in their husbands' ability to participate in conventionally-oriented forms of recreation. Yet, these men came to realize that, because of lack of money, they could not participate in activities they had fantasized about during imprisonment except by eating into scarce family resources. Wives reported that they could see that many of their husbands got so frustrated by this that they resumed some of their criminal activities.

In contrast, wives of conventionally-oriented husbands were concerned about maintaining their own sense of independence. Six women indicated that they had learned to manage their lives and households to their satisfaction during separation. This gave them satisfying lifestyles as well as a sense of independence and competence. Many husbands were unwilling to accept the changes that this implied. The working class women in the study population were most often determined to continue to make decisions about some household and children management problems, to retain the right to choose their own friends, and to decide when to visit relatives and friends. Whenever their men decided to reassert their authority as fathers and husbands, these women were likely to regard their husbands as potentially disruptive forces in their households:

> It's funny but Charles said to me the other day that "I think you have lived alone too long. You don't need a man in the house." I've learned to survive but I do need a man. I can do these things for myself and I have the house the way I like it. He says that I get in the way of his relating to the kids. When he tells them to do something and scolds them, I tend to stick up for them. I try to protect them from him when I think he's not doing it right. He says that I'm always interfering with the children and him and that I am always judging how he is doing with the kids.

As one of the women related:

> I've told him and I'll tell you. He's trying to point out my faults all the time so that he can cover up his. He's like Mr. White Gloves when he came back. He wants to make sure everything in the house is just spotless. He's become like a foreman and is always telling me what to do.

In a few cases, the issue of maintaining a new sense of independence centered around the womens' unwillingness to change the aspects of their "square jane" lifestyles. These wives were quick to point out that incarceration can and did undermine some marital relations. Those women who had lived in common-law relationships before separation, but had not conceived children, found that enforced separation had made it easier for them to move to new communities and establish satisfying life patterns. According to these women, the major issue was not whether their husbands were going to resume their old ways, but whether they themselves could continue to maintain their independence and lifestyles. Another women who is majoring in art at one of the local colleges illustrates this point:

> It's been so helpful to me to be in art school. The atmosphere there is so positive. It's such a creative and stimulating atmosphere. Since I've been in school, I began to feel better about myself and I felt stronger. I feel that I have a stronger self image and identity. Since I feel this way, I didn't want anything to interfere with my growth. Tim interfered. I would like to be in some kind of good relationship but I feel right now that men aren't really that important. I'd rather go home and draw.

Hence, they needed to be assured that their husbands were willing to pursue their wives' lifestyles and to establish more egalitarian marriages. As long as each partner could independently decide to choose their own careers and have equal opportunity in domestic decision-making, marital conflicts were minimal. In most cases, this meant continual negotiation and renegotiation of these issues.

Thus wives' accounts revealed that enforced separation actually encouraged some couples to drift apart so that wives and husbands could pursue their respective lifestyles. Reunion had become a difficult process: having developed divergent lifestyles, spouses could not fall back on old familiar marital patterns.

PAROLE SUCCESS AND PAROLEES' WIVES

The literature indicates that parole success is closely associated with strong family ties. In the early stages of re-entry, there appeared to be differences in the kinds of support the fifteen women provided for their husbands. All not only wanted to help their husbands to keep the conditions of their paroles, but to increase their motivation to settle down. Given their belief in the therapeutic effect of imprisonment, they all thought it would change their husbands for the better. Some women felt that it had encouraged the men to grow up.

Wives' Responses to Settled Husbands

The six women whose husbands adopted a more settled lifestyle claimed that they were not overly concerned about their husbands resuming criminal activities. Instead, they were preoccupied with assisting their husbands to fit into a new pattern.

A year later, not one of these men had been charged with a parole violation or arrested. Although wives of these men were sure that their husbands would stay out of trouble, they also described preventive strategies they employed to prevent any further "troubles":

> If I bring it up and ask, "Reggie what are you doing?" when he's been out, it would make him feel that I don't have any trust in him. I don't worry about it anyway. I don't ask him any questions about where he goes.

All these women also claimed that nurturing served as a preventive mechanism. To reinforce their husbands' conventional behavior, these wives attempted to build up their self-confidence, to assist them in transforming their social identities, to advise them about their character defects, and so forth. One young woman described how she nurtured her husband:

> I give him a lot of positive reinforcement about his job. Anything positive that he does, I try to recognize it. When he told me about going to see the people in Burlington, I interrogated him and he got the full inquisition and I don't let him off the hook. A lot of times he talked to me and as I quiz him, he begins to see the reasons why he got involved in something. But I'm sure all this has to do with trying to rebuild his identity.

Wives also resorted to active resistance as a strategy. All the wives repeatedly pointed out that future nonconventional behavior would result in the loss of their wives and children. Furthermore, these wives undertook at least one of several preventive actions, *e.g.*, not allowing alcohol or drugs in their homes.

Nevertheless, these wives claimed that their husbands' successful parole performance could not be ascribed to any of these strategies. Instead, they saw more important factors at play. First, these husbands had returned home more stable than they were before prison. This stability, they noted, increased their husbands' determination to avoid criminal actvities.

> I know that he won't go back to jail. He won't go intentionally, I know by the way he goes about doing things. Before he didn't

want responsibilities for me or the kids. He was young then too, he was seventeen. Now he wants to better himself right away. It's hard to explain but I know just by talking to him. Jail had done him a lot of good. Before he spent at most two months in jail and now he was in for three years. This was his first big time. His being there helped him and he saw what he was missing on the outside like his kids. It matured him. He had a lot of time to think that he could get a lot more out of life doing things the right way.

Second, some wives reported that prison had equipped their men to avoid "troubles" by providing them with vocational skills and/or educational training. Some gained insights into their drinking problems and others acquired a strong distaste for prison.

Although six men had not been returned to prison for parole violations or crimes, they did not all re-establish stable marriages. Of the six, two wives filed for divorce. According to the wives, they and their husbands had drifted apart as a consequence of the changes in lifestyles during enforced separation. Many patterns established during enforced separation no longer seemed satisfactory to one or both partners and the spouses were unable to adjust. According to these women, the major issue was not whether their husbands were going to resume their "old bags," but whether they themselves could continue to maintain their independence and lifestyles. Over the months since reunion, they had grown increasingly distant from each other. Further, these wives had become increasingly indifferent to whether or not their husbands performed successfully while on parole; their own sense of independence had assumed priority over supporting their husbands.

Wives' Responses to Husbands' Fast Living and Crime

During imprisonment, dreams and promises served as a vehicle for sustaining wives' commitments to their husbands. On release, many wives realized that their husbands were becoming increasingly preoccupied with fast living which they believed to foreshadow criminal involvement. During re-entry, most wives reported that these dreams and promises became tarnished, but, nevertheless, remained a vital mechanism they utilized to reinforce their beliefs in the permanence of their marriages.

In order to maintain these dreams, wives once again employed accommodative strategies designed to divert their husbands away from deviant behavior.

Nine wives had not changed their interpretations of their husbands' criminal activities throughout the stages of the criminalization process. At each stage they were preoccupied with convincing themselves—and perhaps others—that their husbands' behavior could be attributed to external or situational factors. They emphasized that such outside factors as alcohol, environmental forces, family crises, and so forth—alone or together with internal forces such as character flaws—were to blame for their husbands' deviations from proper patterns of behavior. To prevent troubles with the law, the wives frantically searched for some kind of effective strategy. They often tried several. As time went on, wives were less and less likely to respond to their husbands' fast living and criminal behavior with nurturing. In general, old timers were less likely than neophytes to nurture their husbands. When wives engaged in nurturing, it was usually to avoid physical battering, to deal with husbands who were drunk, to deal with the resumption of sexually deviant behavior, and so forth. "Nurturing," in this sense, took the form of providing emotional support, listening attentively to husbands, as well as attempting to strengthen their self-confidence. For instance, one wife describes how she attempted to build up her husband's self-confidence to deter him from further sexual crimes:

> I've got to build his confidence up. He has to feel good about what he's doing. I want him to feel good about masturbating. As soon as he masturbates, he feels guilty and dirty and that keeps him further from me. When we're making love, during the foreplay, I've taken to feeling him and then having him touch himself and I try to make him feel good about touching himself.

Nurturing was generally ineffective in breaking the cycle of arrest, courts, and prison. When wives tried nurturing and found it ineffective, the majority once again turned to active resistance as a strategy. Since all the wives had had experience with their husbands' fast living and criminal enterprise prior to prison, they knew what to expect and acted accordingly. They quickly took control of the family income, hid money, and refused outright to give money to their husbands. For instance, one neophyte explained her reasons for hiding the household money from her husband:

> I got pissed last night and I took all the money in the house and hid it. I hid it because he wanted the money so that he could buy some pot. He knew I needed some things for the house. I have a checking account but he found the money and took it. He's going to share the account. All we need to get is the signature card. He wants to blow the money on pot three or four times a week. I spend $100 or more on food with the food stamps and whatever I have left has to go on other items. He bitches and sneers if I buy some socks for myself. We can't afford movies but we can afford to buy pot.

Wives also report that they attempted to keep track of their husbands' activities outside their homes and the kinds of friends with whom they hung out:

> He either has to do what I ask him to do or I do a lot of yelling or bitching. He doesn't want to hear my yelling and bitching and so he doesn't have a choice. He does it like I want him to do. I also scare him. If he couldn't see the kids, that scares him. I tell him that he wouldn't see those kids himself. He's isolated himself from the people who could get him into trouble. Lately he's been going to his family more because his grandfather is ill in the hospital. I don't like his going but I try to control his visits. He also goes to this guy Doc's house. I don't know him and that's my problem. More or less, I try to meet the guys he hangs with. I go to their homes, try to see their angles, and I try to find out who goes to their house. I want to see where they are at. I do it because I've been hurt too many times now. It's a precaution that I take now. I want to make sure that he's not with another girl. I want to make sure that the people he's with won't get him into trouble.

Some reverted to hiding the car keys or the car's spare tires. A few wives nagged their husbands about maintaining contact with their parole officers. One wife even pinned the parole regulations on the wall so that her husband could continually see them. An old timer described why she actively resisted:

> I just won't stand for Rudi to be drunk. I feel good about that. Since he's been home, he's been drunk twice. And he always has an

excuse for being drunk. I don't take it. I blow up. He came home drunk and he gave me a lot of crap. I told him to suffer. I said, "Just suffer!" We went to court about my daughter and after court he went out and celebrated. When he got home, I told him to suffer. And then I gave him some Di-Gel and he got terribly sick. He suffered.

Frustrated and fearful, these wives argued with their husbands in the hope that this strategy would change their behavior. Arguments centered around their husbands' failure to provide satisfactory incomes and around their inability to fulfill their dreams for a conventional lifestyle.[9] Marital conflicts also erupted around the wives' fears that their husbands would return to prison. Accordingly, they were more likely to escalate their demands as time went on. Their increasing frustrations were often expressed in angry outbursts and statements that came as a surprise to their husbands:

A lot of us assume this mother figure position with our men. We keep telling them all the things they can't do because they could get in trouble. We get so uptight over what they do and so fearful that they are going to get back into trouble again that we end up nagging them about all the things they shouldn't be doing. So to them it feels like they're still in prison because they have someone else who is telling them continually. And the more you tell them what to do, the more they rebel.

In some cases, the more argumentative the women became, the more their husbands got into fast living and crime. Seven wives considered informing parole officers about their husbands' violations. Two were afraid to do so. Four actually did. They thought that parole officers could relieve them of some responsibility for their husbands' behavior and also control their husbands to the point where they could not get rearrested. Initially two old timers attempted to abide by the prison code of "no snitching." But once their husbands' behavior began to interfere with their roles as mothers, they used parole officers as a last resort:

BEA. Rudi was drinking heavily the last time, when I had to take care of my mother. He started drinking and going around with these floozies [women]. But if I ever said anything to the authorities, I'd get killed. I come from the old school. Your lady don't ever rat on you.

ARLENE. I come from the old school too. You young women don't
know about these things. But that one time, I just feel that I had to
get him some help and St. James was the best place for him.

These wives reported that parole officers did not respond as
they expected. Many wives complained that parole officers were
indifferent to their situations and did not even attempt to pressure their husbands into changing their behavior. None of the
men involved returned to prison for parole violations. As one
old timer said of parole officers:

Some I've had no contact with at all, and others weren't worth the
power to blow them to hell. One parole officer had me report in
for Frank if Frank didn't feel like it. Once Frank was gone for two
months and the guy didn't know it as long as I kept reporting for
Frank.
    They'd say, "How is he doing, is he drinking? No? That's
good, see you next month." I get sick of trying to deal with them.
A lot of times I asked them for help. Before I had Frank committed, I called to have it put in a stipulation that Frank has to go to
AA or get in some kind of an alcoholic program. They say, "Yup,
yup" and I never hear anything more about it. Anybody in the corrections or probation and parole, if the wife calls and says she's
having problems, thinks she doesn't want her husband around.
They just don't do anything. They think that when the wife calls
for help she can see problems starting and she wants them to stop,
but they take the attitude that she just doesn't want them in the
house and that's it.

In only one instance did an officer put pressure on a man to
abide by parole rules and regulations. Only one husband was
charged with parole violation. From wives' accounts, it appeared
that parole officers were more likely to respond when an event
had blown up than they were before this had happened. In one
instance, the wife, whose marriage has been conflict-ridden, described how she and her husband argued at a night spot. The
husband, quite drunk, damaged his wife's car when she attempted to leave. While staying at a friend's home, her husband
called her to inform her that he was destroying their home. She
promptly called the police. Later, he called her again:

I got on the phone and he told me to get my ass home. I said,
"Where are you?" He said, "I'm at your house." I told him that I

was afraid of him and that I wasn't going near him. He told me to come home or he'd kill me. I told him not to come here. Then I heard all this crashing and he came back to the phone and said, "There goes your stereo, you'd better come home." Then he changed his tune and started pleading, "Please come home." And he kept going back and forth like that: from violent to pleading. He wouldn't hang up the phone. I could hear all the noise and crashing. Then he picked up the phone again and said, "Are you coming home now? I'm making a nice wreck here!" Then he said, "OK, I'm gonna kill myself!" And he hung up. I called my neighbor Bruce, and asked him to check on Tim for me. He said he would but then he came back and said that he wouldn't go in there with a ten-foot pole with all that noise. It was then I called the police.

The parole agency recommended that this man's parole be cancelled and that he be sent back to prison. His wife filed for divorce.

Separating from their husbands was not a new strategy for most wives. Flight was one seemingly logical way to control what they perceived as their husbands' failure to fulfill their expectations. All these wives had tried separation; sometimes more than once. However, they had usually returned to their husbands within a few weeks.

Separation served several functions for wives. First, it appeared to be a way out of the cycle of arrest, courts, and prisons. Second, they thought that separation might teach their husbands the value of family life, and therefore encourage them to renew their commitments to the dream of settling down. Finally, it was used to make a strong statement that the wives would no longer tolerate their husbands' behavior.

Enforced separation contributed to wives' ability to initiate separations. During their husbands' imprisonment, they saw how manageable life could be without them. This encouraged wives to believe that their husbands were "luxuries" they could no longer afford:

I have my own furniture and I still have welfare. I don't need no guy. I can live without a guy. It doesn't bother me any more. Him being in jail so long. He's been in and out of jail these seven years. I'm used to living without a guy.

All these ways of actively resisting usually brought some relief. But they also yielded only temporary results. For a period of time, household money was more effectively controlled. For varying periods, husbands were reminded that they could be returned to prison for parole violations. Some stopped their "troublesome" activities. Yet the costs of actively resisting were high. When wives employed this strategy, their husbands became increasingly resentful, further alienated from their wives, and eventually resumed criminal and fast-living activities.

When their husbands did this, five wives then reverted to another familiar strategy: passive distance. By withdrawing into silence, these wives avoided arguments that could lead to violence. However, in assuming this coping strategy, they once again encountered their husbands from a position of perceived powerlessness:

> Mostly, I keep my mouth shut. And I'm not a person to keep my mouth shut. He comes and goes as he wants. When he is home, we sit here at night and we don't talk. I'm doing this for the kids. I don't want the kids without a father. I was brought up without a father.

Once the wives employed this strategy, they had given up any responsibility for their husbands' actions; as far as they were concerned, their husbands were out of control.

One of the least frequently employed strategies was co-participation. To preserve her marriage, one woman resumed the pattern prior to her husband's arrest: drinking heavily with him, and issuing bogus checks to raise money for alcohol and drugs. Co-participation allowed this wife, once again, to normalize her husband's behavior by joining him in his marginal status. Finally, one wife hoped to deter her husband from participating in criminal activities by independently initiating her own. This woman talked about her reasons for shoplifting:

> I've started shoplifting for Rex. I started because he made these promises. We needed money to go to Virginia. And I was buying his life for me. Men have this incredible way of manipulating their women to get money. These are welfare women and they have to take money from them. I have gone without so that he could have what he wanted.

I was afraid he'd go back to doing B & E's since he got out of jail. But then again, why should he? I was handing him enough money every week. I could average $200 a week from stealing cigarettes, plus the welfare check and food stamps. I handed everything to him. In the month of January I made over $1,000 in cigarettes.

But I did these things for love. I stole for love or what I thought was love.

Wives' Reactions to Re-Arrest

Re-arrest therefore came as no surprise to the wives involved. Of the nine husbands who gravitated towards fast living and criminal activities, seven were arrested again. Five of these husbands had subsequently been imprisoned, while two had charges dropped. All these men and their wives were old timers, except for one neophyte who was instrumental in having her husband's parole revoked.

Although their husbands' arrests were generally anticipated, these seven wives faced them with mixed emotions. The feelings of grief and sadness at involuntary separation were similar to the kind of grieving these wives experienced during previous arrests. At the same time, their husbands' arrests were also welcomed with relief, anger, and resentment.

Wives' accounts provided several reasons why their husbands' arrests would be greeted with some degree of relief. First, wives perceived that arrest would break the cycle of alcohol and drug abuse, battering, and irresponsible behavior and might return their families to some degree of economic solvency. Their husbands' return to prison was felt to remove what had become a destructive force within their households. Re-arrest appeared to be functional. On the one hand, husbands were no longer being reminded that they had failed to achieve their dreams and promises. On the other, wives gained some relief from having to deal with their husbands.

Second, seven wives indicated that, prior to re-arrest, their husbands had begun to lead somewhat segregated lives, *i.e.*, their husbands began pursuing fast living while the wives remained caught up in child care and other domestic concerns. Their husbands' arrests and imprisonment brought with them the satisfaction that they and their husbands, could, once again, have a *common interest*. They had previously discovered that the criminalization process became one of the few major ongoing events which they could share with their husbands. With re-arrest, they could, once again, share their husbands' passage through the criminal justice system, shape future plans, and renew faith in their marriages. The new sentence and incarceration served as a welcome reprieve from having to assess how realistic their dreams were and how likely it was that their husbands would change.

Three old timers also reacted with relief, but for somewhat different reasons. These wives epitomized the service wife syndrome: they had discovered that they were uncomfortable in their roles as wives whenever their husbands were in their households.[10] They reported that their husbands' presence interfered with their performing their roles as wives to their satisfaction. For these women, their husbands' arrests came at an opportune time. They were ready to resume, once again, their lives as independent wives with all the privileges of having absent husbands, but with few responsibilities to them. Enforced separation would allow them to reduce friction in their marriages. Marital relations were reported as more satisfying. They were more likely to enjoy their husbands and feel closer to them once they were at a confortable distance:

> I don't have a hassle and no one to answer to except myself when he's in jail. I feel like a martyr. I enjoy it. [When he's out] I'm still a martyr. But I'm not as happy a martyr as when he's inside. When he's out, I can't seem to control anything and usually I can control anything. He's a sleeping partner—my stud service. That's about it. It's true that I get greater payoffs when he's in than when he's out.

As with this wife, two other old timers also reported that imprisonment provided them with the opportunity to resume some satisfying patterns. First, their husbands' imprisonment provided them with a chance to "get out socially" by visiting their husbands at prison, and once again see old acquaintances, both prisoners and their wives. Further, they could once again "serve time" which, for them, was a pleasant, although somewhat annoying experience. They now had a goal which they could reach with some degree of satisfaction: they could begin, again, to control their own lives, mark off days of having lived alone successfully, and gained some satisfaction from their ability to visit their husbands faithfully. This old timer's statement clearly illustrates this point:

> I'm used to doing time. I'm the sole support of my daughter and myself and when he's in jail, I can go and make my weekly visits and pat him on the back and say, "Poor Frank, poor little Frank." I can be the devoted, long-suffering wife again. I never had to give him my money when he was in jail. He took good care of me when he was in jail. He sent me about $200 a week. He sold dope and ran the numbers. He always had some scheme going. He only kept $5 for himself and always sent the rest home. He always got a scam going.

They derived, in the final analysis, satisfaction from observing their husbands' progress within the prison community, *e.g.*, the number of prison activities in which their husbands participated, their husbands' movement from one classification level to another, etc. When these men were on the outside, their reintegration into society was fraught with failure, *e.g.*, the struggle to survive financially, drinking, and bickering with their wives. Prison offered these wives, as well as their husbands, an opportunity to forget struggle. For instance, one old timer commented about her husband's progress:

> The biggest thing for me is that he's taking anti-bus and joining programs. In the past he'd say that he doesn't need them. Before the stipulations were given, he told me he'd try anything to be able to stay on the streets. He never said that before. It came from him and I didn't put it in his mouth or anything.

Despite these "benefits," all seven wives reacted with anger and resentment when they learned about their husbands' re-arrests. In some cases husbands' departures from conventional lifestyles significantly eroded wives' support and ultimately led them to consider divorce. Previous separations and reconciliations had encouraged many wives to establish their own lives. These wives were not sure that their marriages were going to last. However, they were accustomed to separation and more sure after re-arrest that they could establish satisfying lives for themselves once their husbands were removed from the scene. Only one woman, who had reported her husband's violations to his parole officer, did initiate divorce proceedings. She had relegated her man to a status of "differentness," and saw him as incapable of changing because of his inherent character flaws. To minimize her husband's potentially disruptive influence on her own life, she divorced him. Of seven wives, only this neophyte actually carried through.

No matter how many separations and reconciliations occurred, and no matter how many times the men had gone through the criminalization process, old timers struggled to remain committed to their men. According to them, they had no security other than what they could obtain through a permanent "love relationship." Reconciliations were, therefore, primarily based on the notion that they really loved their men, and that "this time" was going to be different:

> I feel lonesome. But I know that I can make it on my own. I have done it when he was in jail . . . I'm hoping we can work out our problems and that he comes home and gets a job. That's what I'm hoping for. I even hope that some day we can own our own house.

The wives also mentioned that they were determined to remain in what they considered to be not-so-satisfactory marriages for the sake of their children. This motivation was, perhaps, understandable since these wives had often been deprived of one of their own parents due to death, divorce, or desertion. Thus, wives' accounts agree that prison marriages were remarkably resistant to such crisis-provoking events as re-arrest and reincarceration. Of fifteen women, only two filed for divorce. Although their marriages were fraught with difficulties, and although their men repeated the cycle of crime, arrest, and imprisonment, most of these prisoners' wives remained committed to their men and their marriages endured.

CHAPTER X

The World of Prisoners' Wives: Conclusions

I get so mad when I look at how the TV stereotypes prisoners' wives. These movies that were done in the fifties really make me mad. They show the wives as playing one guy against another guy. They show the wives as either cheats or as illiterates who are browbeaten and cringe from their husbands. You never see the woman who makes it even though her husband is in prison. They're shown as either know-nothings or tramps. Every time I watch I get angry inside.

—A Prisoner's Wife.

Male criminality is a vital issue with which prisoners' wives struggle at home, with their children and parents, and in their communities. Wives must enter into painful interpersonal negotiations about what is or is not acceptable about their husbands' behavior. The purpose of these negotiations is to limit opportunities for encountering stigmatization and to normalize both their husbands and themselves.

Earlier research on wives of alcoholics and batterers has shown that wives are likely to hold a traditional view toward their roles as wives and mothers.[1] What has been learned about prisoners' wives fits well with what is known about "traditional" women who endure their marriages no matter how unsatisfactory they may be. They readily accept its permanence, the view that a "woman's place is in the home," that men ought to be the breadwinners, and the belief that males ought to be heads of their households. Their marital expectations are similar to those of the women from similar social backgrounds: stable, conventional lifestyles. They want their husbands to work. They want material goods. They want companionship. Unfortunately, neither they nor their husbands have, as a rule, the kinds of skills that would enable them to pursue this kind of conventional lifestyle. Instead, they often find themselves living fast; fast living provides men with a means of avoiding the pressures and difficulties involved in settling down.

To cope with this contradiction, wives expected that through love and forbearance, they would be able to induce their men to settle down to a traditional and conventional lifestyle. In this context, accommodations served as attempts to normalize their husbands' behavior and prevent their getting into trouble with the law as well as to integrate their husbands into their households. Similar to spouses of prospective mental patients,[2] these wives were reluctant to contact the police or social agencies even though they found their husbands' behavior intolerable. Instead, the majority of women believed that their husbands would get arrested eventually and anxiously awaited this event.

What is particularly interesting here is that, almost universally, it is *women* who must cope with *men's* problems. Throughout their lives, these women have been faced with difficulties arising from male criminality. These problems do not end when husbands are incarcerated. They do not simply vanish when the men disappear behind prison walls. Husbands continue to have a significant impact on their wives' daily lives which is as important as that generated by dramatic encounters with police, courts, and prisons. Prisoners' wives are not simply "separated" from their husbands—although they share similarities with others facing "crises of separation." They must also continually deal with the problems of minimizing opportunities for stigmatization, particularly in prison towns and in the various prisons. Old timers also often face hostility from their families, who feel betrayed by husbands' histories of imprisonment.

The accommodative strategies these wives adopt are those suggested by their own backgrounds and social groups. While the social pressures with which prisoners' wives must cope depend, in some measure, on whether or not they live in crime-tolerant communities, all wives have a sense that they are "different" from those around them. It is this sense of differentness that underlies their stance toward the larger social world and toward the criminalization process.

THE LARGER CONTEXT

Domestic Life and Arrest: Interpretations of Male Criminality

It is known that families' interpretations of a deviant member's behavior frequently changes in response to changing situations. Similarly, wives' definitions of male criminality are often altered in the face of their husbands' gravitation toward criminal activities, arrest, imprisonment, and release.

During courtship, many women raised the issue of their husbands' stigmatized status. To solidify their intent to marry them, the women who later became prisoners' wives devised various apologia that rendered their potential husbands not fully responsible for their criminal activities; either they disavowed this criminality, (*e.g.*, "It's the man who counts and not his criminal record."), or they devised "sad tales" that conveyed an image of their men as pathetic and in need of being rescued, or they avowed their husbands' behavior, and thus presented their criminal activities as non-threatening.

Wives' accounts reveal that their responses to male criminality were not unique. There is an increasing body of literature that describes the kinds of reactions wives formulate toward husbands who pursue some deviant lifestyle. The findings reported here are consistent with rationalizations devised by wives of alcoholics, mentally ill, and physically abusive husbands.[3] After marriage to these men, a distinct pattern emerged. Most wives continued to delay assigning a criminal label to their husbands. Unlike courtship, however, these post-marriage interpretations more often centered around placing blame on such "outside" forces as alcoholism, environmental factors and significant others. Other interpretations located the source of blame within their husbands' characters, *e.g.*, immaturity. Many wives searched for the causes of their husbands' criminality within themselves, feeling that, somehow, they were inadequate as wives and women.

Similarly, wives' definitions of male criminality were often altered in the face of their husbands' arrest. Through the telling of sad tales, these wives ascribed blame to a variety of external circumstances (often extraordinary situations, seen as unlikely to recur) and sometimes assumed blame themselves in order to absolve their husbands of responsibility for criminal acts. Moreover, once their husbands were arrested, most wives still did not concur in assigning criminal labels, such as "accused offender," to them. The evidence presented here clearly indicates that a "vocabulary of motives" serves to perpetuate an image of their men as basically conventional or normal. Such interpretations allowed women to continue to interact with their husbands without their husbands' criminal behavior and status as accused offenders becoming a vital factor in future marital relations.

Of significance here is the finding that, as traditional women, prisoners' wives believe that, through love and marriage, their husbands can change and it is up to them to support them so that desirable changes will take place. It is also interesting to note that some wives persist in these visions throughout their marriages and the events which surround arrest. Hence they employ definitions which suggest that their men's criminality is not permanent, and not centrally important. With encouragement from their husbands, most wives manage to reinforce their beliefs that change is imminent. As traditionalists, wives view marriage as a career and believe that they are somehow responsible for the criminal acts perpetuated by their husbands. This serves to reinforce their determination to maintain conjugal relationships despite unemployment, fast living, criminal activities, arrest, and re-arrest.

Domestic Life, Arrest, and Re-Entry: Accommodation Patterns

The accommodative strategies employed by wives also change in response to such changing situations as: (1) their husbands' gravitation into criminal activities and fast-living lifestyle patterns as well as; (2) their encounters with two specific stages of the criminalization process, prior to arrest and re-entry. During their marriages many wives attempted to understand and cope with their husbands fast-living and criminal escapades. They devised a succession of accommodative strategies directed at changing or ameliorating the situations they faced so that they could remain married to men who were less able to perform conventional roles than they had expected. Wives usually oscillated between nurturing their men and taking more assertive and punitive actions. When these strategies proved futile, many wives then shifted toward passive distance.

By employing accommodative strategies, wives hoped to pressure their husbands to cease their illegal activities, but these strategies were seldom effective in deterring the husbands' deviant behavior. This is consistent with previous research.[4] At best, wives were able to achieve a momentary attenuation of some of the fast-living or criminal activity they found most difficult to cope with. The majority experienced an overwhelming sense of powerlessness as a result of trying to deal with their husbands during this stage in their lives. Linked to this was a sense of inevitability about their husbands "getting into trouble with the law." This undermined the effectiveness of the strategies adopted, and made the task of steering the men away from criminal acts and fast living—and thereby preserving their marriages—even more difficult than it might have been.

Several studies have indicated that post-prison success is associated with marital harmony.[5] The wives' accounts related here suggest two significant factors that contribute to marital discord: the task of household reorganization and the accommodative strategies adapted by wives. After their husbands' release from prison, reorganization was seen by the wives as essential for establishing conventionally oriented lives. Couples undertook reorganization either by settling down or by resuming fast-living lifestyles with criminal activities.

Most women expected their husbands to establish conventional lifestyles after their release. Within seven months, nine of the fifteen men were unemployed and gravitating back toward their pre-prison patterns: fast living and crime. Wives quickly moved toward the active resistance accommodative pattern to deter their husbands from further fast living and crime, and to encourage them to reintegrate into their households. Arguments most likely between spouses whenever wives used this strategy.

In contrast, some wives reported that their households had been reorganized on the basis of conventional patterns of living. Their husbands were steadily employed or highly motivated to find work and they conformed rigorously to a conventional lifestyle. There was wifely support for settling down. To reinforce their husbands' conventional behavior, these wives nurtured their husbands and refrained from criticism or threats.

It is interesting to note that wives did not appear to have much influence on whether or not their husbands participated in criminal behavior, got arrested, or went to jail. In fact, it appears that there is an important, unintended consequence of the active resistance strategy. Wives actively resisted *in order* to deter their men from elements of fast living and crime. While criminal and fast-living lifestyles are characterized by conflict-ridden marriages, in many cases these troublesome behavior patterns precipitated such conflict, rather than the reverse. Marital conflict, in turn, encouraged further norm-violating activity by husbands.

Prior to their husbands' release from prison, the majority of wives expected that their husbands' criminal activity was a "thing of the past" and that they were ready to settle down, obtain jobs, and provide adequate incomes to support their wives and children. Re-entry, however, presented wives with some difficulties in establishing stable and conventional lifestyles. It is important to note that the problems encountered by prisoners' wives, almost universally, are reported as stemming from their husbands' failures to establish conventional lifestyles for themselves. Given this, their husbands' unemployment was most worrisome for the women. When unemployment was combined with such elements of fast living as financial irresponsibility, drinking and drug habits, physical assaults and crime, there was cause for the women to be alarmed. These failures on the part of their husbands were seen by the wives as a threat to the conventional lives that they generally established for themselves during imprisonment. Upon perceiving their husbands gravitating back to their "old tricks," all these women were afraid that their husbands would return to prison. These findings are consistent with observations that unemployment is a crucial issue in parolees' post-prison performance[6] and further show that unemployment is also a crucial issue for wives of parolees.

It is interesting to note that many wives' lifestyles shifted dramatically from fast to conventional living in response to the presence or absence of their husbands. These findings confirm Howell's (1973) observation that life events can cause shifts in working class lifestyles. However, a theme emerges from wives' accounts to which Howell (1973) has only alluded: the majority of working-class wives longed to be able to live traditional lives. Their failure to do so stemmed partly from the fact that conventional norms prescribe ways of living that did not fit their circumstances. The major factor that kept them from achieving their desired lifestyles was a lack of opportunities for the development of marketable skills, and the acquisition of significant amounts of capital.

Arrest, Sentencing, and Courts

Wives were often called upon by their husbands to play new and unaccustomed roles, *e.g.*, acting as emissaries to lawyers, visiting their husbands in jail, responding to inquiries about their husbands' situations, and attending court sessions. Most wives knew that their husbands were guilty and expected them to be sentenced and incarcerated. As with male defendants,[7] these wives were more concerned with penalties than issues of justice. However, wives' views of penalties were unique to their position as wives of offenders. As they viewed it, penalties determined time separated from husbands and time coping with a frightening and unknown future. Wives generally reported that they did not want absentee husbands nor did they want to manage on their own. Within this context, wives wanted court personnel to take their fears and anxieties about being on their own into consideration upon determining their husbands' sentences. Anger and resentment about their husbands' sentences were related to their belief that no one agonized about their predicament as wives of the accused.

As did the defendants in Casper's (1970) research study, these wives reported that their husbands (as well as themselves) were treated as objects by court personnel whom they perceived to be more concerned with keeping the assembly line operating than with providing individualized attention. Wives wanted individualized justice; that is, they expected both the court system and the judges to pay attention to their men as individuals and, therefore, take their social backgrounds, the circumstances of the crimes, marital histories, etc., into consideration.

The results here further suggest that the wives wanted some authority figures—whether it be lawyers, prosecutors, or judges— to care about them and to address some of their needs. Most wives come to court not particularly satisfied with the kinds of lives their husbands lived or the content of the crimes their husbands committed. Wives wanted someone to consider why their husbands had engaged in criminal activities and to recommend some form of treatment that would enable their husbands to engage in conventional behavior. Finally, they wanted someone to care about them and thus consider the impact of sentencing on their own and their children's lives.

Living Alone

Whether men are voluntarily or involuntarily separated from their families, their wives find that they must adjust to their husbands' physical absence. In order to make this adjustment successfully, wives must be willing to shift roles and take up many of their husbands' responsibilities. They must often also maintain their husbands' place in the family circle by correspondence, telephone calls, and visiting. Within this context, prisoners' wives must therefore be able to gain a measure of independence in making decisions. While enforced separation engenders hardships, it also seems to provide its own unique opportunities for women to begin playing a larger role in directing their own lives.

While most women experienced problems typical of those faced with enforced separation (social, emotional, and sexual deprivation, financial difficulties, and child management), a significant number also reported difficulty coming to terms with the prospective duration of the separation and a feeling of being, themselves, imprisoned. Although not widely discussed in the literature, this phenomenon is reminiscent of Swan's (1981) concept of "transfer of punishment." While some wives might have identified with their husbands' situations or felt that they themselves, were being punished, it is also likely that some, in effect, created their own prisons by putting their lives "on hold" until their husbands could return.

Stigmatization and Feelings of Shame

The stages in the criminalization process—from arrest, to sentencing, incarceration and release—set up a series of changes in the roles these wives found themselves enacting: "wives of accused," "prisoners' wives," and finally "wives of ex-convicts." The current literature has primarily documented the extent to which stigma is displaced to wives enacting roles of "wives of accused" and of prisoners. It has been assumed that whenever wives fill these roles they become stigmatized unless they live in crime-familiar communities. The present study supports earlier research findings that wives who reside in crime-familiar communities do not appear to encounter stigmatizing situations.[8] However, the wives in this study reported numerous stigmatizing situations when they lived in prison towns.

These results suggest that at the time of their husbands' arrest and initial incarceration, shame and stigmatization were not central but rather situational issues in wives' lives. They were more likely to worry about the possibility of stigmatization within their communities than actually to experience it. Feelings of shame appeared to dissipate quite rapidly, since these women had more pressing concerns to handle (*e.g.*, their husbands' legal affairs, their own lives, their households, and their children).

Wives' perceptions of stigmatization when dealing with the prison systems were found to be of crucial importance. Their accounts revealed that the extent to which they felt shamed and discredited varied with the kinds of house rules prisons established for visiting. Responses of prison guards were perceived to be stigmatizing by most wives.

The findings presented here, therefore, extend Goffman's (1961) observation that, upon admission to a total institution, inmates are subjected to a series of abasements, degradations, humiliations, and profanations of their selves. Wives, too, are subjected to mortification by such contaminative exposure as forced interpersonal contact with other prisoners' wives, searching of their possesions, strip searches, closely supervised visits, and so forth. Their self-respect was assaulted whenever they interacted with prison guards who categorized wives as "the good wife" or as "the whore," and who discriminated among them on this basis, making derogatory statements, or treating them in a disrespectful manner. House rules for visiting and the treatment by prison staff were perceived as ever-present reminders that wives shared their husbands' stigmatized status.

The findings add to a growing literature that argues that imprisonment of husbands had deleterious effects on the wives. On the basis of the present study, it is concluded that prison policies believed functional for the institution can have dysfunctional consequences for prisoners' wives. Specific prison policies can set the wives up for encounters that they find extremely distasteful. For instance, the policy permitting prisoners to visit and maintain contacts with their wives includes "house" rules for visiting that restrict the women's behavior. The wives claimed that these rules and regulations created situations in which they felt personally diminished. Even the policy permitting prisoners to have "legal goods" made wives vulnerable to stigmatizing and punitive encounters with prison personnel.

Wives came to believe that they were treated as criminals and punished for wanting to see their husbands in order to reaffirm their marital ties. If one can assume that visits serve to preserve prisoners' marital ties, then those security measures that include demeaning or degrading actions should be closely examined. Such security measures do not, according to many wives, encourage families to maintain close ties but inadvertently work against the family keeping close contact with its imprisoned member.

Although stigmatization was not central to their lives, wives attempted to insulate themselves from it by controlling information about their husbands' situation, by employing accommodative strategies to reduce its effects or turn them aside, and by participating in a normal round of life. Wives also actively avoided labelling themselves as "wives of accuseds" and "wives of prisoners." They had a stake in maintaining their identities as "normal" in order to sustain their relations with others and to reinforce their own notions that they are "ordinary" wives and mothers. Participating in a conventional lifestyle not only provided a sense of normalcy, but allowed them to resist stigmatization. Other wives resisted the application of stigmatizing labels by simply terminating their affiliation with their officially-labeled husbands and dropping out completely. Those not committed to being prisoners' wives resisted learning how to make the psychic adjustments needed to perform this role.

Larger Impact of Prison on Wives' Lives

Recent research suggests that prison systems may not be as closed as previously assumed. Many studies have specifically focused on the extent to which prisoners are able to maintain relationships with their families on the outside. Some attention, although fragmentary, has been given to the kinds of contacts that prisoners maintain with their wives.

The findings presented here, however, elaborate upon these earlier research findings. The present research has specifically examined the role played by patterns of interaction—such as courtship, business arrangements, sharing household decisions, and performing personal services—during prison visiting. For instance, prison romances and renewed courtships flourished as a result of prison policies allowing women to perform personal services for their men and to deliver approved material goods and/or contraband to them. Both forms of interaction provided the husbands with opportunities to enact dominant roles, while the women could defer. These accounts also revealed that these same patterns of interaction could produce their own stresses and strains. Courting could erupt into arguments revolving around husbands' jealousies and anxieties about their wives' infidelity or their decision to limit the supply of contraband or other goods they delivered to the prison.

Several investigators have suggested that maintaining family ties contributes positively to successful rehabilitation.[9] Accordingly, many prison systems have established visiting policies that encourage ties with family and friends. However, the findings reported here suggest that interactions between inmates and their wives are perhaps not optimal. Constant surveillance and frequent disruptions may inhibit all but superficial communication. Also, these interactional patterns recounted by the wives suggest that an air of idealistic romanticism pervades these visits. Conversations rarely included realistic appraisals and plans for the future.

The wives also had considerable contact with their husbands through telephone conversations and home visits, modes of communication that substantially alleviated some of the difficulties associated with separation. While telephone conversations often strengthened marital ties, home visits even more dramatically improved family morale, since they were intensely and almost entirely pleasurable. In particular, they served to promote feelings of well-being for both husbands and wives, reinforcing marital and family commitments. Telephone calls and visitation further provided the wives with a respite from their own sense of imprisonment.

Despite the obvious benefits of such communication, it should not be overlooked that, more often than not, men used telephone contacts to place restrictions on their wives, to make demands and to maintain their authority and dominance. Also, a significant proportion of these men used the telephone to check up, periodically and unpredictably, on their wives' activities. In response, the wives reported that they had no lives of their own and were forced to create "prisons" for themselves.

It should also be noted that, despite the several positive aspects of home visits, these furloughs did not appear to accomplish their intended function as dress rehearsals for later reintroduction into the community, with its attendant duties and responsibilities. On the contrary, husbands were carefully shielded, by their wives, from domestic pressures, stresses, demands, and responsibilities. Moreover, the nature of such visits might well have perpetrated idealized or unrealistic expectations of how life together would be in the future.

The current literature indicates that prisoners' attitudinal and behavioral changes are more closely related to men's adaption to the prison environment than to how they perform once they have been released.[10] It is significant that the wives believed that their husbands had undergone sufficient attitudinal and behavioral changes to be released and to lead conventional lives. Prison visiting was a time when the wives searched for clues indicating significant behavioral and attitudinal change. The findings suggest that prison, an institution that emphasizes punishment, unintentionally encourages men to be contrite and repentant, to make promises never to get into trouble again and to make future plans with their wives for release and renewal. In turn, most wives believe that these promises are viable, unaware that they have been made in response to prison life, and not as a consequence of a realistic appraisal of what the men could achieve later. Certainly, the fact of imprisonment makes it impossible for husbands to engage in criminal activities which had been the root of many domestic quarrels on the outside. In the absence of such conflict-producing episodes, it makes sense that relations between the spouses would be less strained and that wives would be more willing to believe that their husbands had reformed. However, the reports of wives whose husbands had been imprisoned previously (old timers) make it clear that such perceptions were frequently naive or idealistic. Old timers were far less likely than neophytes to believe that their husbands had truly reformed and would lead conventional lives upon their release.

Male Criminality, Involuntary Separation, and Poverty

In many respects, the experiences these prisoners' wives encountered during involuntary separation parallel those of single mothers who live at the edge of subsistence. Prisoners' wives share many experiences with women whose husbands are absent due to separation, desertion, divorce, and so forth.[11] The women interviewed recounted numerous problems centered around finances, loneliness, anxiety and stress, stigmatization, and child management. Rather than feeling "liberated," they were emotionally and socially isolated, as well as overloaded with demands on their time and energy.

Some wives also derived real benefits from their husbands' imprisonment. These women mentioned release from marital disruptions and its impact on their roles as wives and mothers, feelings of a sense of personal autonomy, increased control over their lives, household finances, and children. Many reported that they felt increasingly competent to cope, as wives and mothers, with difficult circumstances.

Most wives revealed that financial insecurity and hardships were not unfamiliar to them. Most did not experience a drop into poverty upon their husbands' removal from their households, although this phenomenon was reported by square janes. Rather, most of the wives had lived at the edge of subsistence during their growing years and their marriages simply meant a continuation of persistent financial hardships. Within this segment of the population of poor, single mothers, transition in family status (*i.e.*, their husbands' enforced separation from their households) appeared to have little bearing on their continuing impoverishment. The observation that a fundamental cause of poverty among female-headed households is due to familial changes (*e.g.*, divorce, widowhood, etc.) perhaps is more relevant for middle-income white women than lower-income white women.[12]

The literature on the poverty of women offers a related and important factor to explain the increasing poverty among female-headed households: the male flight from responsibility. Ehrenrich (1983) claims that the majority of men who are not living with their wives and children have abdicated their familial responsibilities. Study upon study[13] reveal that most divorced men neither financially support nor directly care for their children after separation or divorce. There is little doubt that this analysis of women and poverty is valid, but it is not the whole story. Although Ehrenrich and others speak of the males' abdication of family responsibility after divorce, the present research suggests that this abdication, for at least this segment of the American population, occurs during the early years of marriage.

According to wives' accounts, their husbands' pursuit of a fast-living lifestyle and criminal escapades can be equated with an abdication of familial responsibility. They also reported that prior to arrest and imprisonment their men further abdicated their responsibility by being unemployed or intermittently employed and thus contributing little income to their households. In response, wives reported that they received some form of governmental assistance and/or participated in some form of quasi-illegal and/or illegal activities in order to make ends meet.

Furthermore, the findings strongly suggest that imprisonment is an important family structural change that has been ignored by literature. Wives' accounts showed that imprisonment inadvertently kept most wives at the edge of subsistence while legitimating the male flight from economic support of their wives and children. Imprisonment thus reinforced male irresponsibility. Most women in the study believed that their incarcerated husbands did not suffer the hardships that characterized their own lives; their husbands did not have to worry about children or how the bills were going to be paid, or the food placed on the tables. They had many and sometimes more of the comforts of living than the wives and children. They had the time and energy to pursue various personal interests and activities. And finally, unlike their wives, the prisoners had constant companionship. The gap between the experiences of these women and their husbands continued to widen as the years passed.

Imprisonment thus sets men up to persist in their flight from commitment insofar as men who are paroled from Vermont prisons are quite likely to reencounter unemployment, underemployment and life at the margins of society. It is not surprising that a significant number of paroled men become further entrenched in such irresponsible behavior as participation in the cycle of unemployment, fast-living and criminal activities.

Prisoners' wives reported that such hardships as increased parenting responsibilities, providing their incarcerated husbands with material goods, the financial costs of communicating with their incarcerated husbands, and loneliness created a socioemotional impoverishment directly related to familial structural change that occured after their husbands' imprisonment. Nevertheless, although most women found themselves carrying burdens that they expected their husbands to assume, they were strongly committed to their marriages. Several factors emerge from the wives' accounts that provide some important insights into the wives' marital commitments.

These wives remained in their marriages because they had few other alternatives, particularly if they had children. Most of the women who considered dissolving their marriages reported that, if they did so, they would remain hopelessly impoverished. They usually had few financial resources, few marketable skills, and little community or family support to lift themselves out of poverty.

Many wives maintained the belief that they would, some day, be taken care of by their men and thus did not need to prepare themselves to be fully independent. They believed that their hus-

bands should and would support the family financially and that
their own equally important contribution should center around
caretaking.

During involuntary separation many wives gained insight
into the actual inequalities of the gender roles in the family.
However, this did not encourage them to dissolve their marriages. Wives of prisoners knew that they had more to lose economically and emotionally through divorce and thus they had
more at stake in marriage. Wives reported that these burdens—
especially the financial burdens—they carried during imprisonment were heavy and far outweighed any benefits that they
might have gained from the temporary separation from their
husbands. These insights and experiences reinforced their determination to establish stable and conventional lifestyles for themselves and their children, no matter what the costs. Whatever
conventionality they achieved during this period, however, was
perceived as temporary. Most wives believed that such a lifestyle
could only be secured upon their husbands' release from prison
and subsequent employment. Increasingly, their husbands' return
seemed attractive to these women because it might provide a
more secure economic foundation for a conventional lifestyle. In
this sense, then, imprisonment inadvertently functions to keep
married women "in their place"; that is, married.[14]

Nevertheless, the extent to which the women in the study
population were resistant to extricating themselves from their
marriages was startling. These women, therefore, challenge the
public image of prisoners' wives as women who walk out on
their husbands the first time they get arrested and imprisoned.
The accounts of these women also contradict the public image of
prisoners' wives either as stoic women who passively and help-
lessly stand by their troublesome husbands, or as fast livers.
Rather, they are seen as traditional wives who actively manipulated their environments, continuously attempting to establish stable conventional lives for themselves. In so doing, they
displayed both a remarkable variety and similarity of coping
strategies.

Throughout this book, an attempt has been made to explain,
illuminate, and generally make sense of the careers of prisoners'
wives as they do their own time on the "outside." The women

who participated in this study wanted to be a part of it in order to "tell it like it is" to people who would come to know exactly who they were—and the texture of their struggles.

APPENDIX A

THE LITERATURE

The strong bias in the criminalization literature is toward studies of the *official* legal process: how criminal laws are created and enacted, the relationship between the law and the offender, and the kinds and quality of interaction between offenders and agents of the criminal justice system. Comparatively little attention has been paid to unofficial processes and, hence, to the impact of criminalization on those closely connected with the accused. Studies of prisoners' wives have overwhelmingly focused on incarceration as the single most important crisis point in the relationship between husbands and wives and hence, as the touchstone in the long-term development of their relationships.[1]

Moral Careers and Deviant Identities

Goffman's essay "The Moral Career of a Mental Patient" provides an important point of departure for the research reported here.[2] Goffman discusses ways in which institutional settings—in particular, "total institutions"—shape the identities of actors within them. He uses the term "moral career" to refer to that sequence of experiences that transforms a mental patient's social identity and imagery for self-assessment through the phases of "pre-patient," "in-patient," and "out-patient." Goffman argues that the shape and content of this moral career ultimately depend on the organization and practices of mental hospitals. These, in turn, structure deviant identities for patients and create a framework for interpreting their behavior.

Blumberg's "The Moral Career of An Accused Person" provides a parallel description of the journey of an accused person through stages in the criminal justice system.[3] In this case, if convicted, the accused changes status from "civilian" to "crimi-

278

nal" and eventually, in most cases to "ex-convict." During processing, the accused's public and private identities are subjected to attacks by various institutions and their agents, who often relate to him or her as a "criminal." This sets a dynamic in motion in which the accused often comes to accept this designation even when he or she is not willing to do so. Although a redefinition of self as "guilty" may alleviate an accused's identity crisis, it also enables the police and courts to process a case with a minimum of difficulty.

Both Goffman and Blumberg note that formally uninvolved parties may play important roles in supporting and sustaining stages in the moral careers of those becoming defined as deviant. Blumberg observes that relatives can, in effect, act as agents of the court system by appealing to the accused to "help himself," *i.e.*, plead guilty. Goffman finds that patients often arrive at mental hospitals as a result of family action. Both the "mental patient" and the "accused" are subjected to frontal assaults by institutions, their personnel, and, frequently, by family members. When "mental patients" or "accuseds" accept the labels being applied to them, their social identities become transformed into deviant ones.

While this notion of a "moral career" has been explored in a variety of contexts,[4] most research has been confined to examining the impact of institutional definition and redefinition on those actually being processed through a given system.

Wives' accounts reveal that they, too, have a moral career although they are formally outside of the criminal justice process. Wives' conceptions of themselves become transformed from "wife" to "prisoner's wife" and in most cases to "wife of an ex-convict." These transformations of their social identity have important consequences upon the forms of accommodations wives adopt toward the criminal justice system and the ways that these influence and interact with their lifestyles, backgrounds, and adjustments to separation.

The Criminalization Process

Most work on criminalization has focused on the processes through which criminal identities are defined, affirmed, and reaffirmed as a result of formal interactions between offenders and criminal justice agencies. However, Turk (1969), Harjen (1974), and others have suggested that informal judgments, formed and maintained in the course of face-to-face encounters, also play an important role in criminalization. Since these types of informal interactions would not normally be confined to those being processed by the criminal justice system—but would include members of their families, as well—one might expect similar, if not identical, shifts to occur in the social identities of these closely related kin. Despite this, neither Turk nor Harjen has even speculated on how the criminalization process might affect the lives of relatives of the accused.

The Crisis of Separation School

Following in Hill's (1949) tradition, a number of studies have attempted to integrate the multiplicity of factors involved in prisoners' families' adjustments to enforced separation. While based on quantitative data gathered through questionnaires and/or highly structured interviews in the United States and Great Britain, they have made important contributions to a broader understanding of the larger circumstances resulting from involuntary separation.

Hill's (1949) study of the effects on families of war-time separation provides an important set of theoretical tools for understanding these kinds of circumstances. Hill defines a crisis as an event which creates a sense of sharpened activity, or which blocks customary patterns of behavior and requires new ones. He argues that three factors jointly determine whether or not a given event becomes a crisis for a given family: (1) the hardships of the situation itself; (2) the resources of the family, its role structure, flexibility, and previous history of dealing with crises; and (3) the way in which a family defines the event, that is, whether or not members treat it as a threat to their status, goals, and objectives. Hill points out that the war-time separation of husbands from their families required new patterns of family action because customary patterns had been disrupted. Family adjustments, he observes, required shifts in members' activities and responsibilities in order to accommodate to the realities of separation. For families to hold together, their routines had to continue and positive relationships had to be maintained or established with friends and neighbors.

A number of researchers have replicated Hill's "crisis of separation" model in order to predict how prisoners' families will adjust to involuntary separation.[5] These studies have concluded that family relationships following conviction and imprisonment follow patterns established before these events occurred. Thus, where marital relationships were good before imprisonment, there is almost no likelihood of marriage breakdown during this period. Where marital relationships were seriously strained before imprisonment, marriages may break up, but even in this case the numbers are relatively small. Indeed, where strained relationships exist, imprisonment may lead to improvements in the situation. A more recent study[6] has concluded that wives' *perceptions of crises* bear directly on the kinds of adjustments they will eventually make to enforced separation. Their experience with crises, moreover, is not cumulative.

These findings presented here are consistent with observations that: (1) imprisonment does *not* necessarily constitute a crisis for every wife; and (2) that crises are not cumulative and that, therefore, wives' experiences in coping with one crisis situation may not bear directly on how they deal with another.

The Accommodation Literature

While it is possible to construct an account of the relationships between prisoners' families and the criminalization process that focuses only on such dramatic moments as police arrests and courtroom encounters, a more balanced view must include information about how prisoners' wives live with troubles and with their husbands' criminal behavior on a daily basis. There is almost no detailed literature on how crime and social control specifically impinge on the ordinary lives of the wives of men being processed by the criminal justice system. However, a related area of research treated in the literature on accommodation is relevant here: how wives' definitions of husbands' deviant behavior and accommodations are used in making relations with husbands more bearable.

A consistent finding emerges from recent work on family re-actions to alcoholism, mental illness, and battering.[7] There is of-ten a considerable delay between the time when potentially deviant behavior first appears and the time when families accept the definition of one of their members as mentally ill, alcoholic, or physically abusive. Families frequently find ways of postpon-ing this recognition by *normalizing* a member's disturbing be-havior and thereby making their own lives more bearable. In many cases, as these studies note, there is a sequence of changes in families' interpretations of their members' difficulties, with re-definitions occurring as situations change or as a family mem-ber's behavior changes.

Research on family accommodation to other "troublesome spouses," including alcoholics, the mentally ill, batterers, and gamblers has documented the extent to which the continuation of such marriages depends upon the development of numerous coping strategies. Such coping strategies include listening and ad-vising, humoring the troublemaker, taking on the troublemaker's responsibilities, isolating and avoiding troublemakers, and play-ing out a "spy game" to control the troublemaker. Such studies suggest that families frequently employ a sequence of different coping strategies to deal with a member's difficulties. New ac-commodations are likely to occur as situations change or as fam-ily members' behaviors change.

The existing literature on accommodation to problem family members also suggests several patterns that might be expected to emerge in the coping styles of wives of active criminals. For ex-ample, families frequently appear committed to insulating the deviant member within the highly tolerant household, contacting appropriate authorities or agencies only as a last resort when overwhelmed by the deviant's disruptive behavior. Several authors[8] have suggested that such tolerance may be a source of delay in the identification and treatment of mental illness and alcoholism. A more recent study[9] has pointed out that, while "troublemakers" may not be overtly sanctioned, families often attempt to shape and guide their behavior through normal inter-action. Both family members and close associates may try to pro-mote the deviant's integration into society.

There are important gaps in this literature. Virtually no attention has been paid, for instance, to how prisoners' wives accommodate to the entire *range* of stages in the criminalization process. Yet the shifts involved are enormously important to the daily lives of these women. Where researchers have examined the accommodations surrounding a *particular* stage, the interpersonal mechanisms and strategies used by wives have been largely ignored. Yet, prisoners' wives engage in consequential and often painful interpersonal negotiations about what is or is not acceptable behavior at different stages in the process.

Conventional Social Psychology

A small but growing literature has begun to document the impact of imprisonment on prisoners' wives and to explore the nature and quality of marital relationships from the wives' perspectives. One pervasive theme in this body of work is that of the "transfer of punishment." Swan (1981), for instance, observes that a number of wives believe that their husbands' punishments were directly imposed on their families—on the innocent as well as the guilty. The form and extent of this perceived punishment is closely related to the kinds of hardships such wives experience during involuntary separation. Such perceived hardships typically include financial status (too little money), sexual-emotional effects such as loneliness and depression, and child care or discipline problems.[10] However, Swan (1981) also notes that there are not only costs but benefits to be derived from enforced separation:[11] improved finances, peace of mind, being able to receive AFDC, freedom from husbands' drinking, and "peace and quiet." *Temporary* removal of husbands thus can enhance the quality of life for some families.

Much of the literature to date appears to rest on an underlying assumption that prisoners' wives experience the effects of involuntary separation in complete isolation from their husbands, with the exception of occasional visits. However, it is clear that ongoing communication between husbands and wives colors the daily lives of those both inside and outside the prison walls, affecting the quality of marital relationships, as well as the texture of social and domestic life. Thus, a thorough understanding of wives' adjustments to their partners' incarceration requires consideration of the nature of their continuing contacts, and how these contacts are shaped by various prison systems.

Stigmatization

A search of the relevant literature on prisoners' wives indicates that stigma is usually discussed in vague and general terms. A chief difficulty with this literature, Davis (1980) contends, is that it does not always accurately discriminate between the concepts "stigma" and "shame." There is thus a confusion between the subjective feelings of shame (or fear of being ostracized) and actual hostility. In the present study, then, stigmatization refers to wives' perceptions of actual hostility and lack of respect directed toward them as prisoners' wives. The present study also examines wives' subjective feelings of shame as well as wives' fear of being shamefully ostracized (treated with hostility) as distinct areas of concern.

Attention has primarily been given to wives' feelings of shame and encounters with stigmatization within their communities. In the literature there is some agreement that during the initial stage of their husbands' incarceration, wives' feelings of shame tend to dissipate quite quickly. These findings hold up among diverse populations of prisoners' wives.[12] For example, Morris (1965) in her study of the effects of involuntary separation on British prisoners' wives, found that when wives do report feelings of shame or disgrace, their reactions appear to be related to their husbands' offenses. Wives of sex offenders and white-collar criminals tend to suffer shame, while wives whose husbands are imprisoned for other crimes tend not to do this. In either case, wives' resentments are more clearly related to their husbands' arrests and incarceration than to the criminal behavior itself.[13]

Dealing specifically with wives' fears and anticipation of stigmatization, Morris (1965) also reports that only at the initial stage of incarceration do wives of first-time offenders fear gossip. In response to this fear, these wives recalled that they dared not go out of the house and feared meeting people. These fears, however, quickly wore off.

According to more recent research findings,[14] only a small number of prisoners' wives recall that friends and neighbors view them differently upon learning about their husbands' imprisonment, treating them as if they are also criminals. Other investigators[15] found that some women specifically recalled community reaction to the man's offense as those of disgust, curiosity, pity, and fear, and felt that these reactions were transferred to themselves. Schneller (1978) elaborates on these findings, arguing that the extent to which women report experiencing stigmatization of some form or another depends, in no small way, on the communities in which they reside. Hence, the management of stigmatization was not a great problem for the black families in his sample given the types of neighborhoods in which these families normally reside and the fact that criminality and imprisonment are almost accepted as a part of life by community members.

The findings reported here are consistent with these earlier observations. At the time of their husbands' arrest and initial incarceration, shame and stigmatization are not central but rather situational issues in wives' lives. Also, wives who reside in crime-familiar communities do not appear to encounter stigmatizing situations. However, the wives' accounts reveal an additional dimension in the study of stigmatization. Their accounts provide a detailed picture of how their feelings of shame and humiliation tend to be the result of the stigmatization experienced within the prison system rather than from reactions of their communities or from the violation of internalized norms and mores.

The Prison Literature

Much of the prison literature is not relevant here. However, a number of recent studies have specifically dealt with the kinds and qualities of relationships prisoners are able to sustain with family and friends on the outside. As a rule, these studies have tended to emphasize contacts maintained through visiting and/or letter writing, and to give less attention to other modes of communication, *e.g.,* phone calls, home visits, and work release.

Since in-prison visitation has traditionally been the major form of contact between prisoners and their wives, it has received the most attention in the literature on inmates' ties to the outside. However, given the recent increase of telephone access and home visits permitted, there is a need to examine the ways in which these kinds of contact also affect the marital relationship during the husbands' confinement and the ways in which wives respond to such contact.

Several recent studies have observed that in-prison visitation can encourage couples to revert to patterns of communication reminiscent of courtship, through which marital ties are reaffirmed by reinforcing their former roles as husbands and wives. Holt and Miller (1972) observe that formal visitations can encourage couples to experience renewed courtship and that this form of courtship can be satisfying for both parties. Because of this, visiting can become an important event to which wives can look forward. Schwartz and Weintraub (1974) complement these findings. They describe how couples reaffirm their marital ties during prison visiting by reinforcing their former roles as husbands and wives. Husbands, for instance, can reassert their authority over their wives and wives can defer decisions to their husbands.

More recent studies, documenting interactional patterns, support this observation. For example, research studies[16] exploring the topics of conversations in which prisoners and their wives engage, report that a prominent topic is concern about the future, including hopes, dreams, and aspirations. Such conversations, suggest Koenig and Gariepy (1985), can provide relief from daily stresses for both partners. Several writers[17] have noted that not all marital ties are strengthened as a result of one partner's being incarcerated. Some marriages deteriorate, either because of the imprisonment, or the prison system's structure, or policies regarding communication. Freedman and Rice (1977) have also reported that forms of contact such as prison visiting or telephone calls may serve to renew faith in marital relations or to set in motion events that will undermine them. These authors suggest that the limitations inherent in available forms of communication might frustrate interactions and become destructive to the relationships they are intended to strengthen.

Relevance

Each of these bodies of literature has contributed in important ways to the present study. The "crisis of separation" model, for example, provides an overarching paradigm for understanding the impact of separation, *per se,* on family ties independent of the legal connotations surrounding arrest and imprisonment. The extensions of Hill's (1949) basic model to enforced separation through imprisonment which have been made by other researchers frame a set of problems involving crises and crisis management. Work by Morris (1965), Schneller (1978), Struckhoff (1977), and others has set the stage for an examination of the conditions under which stigmatization and transfer of stigma may occur and the consequences it may have for prisoners' wives. Conventional social psychological studies have provided insights into the emotional dynamics involved in the relationships wives develop both to their husbands and the criminalization process. The accommodation literature has been a rich source of insights into the strategies and coping mechanisms prisoners' wives use in coming to grips with criminalization and making their lives more bearable while it is going on. The prison literature has underscored the dual nature of contacts between prisoners and their wives, given the means of communication available to them for maintaining marital ties.

A number of these ideas have been integrated into a larger framework which stresses the stage-dependent nature of the forms of accommodation prisoners' wives adopt towards the criminal justice system. The present research offers an intensive description of the world of thirty prisoners' wives "doing their time on the outside." The perspective of prisoners' wives adds another dimension to the study of the criminalization process.

APPENDIX B

NOTES ON RESEARCH METHODOLOGY

Finding the Women

With the cooperation of the Vermont Department of Corrections, I was able to make extensive use of the prison population listings as well as all other official records needed in order to gain a reliable and complete listing of married prisoners incarcerated within two facilities—Londonderry Correctional Facility and Newport Community Correctional Center. The prisoners included were married, had received at least a six-month sentence, and had been living with their wives at the time of their arrest.

For the purposes of this study, prisoners were deemed to be "married" if they had been living consensually with a woman for at least six months prior to their arrest. Search of the relevant central prison records, and cross-checking these with Corrections personnel, disclosed that fifty-three male prisoners then held at Londonderry had fit this definition of "married" at the time they were convicted and sentenced. And at Newport, twenty-nine met these criteria. Since no official statistics were compiled on this basis, there was no way to determine if the ratio of married to nonmarried prisoners in these two facilities was different from that in the Vermont prison population as a whole. There was, however, no reason to believe that it was.

After the final list of married prisoners was compiled for each center, I made arrangements with the prison staff to interview all the married prisoners. This was necessary to: (1) inform them of the project; (2) request their informed consent as to what they might have seen as an invasion of their privacy; (3) ask their help in locating their women, and obtain their written consent to contact them; and (4) gather information about their offenses and sentences, and learn something about how they perceived their wives' accommodations to their criminality and imprisonment.

All the men who participated in this study did so voluntarily. They were assured of complete confidentiality. All interviews were administered in various private offices, meeting rooms, and empty cafeterias provided by prison personnel.

One can only speculate as to why they appeared so willing to cooperate. Most prisoners are quite accustomed to being "called up" to see a variety of people during a given day. They are rarely told why they are wanted. Thus, being "called up" to see me did not strike them as unusual. Moreover, apart from female staff, women are rarely seen in men's prisons. Thus, an interview with one probably helps to break the prisoners' routine and to give them a chance to "shoot the breeze" with a new "face."

At the start of each interview, I informed the prisoners of the broad goals of the study, about elements of my own history, and about my dual position as a university teacher and a graduate student working on a dissertation. All prisoners were therefore aware that I came to the interview situation with a "streetwise" familiarity with crimes and prisons.[1] I also explained that I came to this research in part as a consequence of my own experiences as the former wife of a white, Jewish prisoner. Thus, they could anticipate that I would share the world in which prisoners and their wives live to a greater extent than many university researchers.

Surprisingly, I found that the fact that I am a black woman did not seem to engender either hesitation or hostility. Rapport seemed good, and I have every reason to believe that the men viewed me as a legitimate type (university teacher, etc.) whose feet, nonetheless, remained in a world with which they were familiar. With the exception of nine men, all the prisoners agreed to be interviewed. Of these nine, seven were about to be granted extended furlough or parole, and one was about to be transferred to a Federal prison. In effect, only one of these nine could not be interviewed for reasons germane to the study.

Structured interviews were then administered to each prisoner. I conducted a majority of these interviews. However, I received some assistance from work study students at the University of Vermont whom I trained for this purpose. These interviews ranged in length from 45 minutes to over an hour. In addition to receiving permission to contact prisoners' wives—and, in many cases finding out how they could be contacted—I used these sessions to obtain information regarding the men's family backgrounds, prior arrests and convictions, and how they perceived their wives' abilities to cope with enforced separation. I also tried to determine whether or not they believed that their marriages had changed since incarceration.

Sixty-five prisoners signed the agreement to participate and were able to provide their wives' addresses. Eight men refused to participate in the research project. Seven felt that the study invaded their privacy or they could not locate their wives, or a combination of these factors. Only one refused on the basis that he could see no direct benefits from it either for himself or his wife. Those who did participate seemed to accept the notion that indirect benefits might result from it.

At this point, the process of making initial telephone contact with the wives began. In all, fourteen of the sixty-five wives could not be located; nine additional wives made appointments to be interviewed but were not home at the designated times. There were seven noncontacts who had left the state, and five wives refused to cooperate, largely due to the emotional stress of dredging up unpleasant memories. The wives who were the most difficult to contact were heavily involved in the drug and/or criminal subculture. My final study sample, therefore, consisted of thirty wives who were initially enthusiastic about the goals of the study and who readily agreed to be interviewed.

Representatives

In a small qualitative study of this kind, where random sampling methods are not used, the question of representativeness of the study population always arises. Although the term does not mean quite the same thing in this context as it does where quantitative methods are involved, it is still useful to explore the issue.

In comparing the women in the final study population to others, it is striking that, in what is considered to be a rural state,[2] only four prisoners' wives lived in rural areas. Twenty-six resided in urban or suburban centers. This was probably because the study was conducted in Chittenden County, one of the more heavily urbanized areas in Vermont.[3]

All wives were white. This is consistent with the composition of the population of the state which includes few minority groups. Most were wives of prisoners serving relatively short sentences—on average, between six months and two years. Most of the sentences were for alcohol-related property crimes. Few men had been convicted of crimes of violence, possession of heroin, or other more serious offenses. In this sense, these wives were *not* representative of women associated with men in the American prison population generally. But, given the community-oriented correctional philosophy at work in Vermont, the experiences of these wives were probably representative of those women facing similar circumstances. The prevalence of alcohol-related offenses among married prisoners is consistent with what we know about the population of medium and minimum security prisons as a whole.

Since participation in the study was voluntary, the final study sample included more respectably and conservatively-oriented wives than one would find under other circumstances. It is probably true that the study group under-represents prisoners' wives who are drug users or are, themselves, active participants in criminal activities. But this is probably a limitation common to all studies in which participation is voluntary, whether the participants are recruited through random sampling techniques or not. At some future date, however, it would probably be useful to study the reactions and adjustments of criminally-involved wives.

For present purposes, the study group seems adequately "representative." In a rural state, the wives appear to be more urban than others. But the majority of the U.S. population lives in urban or suburban centers and this is reflected in the composition of prison populations. While living in a major metropolitan center may not be quite the same thing as living in a metropolitan center in Vermont, we have no reason to believe that these women's experiences are qualitatively different from those in more metropolitan areas.

While these women were exclusively white, there is little reason to believe that their experiences are, in kind, different from those of black wives.

The Vermont prison system, of course, is not representative of all prisons in that inmates who are considered "security risks" are placed elsewhere or transferred out. It also probably contains proportionately fewer prisoners incarcerated for drug or drug-related offenses than other prison systems in the United States. In this sense, it is not representative of the closed, maximum security systems that usually house populations of this kind, and that are probably more typical of those with which prisoners' wives most often have to deal. But this study group may well be representative of prisoners' wives who live outside the nation's major cities in states with established community-based prison systems. This is a population about which little is known, but we have no reason to believe that, in fundamental respects, the experiences of these wives with crime, arrests, courtrooms, and prisons are markedly or systematically different from those of other prisoners' wives in similar situations.

Data Collection

In order to represent the processes whereby prisoners' wives accommodate to the circumstances surrounding their husbands' arrests and imprisonments, I have attempted to integrate data collected from a variety of different vantage points using a number of different methodologies. In many cases, this has allowed me to engage in what Denzin (1978) refers to as "triangulation": deriving the "best" over-all interpretation of a social situation from a series of overlapping measurements or observations. As a result, I have been able to cross-check and reexamine data in the interests of improving their reliability and validity.

For example, I have integrated data drawn from in-depth interviews of prisoners' wives with those obtained through structured interviews with their husbands and with data extracted from summaries of prisoners' wives' "rap" sessions. All of these data, in turn, have been compared to pertinent information concerning married prisoners' socio-demographic backgrounds, conviction records, etc., gathered from prison records.

In gathering information about the lives of these thirty women, I have primarily relied on in-depth interviews corroborated by additional data drawn from prison records, structured interviews with incarcerated husbands, summaries of meetings with small groups of prisoners' wives, and notes on telephone conversations. Not only have these additional sources of data generally corroborated information provided by wives during the interview situation, but they have helped to place it in context and have added depth to the insights gained from these more direct accounts. By cross-checking these sources and following up on "leads," it was possible to illuminate the changes, both subjective and situational, that prisoners' wives undergo upon encountering the criminalization process. Thus, this combination of research methods has yielded a rich source of data with which to capture the fullness of the lives of these women and thereby contribute to our understanding of the ways they interpret and give meaning to their social worlds.

In the present case, while the interviews conducted with prisoners' wives followed no rigid or fixed sequence, an interview guide was used to make sure that, while sequences might vary, the same basic topics were raised with each respondent. Nine areas were covered: family life prior to arrest; husbands' and wives' history of illegal activities; arrests and convictions; managing stigmatization; husbands' adjustments to prison; accessibility of husbands by means of telephone calls, prison visits, and home leave; "managing alone"; marital relationships during separation; and reunion. While the gross outlines of this guide remained unchanged, specific topics were added or deleted as I discovered more about the wives' experiences. Moreover, as the field research progressed, closure was achieved in several areas and these were deemphasized in the remaining interviews. Thus, the use of an interview guide allowed me to retain control over the interviewing process but, at the same time, facilitated the spontaneous and uninhibited expression of the wives' perspectives and feelings.

All interviews were focused, in-depth discussions lasting no less than three, and often as many as ten, hours and sometimes required more than one visit.[5]

During a 24-month period, all thirty women were inter- viewed at least once. However, there was considerable variation in the number of sessions. Thirteen wives were interviewed from three to as many as seven times; twelve wives were interviewed twice; and five wives only once.[6] Repeated contacts with respon- dents made it possible for me to resurrect previous topics and to resolve, if possible, contradictions. All told, this phase of the re- search involved some eighty-five separate sessions.

Most of the interviewing took place in the women's homes. Only two were conducted in my office. Every effort was made to conduct interviews in private. However, privacy was not always possible. If wives had children, it was sometimes impossible to prevent them from being present during at least part of the in- terview. Usually we tried to arrange interviews during times when children were not at home. When wives lived with their parents, one parent was sometimes present during part of a ses- sion. When husbands had been paroled, they sometimes dropped in as well. This was also true of friends. I recognized that in- formation about marital relations given on some of these occa- sions could be unreliable since it might reflect what wives knew their husbands and/or relatives and/or friends might want them to say. When I felt this might be the case, I attempted to verify information in subsequent interviews or through telephone conversations.

All the women in the study were volunteers who came to the interviews with some understanding of my research goals. As mentioned earlier, the rapport between myself and most women exceeded my original expectations. Most women expressed a genuine interest in participating in additional interviews for the following reasons. First, they felt that with me, a former wife of a prisoner, they could share some unsharable aspects of the problems that they encountered as prisoners' wives. Often they mentioned that they felt as though they had broken through a sense of isolation that they felt as prisoners' wives. Second, the time spent during the interview provided them with the oppor- tunity to express a whole spectrum of feelings about their situa- tion. Third, these women, who felt marginal to the criminal justice process, reported that these interviews gave them some hope that they might be heard and/or that social control agencies might become more sensitive to their situation as prisoners' wives. Fourth, the interviews helped them to feel validated as women who have something to offer to a society that they believed treated them as "discredited women." Finally, many said that the interviews offered them a rare opportunity to reflect on their lives and their futures as well as to think of things that they never considered.

Given the development of this rapport, it would have been extremely difficult—perhaps impossible—for me to maintain the role of a completely "objective," detached observer. Many wives expected that, as a university teacher, I would be in a good position to mobilize societal resources on their behalf. I, in turn, tried to learn more about the availability of certain kinds of community aid and, on occasion, I was able to act as an intermediary between various agencies and those wives in need. Sometimes I lent them emotional support, visited them in the hospital, or attended funerals, celebrations, their husbands' court appearances, or accompanied them on prison visits.

Despite apparent reliability and face-validity of the information I gathered from these in-depth interviews, they were not, of course, my only source of data. Large portions of wives' accounts could be, and were, corroborated with prison records and information gathered through structured interviews with prisoners themselves. These records included information about the men's previous convictions, how they interacted with their wives, and how they perceived their wives as managing on their own. In addition, the prison records sometimes included assessments made by probation and parole officers, pre-sentence investigators, and observations made by psychologists and other prison personnel. Such materials were very often highly subjective and unsystematic.

Another source of data evolved out of my initial contacts with respondents. After I began my research, groups of wives began to meet irregularly over the period of a year and a half to share common experiences and feelings. These meetings included from three to eight women and took place around their kitchen tables, in their living rooms, and in my department's offices. In all, ten meetings took place. Those wives who lived closest to the Burlington area were most likely to attend.

As it evolved, my role at these meetings was to provide refreshments, lead discussions, and to keep records of what was discussed. Often these "rap" sessions began with wives' complaints about their status as single-yet-married women, about their husbands, or about the prison system. In the course of a session they might share specific information about the prison system, provide emotional support for one another, or simply air their feelings. Conducting these sessions was especially useful in providing me with opportunities to discover which issues or problems were most salient to wives and to revise and reformulate my impressions accordingly.

Although less systematic, telephone calls were another important source of information. After each interview, I left wives with my telephone number and suggested that, if they wanted to talk further, I was always available. Twelve wives responded by contacting me at least every two weeks. These telephone conversations typically lasted from 15 minutes to an hour, during which I kept careful notes. Sometimes wives simply treated these calls as an opportunity to "sound off" to a sympathetic listener. At other times they were seeking help in solving particular problems, trying to mobilize resources, etc.. Although I made less systematic use of information gathered in this way than others, often these conversations helped me to get a sense of the texture and tempo of the wives' experiences.

Making Use of the Data

The data collected through these methods were analyzed with the "grounded theory" procedure articulated by Glaser and Strauss (1967) and elaborated by Charmaz (1983). Information from data sources has been subjected to rigorous comparisons, cross-checking, and validation with respect to the experiential frame and lifespace of the prisoners' wives, themselves. In doing this, the "constant comparative" method of analysis (Glaser and Strauss (1967) was followed. This method involves juxtaposing categories of data and searching for similarities and differences. In this fashion, "old timers" have been compared to "first timers," wives with children to wives without children, wives married to husbands who lived fast to wives married to husbands who pursued a conventional lifestyle and wives of property offenders to wives of personal offenders. Other comparisons also have been made along a variety of dimensions.

In order to accomplish these comparisons more effectively, the data were transcribed and coded according to a series of general categories. These categories continually evolved, since they were based on what seemed to be the most salient aspects of the data. In the course of the research, for instance, general categories were divided into subcategories based on topics mentioned by respondents, *e.g.,* "domestic life prior to arrest" was divided into "spouses' employment history," "spouses' criminal enterprises," "prison visiting" was divided into "prison rules and regulations for visiting," "treatment by guards," "strip searching," "contraband," "sex in the visiting room," "conversations," "future plans," "difficulties in visiting" and so on. These categories then served as a guide for information used in comparisons. By making these comparisons, for instance, I found that neophytes had special problems not encountered by old timers, and that some crimes committed by husbands were more easily justified by wives than others.

In creating an over-all image or representation of the reality depicted in the data, more-or-less finely-cut categories and subcategories were rearranged so as to assemble together material relevant to each topic. New patterns appeared and older ones disappeared in the process of determining the final array. Thus, much of the analysis presented here is a product of the continual refinement and reformulation of a series of themes and comparisons implicit in the categories and subcategories.

NOTES

CHAPTER I

1. The concept moral career was elaborated upon by Goffman, 1959, in his research on the mental patient.

2. According to Harjen (1974), the criminalization process consists of a set of actions, beginning with apprehension by the police, through judicial handling, and then correctional handling, that result in the successful application of the label "criminal" to the individuals involved. Each step in this process confronts the affected individuals with drastic changes in their public identities. These changes, in turn, have important implications for the subsequent actions, private identities, and everyday lives of those labelled in this fashion.

3. Such interpretations are what Scott and Lyman (1972) have called "accounts." *Accounts* are both justifications and excuses made by a social actor "to explain unanticipated and untoward behavior" (Lyman and Scott, 1972: 25) whether that behavior is her own or others, and whether the proximate cause for the statement arises from the actor or from someone else. *Justifications* arise in situations, according to Lyman and Scott, in which an actor accepts responsibility for an act, or places responsibility for it on others, but seeks to have the specific instance in question defined as an "exception." *Excuses*, by contrast, occur when an actor attempts to relieve herself or others of responsibility for a deviant act or set of acts.

4. Work on lifestyles such as Howell's (1973) has sensitized us to the ultimate dependence of forms of accommodation on subcultural and cultural patterns drawn from the larger society. The wives' accounts of their concern for fast-living and conventional lifestyles strongly resemble those portrayed by Howell in *Hard Living on Clay Street* (1973).

He has developed a typology of working class lifestyles in which he distinguishes between "hard living" and "settled" living patterns. "Hard living," he says, is evidenced by such things as: (1) a preoccupation with the problems and drama of the day-to-day life, particularly with personal relationships; (2) chaotic work histories, in which families experience recurrent employment and unemployment; (3) marital instability, in which family members have had at least one previous marriage and an unsteady current marriage; (4) general rootlessness, in that families rent their homes and tend to move frequently; (5) toughness, in which hard livers tend to use an abundance of profanity, talk about violence, and generally act tough; and (6) heavy drinking. By contrast, "settled living" families tend to be more conventional and moderate in their approach to life: (1) marriages tend to be long and stable; (2) there is a greater sense of rootedness to their communities; (3) people tend to be more cautious and likely to be steadily employed, while their wives keep homes and children in shining order; and (6) settled livers consider themselves to be "respectable" members of their communities and to be concerned about how they are regarded by others.

5. A "total institution" is one which completely absorbs and structures the identities of actors within it. See Goffman, 1961.

6. See, for instance, Homer, 1979; Adams and Fischer, 1976; Holt and Miller, 1972.

7. Dickinson, 1984; McCarthy, 1979; Schafer, 1978.

8. Gimenez, 1987; McCrate, 1987; Hewlett, 1986; Rogers, 1986; Sidel, 1986; Weitzman, 1985; Ehrenreich, 1983; Nazzari, 1980; Pearce, 1978.

9. Refer to Arendell, 1986, Wallerstein and Kelly, 1985; Anderson-Khleif, 1982; Berman and Turk, 1981; Spanier and Casto, 1979; Weiss, 1979; Brown *et al.*, 1976.

10. Note that this term is used here to refer both to men who are legally married and those living in common law arrangements.

11. The others mentioned by the wives are the St. James and Woodlawn Correctional Centers and Walden Farms.

12. Newfane held males drawn from all parts of the state.

13. Those prisoners classified as too dangerous or too likely to escape to be held in the Vermont System are now shipped off to various Federal prisons throughout the country. The number involved is a small proportion of all those sentenced by Vermont courts. It is interesting to note that wives of Vermont prisoners view all such prisons as

"closed" to them because: (1) they are far from where wives reside; (2) Federal prisons tend to tightly supervise contacts; (3) the men are, in effect, "banished" from Vermont; and (4) most prisoners' wives do not have the resources for frequent visits and closer contact even if they were permitted.

14. All wives were white. This is consistent with the composition of the population of the state which includes few racial minority groups.

15. According to the wives, fifteen men were to serve two years or less, six men were to serve three years while eight were to serve four years or more.

16. Since a voice print can be a valid source of identification, I decided not to use a tape recorder. The decision to hand record was based on the assessment that the wives were likely to be more candid than if a tape recorder was used.

CHAPTER II

1. Paula's experience differed from that of other women in the study in that she was pregnant with their first child when she and Bud were married in Newfane Prison.

2. Researchers in the area have uniformly been struck by the youthfulness of their samples of prisoners and their wives. A disproportionate number of prisoners in penal institutions of the United States are recruited from among younger adults. A similar disproportionate number of prisoners' wives are drawn from this set of age-cohorts. The women in the study population here are no exception to these findings: for example, see Swan, 1981; Love, 1970; Morris, 1965; Blackwell, 1959.

3. This finding is consistent with Blackwell's (1959). He shows that 77.5 percent of the men in his study were products of broken homes, in contrast to 64.6 percent of the wives.

4. Those women and men in the study group who, themselves, were generally oriented toward conventional lifestyles were likely to have had few friends with previous criminal experience, although many of their friends had occasionally deviated from the bounds of "respectable deviance," *e.g.,* recreational use of psychedelic drugs.

5. The conventional breakdown of offenses has not been used here. Offenses have been broken down into: (1) crimes against property; (2) crimes against the person; (3) sexual offenses; and (4) fraud, embezzlement, and other paper crimes. Crimes against property include those felonies where there is no intent to harm people. These include crimes such as theft, burglary, possession and concealment of stolen goods. Crimes against persons include those crimes where there is such intent, *e.g.*, armed robbery, assault, and kidnapping. Sexual offenses include voyeurism, lewd and lascivious behavior, and rape. Paper crimes include such activities as fraud, embezzlement, counterfeiting, and forgery.

6. Refer to Scott and Lyman, 1968.

CHAPTER III

1. The following research studies have focused upon the relationship of specific variables: Swan, 1981; Struckhoff, 1977; Love, 1970; Morris, 1965; Blackwell, 1959.

2. Some prisoners and their wives, of course, are drawn from the middle class. Hence, Irwin's (1970) archetype of middle class lifestyles, the "square john," is also relevant here. Extending Irwin's conception, "square jane," is here used to denote a female counterpart of the "square john." She is characterized by: (1) steady employment in white collar and/or skilled blue collar occupation; (2) strong ties to her community; (3) stable family life; (4) a position as an "upstanding" citizen; (5) the acquisition of the recognized symbols of middle class status; (6) moderate consumption of drugs and/or alcohol; and (7) participation in a middle class round of life.

4. Some wives did not report the fact that their husbands were employed so that they could combine public assistance with income from their husbands' jobs. This is illegal. Women were willing to risk detection since there was no way that they could depend on their husbands' incomes.

5. According to Glaser and Strauss (1965), an *open* awareness context occurs when both the hospital staff and the dying patient openly acknowledge the patient's condition. A *closed* awareness context occurs when the interaction between staff and the dying patient is based on the lack of direct acknowledgement of impending death. A *suspicion* awareness context occurs when the dying patient suspects impending

death and seeks confirmation from the staff. Finally, a *pretense* aware-ness context occurs when both interactants are fully aware but pretend not to be.

6. Glaser and Strauss, 1965.

7. Lesieur (1977) also describes similar patterns of discovery in his treatment of wives' reactions to their husbands' habitual gambling.

8. Glaser and Strauss, 1965.

CHAPTER IV

1. For a discussion of how other wives place blame upon outside forces to justify their husbands' deviant behavior see Ferraro and Johnson, 1983; Pagelow, 1981; Schwartz, 1957; Yarrow *et al.*, 1955; Jackson, 1954.

2. The following research studies have discussed how wives can lay blame on husbands' character defects: Ferraro and Johnson, 1943; Yarrow *et al.*, 1955; Schwartz, 1957.

3. Some exploration also has been given to wives who perceive themselves as the cause of their husbands' deviance: for example, see Ferraro and Johnson, 1983; Pagelow, 1981: Dobash and Dobash, 1979; Schwartz, 1957; Yarrow *et al.*, 1955; Jackson, 1954.

4. Both Jackson (1954) and Walker (1979) mention nurturing as an accommodative practice used by alcoholics' and batterers' wives to influence their husbands to cease deviant behavior.

5. The accommodative literature offers rich insights into a range of active strategies employed by families of alcoholics, gamblers, and the mentally ill (see, for instance, Walker, 1979; Lesieur, 1977; Schwartz, 1957; and Jackson, 1954). These strategies range from nagging and ar-guing to hiding liquor bottles or car keys to controlling money. Some wives threaten to inform the police about their husbands, or in desper-ation they threaten to leave them. Lynch (1983) reported that family members and close associates claimed that explicit confrontations with troublemakers did not alter their subsequent behavior; instead, it gen-erally resulted in misunderstandings.

6. Lynch (1983) noted that family members and close associates frequently sustain efforts to live with mentally ill persons by ignoring them. As an accommodative practice, ignoring involves some interac-

tion, "though of an attenuated and inauthentic kind" (1983: 155). It has the effect of isolating the troublemaker within the organizational or family network. Within this context, the accommodative practice of "passive distance" includes both the act of ignoring and the act of withdrawing from husbands' criminal pursuits.

CHAPTER V

1. In the present study, those wives who have experienced enforced separation more than once are referred to as "old timers." "Neophytes" are those wives who were experiencing enforced separation for the first time. The wives' accounts reveal that seventeen can be considered neophytes while thirteen can be considered old timers.

2. Many men had been charged with more than one offense. Nineteen women said that their men had been arrested for such crimes against property as concealment and/or receiving stolen property, or breaking and entering. Eleven named such crimes against a person as aggravated and simple assault, armed robbery, and kidnapping. Five reported charges of forgery and counterfeiting. Three women said that their men had been charged with sexual offenses such as attempted rape and lewd and lascivious conduct. Four women said that their husbands had been arrested for escaping from prison. Only two wives reported that their husbands had been charged with sale or possession of drugs.

3. Several investigators have pointed out that the aftermath of arrest is generally a period of confusion, pressure, and emotional stress for the wives of offenders: Fishman, 1981; Cobean and Powers, 1978; Schwartz and Weintraub, 1974.

4. Some other studies that show prisoners' wives' disenchantment with their husbands' lawyers are: Fishman, 1981; Swan, 1981; Schwartz and Weintraub, 1974.

5. Casper (1972: 241) suggests that the difference between private attorneys and public defenders is not so much how they behave, but, rather, the nature of the transaction between lawyer and client: the private attorney is paid by his client and, hence, he must be on the client's side. The public defender, by contrast, is paid by the state—and, hence, must be on the state's side.

6. Recent investigators have found that all too often wives whose lives have been severely affected by this system do not receive the min-

imum information to make a reasonable assessment of their situation. And in many cases, lawyers' inaccessibility and/or lack of interest in providing answers to wives' questions contributes to this information "vacuum." These findings have held up across diverse populations of wives of accuseds: see, for example, Koenig and Gariepy, 1985; Daniel and Barrett, 1981; Fishman, 1981; Swan, 1981; Fishman and Alissi, 1979; Schwartz and Weintraub, 1974.

7. Casper, (1972), in his study of defendants' perceptions of the nature of the justice system, observes that defendants based their sense of justice on what they considered to be a fair sentence. Fairness, for defendants, means they either receive a sentence very close to the norm for their particular crime or they "get a good break."

8. Morris (1965) who studied the effects of involuntary separation on British prisoners' wives offers some insights into feelings of injustice. She observes that feelings of injustice about their husbands' sentences are most likely expressed by wives of first time offenders; especially by wives of first timers who were convicted of a sexual offense. Sex offenders, she suggests, tend to receive extremely long sentences which wives compared unfavorably with sentences given to men committing other types of offenses. Few wives of repeat offenders express similar reactions. Instead, they are more likely to complain about what they believe to be overly long sentences for property crimes which they argue are relatively unimportant crimes since no violence is involved.

9. This process reported by the wives is plea bargaining. Generally, the defendants are offered a deal. Charges will be reduced, sentence agreement or both in return for a plea of guilty. The husbands have been offered this deal through their lawyers with assurance that the prosecutor will recommend this deal to the judge. As the defendants, in Casper's 1970 research study, the wives are unaware that judges do not always go along with the prosecutors' deals. Many times, judges may impose longer or shorter sentences than is recommended by the prosecutors.

CHAPTER VI

1. For a discussion of the kinds of accommodations wives make to the hospitalization of their mentally ill husbands, see Deasy and Quinn, 1955. And for a discussion of parents' reactions and accommodations to their children, handicapped by polio, see Davis, 1972.

Another discussion has focused upon parental reactions and accommodations to their mentally retarded children. See Birenbaum, 1975.

2. There has been some relevant work on wives' experiences with stigmatization within their own communities. According to Perry's 1973 and Schwartz's and Weintraub's 1974 findings, only a small number of prisoners' wives recall that friends and neighbors view them differently upon learning about their husbands' imprisonment, treating them as if they are also criminals. Other investigators (Koenig and Gariepy, 1985; Daniel and Barrett, 1981) found that some women specifically recalled community reaction to the man's offense as one of disgust, curiosity, pity and fear, and felt that these reactions were transferred to themselves.

3. Schneller (1978) elaborates on these findings, arguing that the extent to which women report experiencing stigmatization of some form or another depends, in no small way, on the communities in which they reside. Hence, the management of stigmatization was not a great problem for the black families in his sample, given the types of neighborhoods in which these families normally reside and the fact that criminality and imprisonment are almost accepted as a part of life by community members.

4. The present study supports earlier research which found that wives who reside in crime-familiar communities do not appear to encounter stigmatizing situations: *e.g.*, Schneller, 1978; Schwartz and Weintraub, 1974.

5. For a discussion of parents' reaction to their sons-in-law's arrests, see Jorgensen, 1986; Fishman, 1981; Bakker *et al.*, 1978; Schwartz and Weintraub, 1974; Morris, 1965.

6. Some investigators have reported that some wives practice deception in order to maintain a positive image of the father: for example, see Fritsch and Burkhead, 1981; Sack, 1977; Sack *et al.*, 1976; Morris, 1967; Friedman and Esselystyn, 1975.

7. In practice, contraband is anything the prison administrative staff designates as undesirable for prisoners to possess. The list is long-ranging from weapons, alcohol, and hard and soft drugs, to items such as chewing gum, that can be used as escape implements, to items that will eventually clutter the prisoners' rooms.

8. Wives reported that Walden Farms does not utilize metal detectors or strip searches as part of its usual control procedures.

9. Correctional personnel provided the following rationale to the author: the antics and abuses of a few have caused tighter security to be developed. Norm-violating behavior has ranged from visitors and prisoners assaulting each other, visitors verbally abusing or assaulting guards, sexual "hanky-panky" between couples, to visitors passing contraband to inmates.

10. How guards are supposed to perform their duties at the prison entrance has been described to the author by prison staff at the various correctional facilities.

11. For a discussion of wives' encounters with prison staff, see Kotarba, 1979; Cobean and Power, 1978; Morris, 1965. These investigators have noted that prisoners' wives reported being treated with hostility, disrespect, and suspicion by prison staff. According to Koenig and Gariepy, 1985, many wives recalled direct exposure to stigmatization whenever they were searched for contraband by prison staff. Many wives conclude that this process makes them feel like "prisoners."

While this research draws attention to the discomforts of wives' encounters with prison guards, it tells little about the interactional dynamic at work between prison guards and wives. To date, there is little empirical evidence documenting the ways in which wives' interactions with prison guards lead to wives' perceptions that these encounters contaminate them and open them up to feelings of mortification. The existing literature on prison visiting, however, does suggest that prison visitation procedures might be a source of debasement and shame with which wives have to contend.

12. Strip searches are only officially performed at Londonderry when institutional personnel have "reasonable cause" to suspect that visitors may be smuggling contraband. These suspicions are often correct. All nine women who brought contraband into the visiting rooms—as well as one other woman—had been strip searched. By contrast, sixteen women who had never brought in contraband had never been searched. The women's accounts indicate that perhaps the suspicions of prison personnel were valid, and that they were strip searching those people who were doing exactly those things strip searches were intended to prevent.

13. John Edgard Wideman, 1985, eloquently makes a similar observation based on his experiences visiting his incarcerated brother.

CHAPTER VII

1. See Burstein, 1977; Schwartz and Weintraub, 1974; Levy and Miller, 1971.

2. Major attention has been given to prisoners' pre-imprisonment identities—especially to their ethnic and racial components—and how these influence the kinds of adaptations men make to prison. Here it is shown that, in the course of criminalization, men have not been completely "stripped" of their pre-prison identities as husbands. Thus they are prepared to resume these roles when their wives come to visit in their identities as wives. In the course of this, both identities, are reactivated and sometimes redefined. This contributes to solidifying marital relations, as well as neutralizing partners' identities as "prisoners" and "prisoners' wives."

The following researchers have explicitly discussed the relationship between prisoners' pre-prison criminal identities and adaptations made to prison: Irwin, 1970; Irwin and Cressey, 1962. More recent research studies have also explored prisoners' ethnic and racial identities and the kinds of adaptations prisoners make. See Jacobs, 1977; Carroll, 1974; Davidson, 1974; Ianni, 1974.

3. Some attention has been given in the literature to the relationship between the viability of prisoners' marital ties and prison visiting. See, for instance, Burstein, 1977; Brodsky, 1975; Holt and Miller, 1972. Some exploration also has been given to the problems of prison visiting by: Schwartz and Weintraub, 1974; Levy and Miller, 1971.

4. Survey data indicate that prison visiting opportunities in general have expanded in the last two decades: the number of prisons permitting prisoners more than four visits per month, as well as lengthened the time for each visit, has increased. (Dickinson, 1984; Schafer, 1978.)

5. At Walden Farms, all prisoners are permitted to receive visitors during the designated times.

6. At Walden Farms, the most "open" prison, the house rules only pertain to physical contact, to the kinds of clothes visitors wear, and to the handling of packages, gifts, and money.

7. Burstein (1977) also offers some possible clues as to how the structure of formal visiting contributes to or undermines marital stability. Prisoners who receive ordinary (not conjugal) visits are unlikely to report that these visits allow them to achieve stability in or enhance their marital relationships. Therefore, these prisoners are less likely to report such things as intimacy, increased understanding, emotional closeness, and so forth, as outcomes of visits with their wives. These same prisoners seldom offer anything positive about the suitability of visiting places and are most likely to complain. On the basis of this,

Burstein suggests that prisoners' attitudes towards visiting may be largely attributable to the very restricted conditions under which visits take place. Even with the best of intentions, intimacy, self-approval, and planning for the future are all but impossible.

8. Given the constraints upon visiting, the extent to which the women in the study population visited their husbands was startling. Twenty wives averaged two visits every week when the prison was within easy commuting distance from their homes. Of these women, eight claimed to have rarely missed a visiting day. Many of them believed it was absolutely necessary to visit their husbands although it was very difficult at times to make the trip. However, when the prison was located at considerable distance from wives' homes, the frequency of visits decreased. Seven women averaged two visits a month: they claimed that even though they wanted to go more often, they were unable to do so. Four wives reported that they did not visit their husbands. One woman, incarcerated in a correctional facility, had never received permission to visit her husband. Upon filing for divorce, three women ceased to go to see their husbands.

9. Prison visiting itself can be a grim experience insofar as the constraints placed upon visiting can undermine emotionally satisfying interactions between the spouses. The following research studies report three major constraints which can inhibit visiting. Such constraints include rules and regulations for visiting, particularly rules against physical contact, time restrictions, and lack of privacy: Koenig and Gariepy, 1985; Daniel and Barrett, 1981; Fishman and Cassin, 1981; Bakker *et. al.*, 1978; Burstein, 1977; Brodsky, 1975; Schwartz and Weintraub, 1974; Levy and Milelr, 1971.

10. Holt and Miller, 1972.

11. Similar findings are reported by Koenig and Gariepy, 1985.

12. Husbands usually promised to build log houses.

13. Other investigators also suggest that the expression of love, concern, and sexuality might possibly provide the impetus for wives and girlfriends to continue visiting their incarcerated men. For example, see Koenig and Gariepy, 1985; Burstein, 1977; Holt and Miller, 1972.

14. Schwartz and Weintraub (1974) and Swan (1981) have described ways in which incarcerated husbands and their wives reaffirm their marital ties and their respective roles within the marriage. Hus-

bands, for instance, often reassert their authority over their wives and wives, in turn, frequently defer to the husbands in making domestic decisions.

15. Although the prison literature has provided extensive documentation of the flow of contraband goods and services within the inmate culture, limited attention has been given to the ways in which drugs are smuggled into prisons by visitors. The finding that visitors deliver drugs to prisoners during prison visiting hours holds up among diverse populations of prison inmate cultures: Gleason, 1978; Davidson, 1977; Guenther, 1975; Williams and Fish, 1974.

16. More recent research supports this finding. According to Kalinich, 1986, 1985, the visitation facility can be a major leakage point for contraband. For instance, whenever security is lax for the visitation room, contraband is most likely to be transferred to prisoners. Given this, such prison policies which allow contact visitation and laxity in the thorough searches of visitors and of residents before and after visitation can facilitate the smuggling of contraband.

CHAPTER VIII

1. It is worth noting that the difficulties experienced by prisoners' wives are, to a large extent, experienced by other wives under similar circumstances, particularly those with children. The literature documents the kinds of costs that wives incur when their husbands are absent, either temporarily or permanently, *e.g.*, due to service in the armed forces, to divorce, to desertion, and to death. Even though these wives may experience similar difficulties, it must, however, be pointed out that the problems faced by prisoners' wives are different in important ways because of the social and psychological implications of conviction and imprisonment: the "pains of separation" and the "pains of imprisonment" are not precisely the same.

For an extensive discussion of the kinds of hardships divorced wives experience, see Arendell, 1986; Anderson-Khleif, 1982; Wallerstein and Kelly, 1980; Weiss, 1979.

Some research also has documented the problems encountered by military wives when temporarily separated from their husbands: refer to McCubbin et al., 1980, 1974; McCubbin and Dahl, 1976; Montalvo, 1976; Metres *et al.*, 1974; Macintosh, 1968.

2. A few investigators have reported that prisoners' wives most frequently report that they missed companionship, love, a good sexual relationship, and so forth: Koenig and Gariepy, 1985; Daniel and Barrett, 1981; Swan, 1981; Schneller, 1978; Morris, 1965; Anderson, 1964.

3. Here is at least one important difference between the effects of enforced separation on prisoners' wives and those reported in studies of wartime separation or of service couples. In the social environments in which prisoners' wives lived in Vermont they were often the only wives in their particular predicament. In wartime or on military bases, a number of women in the wives' immediate circles shared the same situation.

4. The literature lends credence to the finding that wives, as single parents, must deal with withdrawal or aggressive and acting-out behavior that are common reactions in children whose fathers and/or mothers have been incarcerated: Lowenstein, 1986; Fritsch and Burkhead, 1981; Swan, 1981; Stanton, 1980; Sack, 1977; Morris, 1967; Fenton, 1959.

5. The literature also supports the finding presented here that older children react to the absence of their incarcerated fathers by school truancy and/or a decline in school performance: for example, see Lowenstein, 1986; Fritsch and Burkhead, 1981; Sack, 1977; Moerk, 1973; Friedman and Esselstyn, 1965.

6. An additional impact of incarceration on children is that they can become vulnerable to delinquencies: see Sack, 1977; Sack et al., 1976; Perry, 1973; Friedman and Esselstyn, 1965; Anderson, 1967.

7. For a discussion of the financial burdens placed upon wives during their husbands' imprisonment, see Koenig and Gariepy, 1985; Daniel and Barrett, 1981; Swan, 1981; Bakker et al., 1978; Schneller, 1978; Pueschel and Moġlia, 1977; Morris, 1965.

There is agreement in the literature that the economic status does not appear to change significantly for many families. There are families where the husband has not held a regular job and has not consistently supported the family in an adequate manner. For these families, the very absence of the head of the household may qualify them for public assistance, providing them with a more regular income than they experienced before his incarceration.

8. A few wives also reported that they acquired additional income from occasional participation in such illegal activities as shop lifting, passing "bad" checks, welfare fraud, and drug distribution.

9. Koenig and Gariepy (1985); Daniel and Barrett (1981); and Morris (1965) also reported that prisoners' wives experienced similar emotional reactions to the absence of their husbands.

10. As Goffman (1961: 61) observed, inmates' reaction of restricting their attention to events immediately around their bodies is a radical form of situational withdrawal.

11. The literature lends support to the finding that wives derive some real benefits from their husbands' imprisonment: Swan, 1981; Schneller, 1978; Holt and Miller, 1972.

12. At various intervals during their husbands' sentences, all wives reported feeling that their homes were like prisons.

13. Struckhoff (1977) states specifically that divorce decisions made during this period are based on the history of the marriage rather than the single element of incarceration, and some families use the incarceration as a first step in detaching ties with the offender.

14. Holt and Miller (1972) also have pointed out that not all marital ties are strengthened as a result of one partner's being incarcerated. Some marriages deteriorate, either because of the imprisonment, or the prison system's structure or policies regarding communication. Freedman and Rice (1977) have also reported that forms of contact such as telephone calls may serve to renew faith in marital relations or to set in motion events which will undermine them. These authors suggest that the limitations inherent in available forms of communication may frustrate interactions and become destructive to the relationships they are intended to strengthen.

15. Freedman and Rice (1977) specifically observe that the use of the telephone can set the stage for a powerful emotional crisis for both partners. Both partners can then suffer acute emotional suffering due to their inability to support one another through this means of communication.

16. Prisoners could obtain temporary release on the basis of need and/or merit, but supervised passes were only issued to prisoners who could find a willing guard or approved volunteer to take them into the community. Guards or volunteers were to keep the prisoners under constant surveillance. Prisoners released on unsupervised passes were free to leave prison without surveillance for a day or a weekend.

17. Similarly, Hassin (1977) reported that the greatest value of such home visits lay in their affording male furloughees a respite from the "pains of imprisonment."

18. McCarthy's (1979) observations lend support to the present research findings. She reports that seldom do female furloughees experience home visits as "tests" of free world reality or "dress rehearsals" for re-entry. Rather, she observes that home visits were more frequently perceived as intermissions, or holidays, from incarceration.

CHAPTER IX

1. See McCubbin and Dahl, 1976; Metres *et al.*, 1974; Boulding, 1950.

2. For a discussion of some factors affecting the impact that released prisoners have on their wives, see Curtis and Schulman, 1984; Ekland-Olson *et al.*, 1983; Liker, 1980, 1981; Cordon *et al.*, 1978; Waller, 1974.

3. Ohlin (1954) initially found that the positive relationship between parole success and maintenance of family ties holds up across diverse populations and in very different locales. Similar findings have been more recently reported by Morris *et al.*, 1975; Erickson *et al.*, 1973; Holt and Miller, 1972; Irwin, 1970; Glaser, 1969.

4. There is additional evidence that interpersonal networks are an important factor for the prisoner's re-entry from prison to be less stressful: refer to Ekland-Olson *et al.*, 1983; Fishman and Alissi, 1979; Homer, 1979; Erickson *et al.*, 1973; Holt and Miller, 1972; Studt, 1967.

5. The following research studies have focused upon wives' anticipations about their husbands' release from prison: see, for instance, Koenig and Gariepy, 1985; Fishman, 1981; Swan, 1981; Cobean and Power, 1978; Morris, 1965.

6. The "extended furlough" program allows prisoners to adjust to working and living within their communities while still under the general supervision of the correctional system. Extended furloughs can be revoked when prisoners violate community rules. When extended furloughs are revoked, prisoners are returned to prison to resume their sentences.

Parole, on the other hand, allows prisoners to serve the remaining parts of their sentences while living in the larger community. Parole is a privilege and can be revoked if parolees violate conditions of their parole. If it is revoked, they are returned to prison to serve the remainder of their sentences. If parolees commit crimes while on parole, they may be tried, sentenced if found guilty, and returned to serve additional terms.

7. Some other studies show that the newly released prisoner does feel as though he is a stranger in a strange land: Ekland-Olson *et al.*, 1983; Irwin, 1970.

8. Some recent investigators have found that the financial burdens which released prisoners place on their families is a major source of dissatisfaction for their wives: Curtis and Schulman, 1984; Liker, 1981, 1980.

9. The following researchers have explicitly discussed how economic difficulties continued to be a source of tension and marital conflict when husbands get out of prison: Liker, 1981; Morris, 1975.

10. Holt and Miller (1972) notes that the so-called "service wife's syndrome" is one way in which wives derive benefits from enforced separation—such as an increased ability to play out satisfying roles as mother and homemaker without the responsibilities attached to the role of wife.

CHAPTER X

1. The following investigators point out that battered wives tend to be traditional women who have adopted the roles of wives and mothers as primary identities. Thus even when they are gainfully employed, they are strongly motivated to succeed in their domestic roles. Most battered women do remain economically dependent on their husbands, a dependency that provides a strong motivation to cope with violence: Ferraro and Johnson, 1983; Dobash and Dobash, 1979; Walker, 1979.

Similar observations have been made about wives of alcoholics: see, for example, Jackson, 1962; Whalen, 1969.

2. See for instance, Mayo *et al.*, 1971; Sampson *et al.*, 1962; Yarrow *et al.*, 1955.

3. For a discussion of rationalizations devised by wives married to "troublesome" spouses see: Jackson's, 1962, work on family reactions to alcoholism; Yarrow *et al.*'s, 1955, studies of family responses to mental illness; and Ferraro and Johnson's, 1983, and Dobash and Dobash's, 1979, work on wives' responses to battering.

4. Research on familial accommodations to other "troublesome" spouses, including alcoholics (Jackson, 1954), the mentally ill (Lynch, 1983; Schwartz, 1957; Yarrow et al., 1955), batterers (Bowker, 1983; Walker, 1979), and gamblers (Lesieur, 1977), has documented the extent to which the continuation of such marriages depends upon the development of numerous coping strategies. There is agreement that these strategies proved futile in deterring husbands from troublesome behavior.

5. Morris et al., 1975; Irwin, 1970; Glaser, 1969.

6. For a discussion of employment as an important factor in paroled prisoners' post-prison performance: see, Rossi et al., 1980; Cordon et al., 1978; Morris et al., 1975; Waller, 1974; Irwin, 1970; Studt, 1967.

7. See, for instance, Casper, 1972.

8. Koenig and Gariepy, 1985; Schneller, 1978; Schwartz and Weintraub, 1974.

9. Homer, 1979; Holt and Miller, 1972; Irwin, 1970; Glaser, 1969.

10. Refer to Ekland-Olson et al., 1983; Irwin, 1970.

11. For an extensive documentation of the hardships wives encounter due to husband absence, see the more current literature: Arendell, 1986; Berman, 1981; Weiss, 1979.

12. Claude (1986) makes a similar observation in her discussion of the impoverishment of black women. She suggests that for black women poverty is often independent of family patterns. Given this context, there does not appear to be any significant increase in the poverty of black women when they assume the status of female head of their households. The are likely to be poor before a change puts them into a female-headed household. Claude concludes that the feminization of poverty fails to take into account that the experiences of lower-class black women are somewhat different from those of middle income white women.

13. See for instance: Arendell, 1986; Hewlett, 1986; Rogers, 1986; Sidel, 1986; Weitzman, 1985; Stallard, 1983; Anderson-Khleif, 1982; Nazzari, 1980; Pearce, 1978.

14. A similar observation is made by Arendell (1986). She observed that divorced women were in agreement that any satisfactions that they

derived from their status as divorcees paled in comparison to the stress caused by the emotional and economic effects of divorce. She then draws the conclusions that divorced women are more likely to look to remarriage than to themselves if they want to achieve secure lives for themselves and their children.

APPENDIX A

1. However, in most prisoners' writings, the recurrent themes are the men's deep concern for the well-being of their wives and families, their despair at enforced separation, and their resentment toward the justice system and society for imposing this separation. The sociological literature on prisoners' experiences has at least mentioned this facet of the men's prison experience. Nevertheless, the major direction of this literature has centered on developing a more systematic analysis of the "hardships" suffered by imprisoned men who are separated from the wives who are on the other side of this relationship. Prisoners' wives tend to be treated as marginal to this issue even though the effects of imprisonment may be as hard and punitive for women outside of prison as for their men inside.

2. Goffman, 1959.

3. Blumberg, 1980.

4. The following current research studies have contained the concepts of the moral career: Rosenbaum, 1981; Lesieur, 1977; Letkemann, 1973; Waldorf, 1973; Davis, 1972.

5. Blackwell (1959) for instance, was the first to apply Hill's, 1949, "crisis of separation" model in this context. His major findings were that marital adjustment before imprisonment is significantly and positively related to marital adjustment during separation, and that wives who define enforced separation as a crisis become more highly adjusted than wives who do not. A number of investigators have replicated Blackwell's research. Morris, 1965, in her study of the effects of involuntary separation on British prisoners' wives, attempted to integrate the multiplicity of factors involved in prisoners' families' adjustments to enforced separation. Love, 1970, has done further testing of hypotheses regarding families' adjustments to the crisis of involuntary separation. Although Struckhoff, 1977, only sampled prisoners' wives, his approach remains consistent with the context provided by the "family separation crisis" model. These studies conclude that the de-

gree of family solidarity—as indexed by marital adjustment before the crisis experience—is highly related to the level of adjustment during this period.

6. Struckhoff, 1977.

7. Refer to Jackson's, 1954, work on alcoholics; Schwartz's, 1957, Lynch's, 1983, and Yarrow et al.'s 1955, work on the mentally ill; Bowker, 1983, Dobash and Dobash's, 1979, and Walker's, 1979, work on batterers; and Lesieur's, 1977, work on gamblers.

8. Sampson, 1962; and Yarrow et al., 1955; Jackson, 1954.

9. Lynch, 1983.

10. Some exploration also has been given to the kinds of problems prisoners' wives encounter during enforced separation by: Koenig and Gariepy, 1985; Daniel and Barrett, 1981; Schneller, 1978; Anderson, 1967; Morris, 1965.

11. Schneller had similar findings. He also reports that prisoners' wives derive some benefits from involuntary separation. See Schneller, 1978: 70.

12. According to Morris (1965), in her study of British prisoners' wives, feelings of shame are almost exclusively reported by wives of first-time offenders, and then only during initial incarceration. Few wives of recidivists express the same reactions. Instead, wives of repeat offenders have become inured to their husbands' arrests and imprisonments. Similar findings have been reported by the following researchers: Daniel and Barrett, 1981; Schneller, 1978; Struckhoff, 1977; Schwartz and Weintraub, 1974; Anderson, 1967.

13. Kotarba's (1979) research reinforces these findings. He observed that many mothers who brought their children to visit with their incarcerated fathers, did not perceive their husbands' arrest as a source of shame for family members. Instead, they saw it as another facet of lower-class life to be accommodated and accepted.

14. Schwartz and Weintraub, 1974; Perry, 1973.

15. Refer to Koenig and Gariepy, 1985; Daniel and Barrett, 1981.

16. Kotarba (1970) reports that the primary topic of communications between prisoners and intimate visitors (wives, fiancees, girlfriends) is that affirmation of the relationship itself, both through body language that conveys feelings of affection and through conversations

about past and future sexual encounters. A second important topic of conversations is plans, hopes, and dreams for the future (Koenig and Gariepy, 1985; Burstein, 1977). Koenig and Gariepy, 1985, also suggest that these conversations provide a fantasy life for the couple and also provide an impetus for wives to continue visiting their incarcerated men.

17. Koenig and Gariepy, 1985; Burstein, 1977; Brodsky, 1975; Holt and Miller, 1972.

APPENDIX B

1. Most of my life, I have lived near the fringes of various criminal worlds and thus am quite familiar with the numbers racket, juvenile gangs, organized crime, drug dealers, prostitutes, and fences.

2. Until the 1980 census, Vermont was not considered to include even one Standard Metropolitan Statistical Area.

3. Burlington and environs became an SMSA in 1980.

4. In fact, respondents seem to have similar socio-demographic characteristics and marital experiences to those of wives across diverse populations. For instance, see Swan, 1981; Struckhoff, 1977; Love, 1970; Morris, 1965; Blackwell, 1959.

5. Three factors appear to have determined the frequency and duration of interviews: the willingness of wives to share aspects of their lives with me; how close they lived to the research base; and whether or not they were hospitalized during the research period.

BIBLIOGRAPHY

Adams, D. and J. Fischer 1976. "The Effects of Prison Residents' Community Contacts on Recidivism Rates." *Corrective and Social Psychiatry.* 22:21–27.

Anderson, N. 1967. "Prisoners' Families: A Theoretical Consideration of Imprisonment as a Family Crisis." *Australian Journal of Social Issues,* 3:9–17.

Anderson-Khleif, S. 1982. *Divorced But Not Disastrous: How to Improve the Ties Between Single-Parent Mothers, Divorced Fathers, and the Children.* Englewood Cliffs, New Jersey: Prentice-Hall.

Arendell, T. 1986. *Mothers and Divorce: Legal, Economic, and Social Dilemmas.* Berkeley: University of California Press.

Bakker, L. J., B. A. Morris and L. M. Janus 1978. "Hidden Victims of Crime." *Social Work,* 23:143–148.

Becker, H. S. 1958. "Problems of Inference and Proof of Participant Observation." *American Sociological Review,* 23:652–660.

Becker, H. S. 1963. *Outsiders: Studies in the Sociology of Deviance.* Glencoe, Ill: The Free Press.

Becker, H. S. and B. Geer 1960. "Participant Observation: The Analysis of Qualitative Field Data." In R. H. Adams and J. J. Preiss (eds.), *Research: Field Relations and Techniques.* Homewood, Ill: The Dorsey Press, 267–289.

Becker, H. S. and A. Strauss 1956. "Careers, Personality and Adult Socialization." *American Journal of Sociology,* 62:253–263.

Berkowitz, S. D. 1982. *An Introduction to Structural Analysis.* Toronto: Butterworths.

Berman, W. H. and D. C. Turk 1981. "Adaptation to Divorce: Problems and Coping Strategies." *Journal of Marriage and the Family,* 43:179–189.

Birenbaum, A. 1975. "On Managing a Courtesy Stigma." In R. Scarpitti and R. McFarlane (eds.), *Deviance: Action, Reaction, Interaction.* Reading, MA: Addison-Wesley, 347–357.

Blackwell, J. E. 1959. "The Effects of Involuntary Separation of Selected Families of Men Committed to Prison from Spokane

County, Washington." Ph.D. Dissertation, State College of Washington. Blumberg, A. 1980. "The Moral Career of an Accused Person." In D. H. Kelly (ed.), *Criminal Behavior: Readings in Criminology.* New York: St. Martin's Press, 465–471.

Boulding, E. 1950. "Family Adjustments to War Separations and Reunions." *The Annals of the American Academy of Political and Social Sciences,* 272:59–67.

Bowker, L. 1983. *Beating Wife-Beating.* Lexington, MA: Lexington Books.

Brodsky, L. 1975. *Families and Friends of Men in Prison: The Uncertain Relationship.* Lexington, MA: D.C. Heath Company.

Brown, C. A., R. Feldberg, E. M. Fox, and J. Kohen 1976. "Divorce: Chance of a New Lifetime." *The Journal of Social Issues,* 32:119–133.

Burstein, J. Q. 1977. *Conjugal Visits in Prison: Psychological and Social Consequences.* Lexington, MA: Lexington Books.

Carroll, L. 1974. *Hacks, Blacks, and Cons: Race Relations in a Maximum Security Prison.* Lexington, MA: D.C. Heath Co.

Casper, J. D. 1972. *American Criminal Justice: The Defendant's Perspective.* Englewood Cliffs, New Jersey: Prentice-Hall.

Chaiklin, H. 1972. "Integrating Correctional and Family Systems." *American Journal of Orthopsychiatry,* 42:784–791.

Charmaz, K. 1983. "The Grounded Theory Method: An Explication and Interpretation." In R. M. Emerson (ed.). *Contemporary Field Research: A Collection of Readings.* Boston: Little, Brown and Company, 109–126.

Claude, J. 1986. "Poverty Patterns for Black Men and Women." *The Black Scholar,* 17:20–23.

Clausen, J. A., M. R. Yarrow, L. C. Deasy and C. G. Schwartz 1955. "The Impact of Mental Illness: Research Formulation." *Journal of Social Issues,* 11:6–10.

Cobean, S. C. and P. W. Power 1978. "The Role of the Family in the Rehabilitation of the Offender." *International Journal of Offender Therapy and Comparative Criminology,* 22:29–38.

Cohen, S. and L. Taylor 1974. *Psychological Survival: The Experience of Long Term Confinement.* New York: Vintage, 1974.

Cordon J., J. Kuipers and J. Wilson 1978. *After Prison: A Study of the Post-Release Experiences of Discharged Prisoners.* London: University of York.

Curtis, R. L., Jr. and S. Schulman 1984. "Ex-Offender, Family Relations, and Economic Supports: The 'Significant Women' Study of the TARD Project." *Crime and Delinquency,* 30:507–528.

Daniel, S. W. and C. J. Barrett 1981. "Needs of Prisoners' Wives: A Challenge for the Mental Health Profession." *Community Mental Health Journal,* 17:310–322.

Davidson, R. T. 1974. *Chicano Prisoners: The Key to San Quentin.* New York: Holt, Rinehart & Winston.

Davies, R. P. 1980. "Stigmatization of Prisoners' Families." *Prison Service Journal,* 40:12–14.

Davis, F. 1972. *Illness, Interaction and the Self.* Belmont, CA: Wadsworth.

Davis, N. 1971. "The Prostitute: Developing a Deviant Identity." In J. N. Heuslin (ed.), *Studies in the Sociology of Sex.* New York: Appleton Century Crofts.

Deasy, L. C. and D. W. Quinn 1955. "The Wife of the Mental Patient and the Hospital Psychiatrist." *Journal of Social Issues,* 11:33–48.

Denzin, N. K. 1970. *Sociological Methods: A Sourcebook.* Chicago: Aldine.

Denzin, N. K. 1978. *The Research Act: A Theoretical Introduction to Sociological Methods.* New York: McGraw-Hill.

Dickinson, G. E. 1984. "Changes in Communication Policies." *Corrections Today,* 46:58–60.

Dobash, R. E. and R. Dobash 1979. *Violence Against Wives: A Case Against the Patriarchy.* New York: The Free Press.

Edland-Olson, S., M. Supancic, J. Campbell and K. Lenihan 1983. "Postrelease Depression and the Importance of Familial Support." *Criminology,* 21:253–274.

Edwards, P., C. Harvey and P. C. Whitehead 1973. "Wives of Alcoholics: A Critical Review and Analysis." *Quarterly Journal of Studies on Alcohol,* 34:112–132.

Ehrenreich, B. 1983. *The Hearts of Men: American Dreams and the Flight from Commitment.* Garden City, NY: Anchor Press.

Erickson, R. J., W. J. Crow, L. A. Zurcher, Jr., and A. V. Connett 1973. *Paroled But Not Free.* New York: Human Sciences Press.

Fenton, N. 1959. *The Prisoner's Family.* Palo Alto, CA: Pacific Books.

Ferraro, K. And J. Johnson 1983. "How Women Experience Battering: The Process of Victimization." *Social Problems.* 30:325–335.

Fishman, L. T. 1986. "Prisoners' Wives' Interpretations of Male Criminality and Subsequent Arrest." *Deviant Behavior,* 7:137–158.

Fishman, L. T. 1986. "Repeating the Cycle of Hard Living and Crime: Wives' Accommodations to Husbands' Parole Performance." *Federal Probation,* 50:44–54.

Fishman, L. T. 1987. "Patterns of Accommodation Among Wives of Criminals." *Journal of Contemporary Ethnography,* 16:176–204.

Fishman, L. T. 1988. "Visiting at Prison: Renewed Courtship and the Prisoner's Wife." *Free Inquiry in Creative Sociology,* 16:115–121.

Fishman, L. T. 1988. "Stigmatization and Prisoners' Wives' Feelings of Shame." *Deviant Behavior,* 9:169–192.

Fishman, L. T. 1988. "Prisoners and Their Wives: Marital and Domestic Effects of Telephone Contacts and Home Visits." *International Journal of Offender Therapy and Comparative Criminology,* 32:55–66.

Fishman, S. H. 1981. "Losing a Loved One to Incarceration: The Effect of Imprisonment on Family Members." *Personnel and Guidance Journal,* 59:372–375.

Fishman, S. H. and A. S. Alissi 1979. "Strengthening Families as Natural Support System for Offenders." *Federal Probation,* 43:16–21.

Fishman, S. H. and C. J. M. Cassin 1981. *Services for Families of Offenders: An Overview.* U.S. Department of Justice, National Institute of Corrections.

Freedman, B. J. and D. G. Rice 1977. "Marital Therapy in Prison: One-Partner 'Couple Therapy.' " *Psychiatry,* 40:175–183.

Freeman, H. E. and O. G. Simmons 1963. *The Mental Patient Comes Home.* New York: John Wiley and Sons.

Freeman, H. E. and O. G. Simmons 1968. "Feelings of Stigma Among Relatives of Former Mental Patients." In S. P. Spitzer and N. K. Denizen (eds.), *The Mental Patient: Studies in the Sociology of Deviance.* New York: McGraw Hill, 391–401.

Friedman, S. and T. C. Esselstyn 1965. "The Adjustment of Children of Jail Inmates." *Federal Probation,* 29:55–59.

Fritsch, T. A. and J. D. Burkhead 1981. "Behavioral Reactions of Children to Parental Absence Due to Imprisonment." *Family Relations,* 30:83–88.

Gelles, R. J. 1974. *The Violent Home: A Study of Physical Aggression Between Husbands and Wives.* Beverly Hills, CA: Sage.

Gibbs, C. 1971. "The Effect of the Imprisonment of Women Upon Their Children." *British Journal of Criminology,* 11:113–130.

Gimenez, M. 1987. "The Feminization of Poverty: Myth or Reality?" *The Insurgent Sociologist,* 14:5–30.

Glaser, B. G. and A. L. Strauss 1965. *Awareness of Dying.* Chicago: Aldine.

Glaser, B. G. and A. L. Strauss 1967. *The Discovery of Grounded Theory: Strategies for Qualitative Research.* Chicago: Aldine.

Glaser, D. 1969. *The Effectiveness of a Prison and Parole System.* New York: The Bobbs-Merrill Company.

Gleason, S. E. 1978. "Hustling: The 'Inside' Economy of a Prison," *Federal Probation,* 42:32–40.

Goffman, E. 1959. "The Moral Career of the Mental Patient." *Psychiatry,* 23:123–131.

Goffman, E. 1961. *Asylums: Essays on the Social Situation of Mental Patients and Other Inmates.* Garden City, NY: Doubleday.

Goffman, E. 1963. *Stigma: Notes on the Management of Spoiled Identity.* Englewood Cliffs, NJ: Prentice-Hall.

Guenther, A. 1975. "Compensations in a Total Institution: The Forms and Functions of Contraband." *Crime and Delinquency,* 21:243–254.

Guenther, A. 1975. *The Social Dimensions of a Penitentiary.* Report to the National Institute of Law Enforcement and Criminal Justice, Unpublished mimeo. 7:64–71, 78–92.

Guse, S. B. 1970. "Psychiatric Study of Wives of Convicted Felons: An Example of Assortative Mating." *American Journal of Psychiatry,* 126:115–118.

Handler, E. 1974. "Family Surrogates as Correctional Strategy." *The Social Service Review,* 48:539–549.

Harrington, M. 1984. *The New American Poverty.* New York: Holt, Rinehart & Winston.

Hartjen, C. A. 1974. *Crime and Criminalization.* New York: Praeger.

Hassin, Y. 1977. "Prisoners' Furlough: A Reassessment." *International Journal of Criminology and Penology,* 5:171–178.

Hewlett, S. A. 1986. *A Lesser Life: The Myth of Women's Liberation in America.* New York: A Warner Communications Company.

Hill, R. 1949. *Families Under Stress: Adjustment to the Crisis of War, Separation and Reunion.* Westport, CT: Greenwood Press.

Hinds, L. 1981. "Impact of Incarceration on Low-Income Families." *Journal of Offender Counseling Services and Rehabilitation,* 5:8–9.

Holt, N. 1971. "Temporary Prison Release: California's Prerelease Furlough Program." *Crime and Delinquency,* 17:414–430.

Holt, N. and D. Miller 1972. *Explorations in Inmate-Family Relations.* Sacramento: Department of Corrections Research Division.

Homer, E. L. 1979. "Inmate-Families Ties—Desirable But Difficult." *Federal Probation,* 43:47–52.

Howell, J. T. 1973. *Hard Living on Clay Street: Portraits of Blue Collar Families.* Garden City, New York: Doubleday Anchor Books.

Howlett, J. 1973. "Marital Deprivations of Prisoners and Their Wives." *Prison Service Journal,* 12:6–7.

Ianni, F. 1974. *Black Mafia: Ethnic Succession in Organized Crime.* New York: Simon & Schuster.

Irwin, J. 1970. *The Felon.* Englewood Cliffs, NJ: Prentice-Hall.

Irwin, J. and D. Cressey 1962. "Thieves, Convicts, and the Inmate Culture." *Social Problems,* 10:142–155.

Jackson, J. 1954. "The Adjustment of the Family to the Crisis of Alcoholism." *Quarterly Journal of Studies on Alcohol,* 15:562–586.

Jacobs, J. B. 1977. *Stateville: The Penitentiary in Mass Society.* Chicago: Univ. of Chicago Press.

Jorgensen, J. D., S. H. Hernandez and R. C. Warren 1986. "Addressing the Social Needs of Families of Prisoners: A Tool for Inmate Rehabilitation." *Federal Probation,* 50:47–52.

Kalinich, D. B. 1986. *Power, Stability, and Contraband: The Inmate Economy.* Prospect Heights, Illinois: Waveland Press.

Kalnich, D. B. and S. Stojkovic 1985. "Contraband: The Basis for Legitimate Power in a Prison Social System." *Criminal Justice and Behavior,* 12:435–451.

Kirby, R. and J. Corzine 1981. "The Contagion of Stigma: Fieldwork Among Deviants:" *Qualitative Sociology,* 4:3–20.

Koenig, C. and L. Gariepy 1985. *Life on the Outside: A Report on the Experiences of the Families of Offenders from the Perspective of the Wives of Offenders.* Chilliwack Community Services, Chilliwack, British Columbia.

Kommarovsky, M. 1971. *The Unemployed Man and His Family: The Effect of Unemployment Upon the Status of the Man in Fifty-Nine Families.* New York: Octagon Books.

Kotarba, J. 1979. "The Accomplishment of Intimacy in the Jail Visiting Room." *Qualitative Sociology,* 2:80–103.

Lemert, E. M. 1960. "The Occurrence and Sequence of Events in the Adjustment of Families to Alcoholism." *Quarterly Journal of Studies in Alcohol,* 12:679–697.

Lemert, E. M. 1962. "Paranoia and the Dynamics of Exclusion." *Sociometry,* 24:2–20.

Lesieur, H. R. 1977. *The Chase: Career of the Compulsive Gambler.* Garden City, New York: Doubleday Anchor.

Letkemann, P. 1973. *Crime as Work.* Englewood Cliffs, NJ: Prentice-Hall.

Levy, H. and D. Miller 1971. *Going to Jail: The Political Prisoner.* New York: Grove Press.

Liker, J. K. 1980. "Nobody Knows the Troubles I've Seen: Post-Release Burdens on the Families of the Transitional and Research Project."

In P. H. Rossi *et al.*, (eds.), *Monday, Work, and Crime*. New York: Academic Press: 299–317.

Liker, J. K. 1981. "Economic Pressures on the Families of Released Prisoners: Evidence from the TARP Experiment." *The Cornell Journal of Social Relations,* 16:11–27.

Love, J. P. 1970 "Conjugal Family's Adjustment to the Crisis of Imprisonment." Ph.D. dissertation, Florida State University.

Lowenstein, A. 1984. "Coping with Stress: The Case of Prisoners' Wives." *Journal of Marriage and the Family,* 3:699–708.

Lowenstein, A. 1986. "Temporary Single Parenthood—The Case of Prisoners' Families." *Family Relations,* 35:79–85.

Luepnitz, D. À. 1982. *"Child Custody: A Study of Families After Divorce.* Lexington, MA: Lexington Books.

Lynch, M. 1983. "Accommodation Practices: Vernacular Treatments of Madness." *Social Problems,* 31:152–164.

MacIntosh, H. 1968. "Separation Problems in Military Wives." *American Journal of Psychiatry,* 125:260–265.

Markley, C. W. 1973. "Furlough Programs and Conjugal Visiting in Adult Correctional Institutions." *Federal Probation,* 37:19–26.

Mayo, C., R. Havelock and D. L. Simpson 1971. "Attitudes Towards Mental Illness Among Psychiatric Patients and Their Wives." *Journal of Clinical Psychology,* 27:128–132.

McCarthy, B. R. 1979. *Easy Time: Females on Temporary Release.* Lexington, MA: Lexington Books.

McCrate, E. 1987. "Trade, Merger and Employment: Economic Theory on Marriage." *Review of Radical Political Economics,* 19:73–89.

McCubbin, H. I. and B. B. Dahl 1976. "Prolonged Family Separation in the Military: A Longitudinal Study." In H. I. McCubbin *et al.,* (eds.), *Families in the Military System.* Beverly Hills: Sage, 112–144.

McCubbin, H. I., E. J. Hunter and P. Metres, Jr. 1974. "Children in Limbo." In H. I. McCubbin *et al.* (eds.), *Family Separation and Reunion: Families of Prisoners of War and Servicemen Missing in Action.* Washington, DC: U.S. Government Printing Office, 65–76.

McCubbin, H. I., E. J Hunter and P. Metres, Jr. 1971. "Adaptation of the Family to the Prisoner of War and Missing in Action Experience: An Overview." In H. I. McCubbin *et al.* (eds.), *Family Separation and Reunion: Families of Prisoners of War and Servicemen Missing in Action.* Washington, DC: U.S. Government Printing Office, 21–48.

McCubbin, H. I., C. B. Joy, A. E. Cauble, J. K. Comeau, J. M. Patterson and R. H. Needle 1980. "Family Stress and Coping: A Decade of Review." *Journal of Marriage and the Family,* 42:855–871.

Metress, P. J., H. I. McCubbin and E. J. Hunter 1974. "Families of Returned Prisoners of War: Some Impressions on Their Initial Reintegration." In H. I. McCubbin *et al.* (eds.), *Family Separation and Reunion: Families of Prisoners of War and Servicemen Missing in Action.* Washington, DC: U.S. Government Printing Office, 147–156.

Moerke, E. 1973. "Like Father Like Son: Imprisonment of Fathers and the Psychological Adjustment of Sons." *Journal of Youth and Adolescence,* 2:303–312.

Montalvo, F. F. 1976. "Family Separation in the Army: Study of the Problems Encountered and the Caretaking Resources Used by Career Army Families Undergoing Military Separation." In H. I. McCubbin *et al.,* (eds.), *Families in the Military System.* Beverly Hills: Sage, 147–173.

Morris, P. 1965. *Prisoners and Their Families.* New York: Hart Publishing Co.

Morris, P. 1967. "Fathers in Prison." *British Journal of Criminology,* 7:424–430.

Morris, P., F. Beverly and J. Vennard 1975. *On License: A Study of Parole.* London: John Wiley & Sons.

Myers, J. and R. Bertram 1959. *Family and Class Dynamics.* New York: John Wiley and Sons.

Nazzari, M. 1980. "The Significance of Present-Day Changes in the Institution of Marriage." *Review of Radical Political Economics,* 12:63–75.

Newman, D. J. 1956. "Pleading Guilty for Consideration: A Study of Bargain Justice." *Journal of Criminal Law, Criminology, and Police Science,* 46:780–790.

Ohlin, L. E. 1954. *The Stability and Validity of Parole Experience Tables.* Ph.D. dissertation. University of Chicago.

Pagelow, M. 1981. *Woman-Battering: Victims and Their Experiences.* Beverly Hills: Sage.

Pearce, D. 1978. "The Feminization of Poverty: Women, Work, and Welfare." *The Urban and Social Change Review,* 11:28–36.

Perry, P. W. 1973. "The Forgotten Victim." *Mental Hygiene,* 57:12–21.

Pueschell, J. and R. Mogilia 1977. "The Effects of the Penal Environment on Familial Relationships." *Family Coordinator,* 26:373–375.

Rodgers, H. R., Jr. 1986. *Poor Women, Poor Families.* New York: M. E. Sharp.

Romero, M. 1985. "A Comparison Between Strategies Used on Prisoners of War and Battered Wives." *Sex Roles,* 9/10:537–547.

Rosenbaum, M. 1981. *Women on Heroin.* New Brunswick, NJ: Rutgers University Press.

Rossi, P. H., R. A. Berk and K. J. Lenihan 1980. *Money, Work, and Crime: Experimental Evidence.* New York: Academic Press.

Rubin, L. 1976. *Worlds of Pain: Life in the Working Class Family.* New York: Basic Books.

Rubington, E. and M. Weinberg 1981. *Deviance: The Interactionist Perspective.* New York: Macmillan.

Sack, W. H. 1977. "Children of Imprisoned Fathers." *Psychiatry,* 40:163–174.

Sack, W. H., J. Seidler and S. Thomas 1976. "The Children of Imprisoned Parents: A Psychosocial Exploration." *American Journal of Orthopsychiatry.* 46:618–628.

Sampson, H., S. I. Messinger and R. D. Towne 1961. "The Mental Hospital and Marital Family Ties." *Social Problems,* 9:141–155.

Sampson, H., S. Messinger and R. D. Towne 1962. "Family Processes and Becoming a Mental Patient." *American Journal of Sociology,* 68:88–98.

Schafer, N. E. 1978. "Prison Visiting—A Background for Change." *Federal Probation,* 42:47–50.

Schneller, D. P. 1978. *The Prisoner's Family: A Study of the Effects of Imprisonment on the Families of Prisoners.* San Francisco: R. and E. Research Associates.

Schwartz, C. G. 1957. "Perspectives on Deviance: Wives' Definitions of Their Husbands' Mental Illness." *Psychiatry,* 20:275–291.

Schwartz, M. C. and J. F. Weintraub 1974. "The Prisoner's Wife: A Study in Crisis." *Federal Probation,* 38:20–26.

Scott, M. and S. Lyman 1968. "Accounts." *American Sociological Review,* 33:44–62.

Shostak, A. B. 1969. *Blue Collar Life.* New York: Random House.

Sidel, R. 1986. *Women and Children Last—The Plight of Poor Women in Affluent America.* New York: Viking Press.

Spanier, G. and R. Casto 1979. "Adjustment to Separation and Divorce: An Analysis of Fifty Case Studies." *Journal of Divorce,* 2:241–253.

Stallard, K. *et al.* 1983. *When Mothers Go to Jail.* Lexington, MA: Lexington Books.

Stanton, A. M. 1980. *Poverty in the American Dream: Women and Children First.* Boston: South End Press.

Struckhoff, D. R. 1977. *Adjustments of Prisoners' Wives to Separation.* Ph.D. dissertation, Southern Illinois University at Carbondale.

Studt, E. 1967. *The Re-Entry of the Offender into the Community.* Washington, DC: United States Department of Health, Education and Welfare.

Swan, L. A. 1981. *Families of Black Prisoners: Survival and Progress.* Boston, G. K. Hall and Co.

Sykes, G. M. and D. Matza 1957. "Techniques of Neutralization: A Theory of Delinquency." *American Sociological Review,* 22:664–670.

Turk, A. T. 1966. "Conflict and Criminality." *American Sociological Review,* 31:338–352.

Turk, A. T. 1969. *Criminology and Legal Order.* Chicago: Rand McNally.

Waldorf, D. 1973. *Careers in Dope.* Englewood Cliffs, NJ: Prentice-Hall.

Walker, L. 1979. *The Battered Woman.* New York: Harper and Row.

Walker, N. 1983. "Side-Effects of Incarceration." *The British Journal of Criminology,* 23:61–71.

Waller, I. 1974. *Men Released from Prison.* Toronto: University of Toronto Press.

Wallerstein, J. and J. Kelly 1980. *Surviving the Breakup: How Parents and Children Cope with Divorce.* New York: Basic Books.

Waltes, E. A. 1977–1978. "Female masochism and the enforced restriction of choice." *Victimology,* 2:535–544.

Warren, C. A. B. and S. W. Phillips 1976. "Stigma Negotiation: Expression Games, Accounts, and the Drunken Driver." *Urban Life,* 5:53–74.

Weiss, R. S. 1975. *Marital Separation.* New York: Basic Books.

Weiss, R. S. 1979. *Going It Alone: The Family Life and Social Situation of the Single Parent.* New York: Basic Books.

Weitzman, L. 1985. *The Divorce Revolution: The Unexpected Social and Economic Consequences for Women and Children in America.* New York: Free Press.

Whalen, T. 1969. "Wives of Alcoholics." In W. A. Rushing (ed.), *Deviant Behavior and Social Process.* Chicago: Rand McNally.

Wideman, J. E. 1985. *Brothers and Keepers.* New York: Penguin Books.

Williams, E., Z. Elder and S. Y. Williams 1970. "The Psychological Aspects of the Crimes of Imprisoned Husbands on Their Families." *Journal of National Medical Association,* 62:208–212.

Williams, V. L. and M. Fish 1974. *Convicts, Codes, and Contraband: The Prison Life of Men and Women.* Cambridge, MA: Ballinger.

Yarrow, M. R., J. A. Clausen and P. R. Robbins 1955. "The Social Meaning of Mental Illness." *Journal of Social Issues,* 11: 6–10.

Zemans, E. and R. Cavan 1958. "Marital Relationships of Prisoners in the United States." *Journal of Criminal Law, Criminology and Policy Science,* 49:50–57.

INDEX

329